This book is a valuable source of information on the long-term effects of early intervention programs on the education of children living in economically disadvantaged areas and in other contexts. Early intervention programs such as Head Start enjoy popular and legislative support, but until now, policymakers and practitioners have lacked hard data on the long-term consequences of such locally and federally mandated efforts.

Success in Early Intervention focuses on the Child-Parent Center (CPC) program in Chicago, the second oldest (after Head Start) federally funded early childhood intervention program. Begun in 1967, the program currently operates out of twenty-four centers, which are located in proximity to the elementary schools they serve. The CPC program's unique features include mandatory parental involvement and a single, sustained educational system that spans preschool through the third grade.

Central to this study is a 1986 cohort of nearly twelve hundred CPC children and a comparison group of low income children whose subsequent activities, challenges, and achievements are followed through the age of fifteen. The lives of these children amply demonstrate the positive long-term educational and social consequences of the CPC program.

Arthur J. Reynolds is a professor of social work, educational psychology, and child and family studies at the University of Wisconsin—Madison.

University of Nebraska Press
Lincoln, NE 68588-0484

www.nebraskapress.unl.edu

Child, Youth, and Family Services

Success in Early Intervention

The Chicago Child-Parent Centers

By Arthur J. Reynolds

Foreword by Edward Zigler

University of Nebraska Press
Lincoln and London

M W

♾

Library of Congress Cataloging-in-Publication Data
Reynolds, Arthur J.
Success in early intervention : the Chicago
child-parent centers / by Arthur J. Reynolds
; foreword by Edward Zigler.
p.   cm. — (Child, youth, and family services.)
Includes bibliographical references and indexes.
ISBN 0-8032-3936-X (cloth : alk. paper)
1. Child-Parent Center Program (Chicago, Ill.)
2. Socially handicapped children—
Services for—Illinois—Chicago.
3. Socially handicapped children—Education (Early childhood)—Illinois—Chicago.
4. Socially handicapped children—Illinois—Chicago—Longitudinal studies.
5. Early childhood education—Illinois—Chicago.
6. Early childhood education—Parent participation—Illinois—Chicago.
I. Title.   II. Series.
HV743.C5 R48 2000
362.7′086′940977311—dc21   99-045985

To my parents for their lifelong inspiration
To Judy

Contents

Illustrations

ix

PHOTOGRAPHS
Following page 34

Tables

Foreword

America's landscape is littered with social programs for children and families that remain in place for short periods of time. Typically intervention programs, even successful ones, are seen to come and go with the vicissitudes of funding and political fortunes. Yet the federally funded Child-Parent Center Program has persisted in Chicago for 33 years. This project, like Head Start, is a large-scale childhood intervention program with its origins in the War on Poverty begun in the 1960s. Indeed it is the oldest extended childhood program. Although conceptually similar to Head Start (the oldest national childhood intervention program), the CPC project is based in the public schools in high-poverty neighborhoods and provides comprehensive services for children and families, transition to school, and substantial follow-up through the early years of school. It thus allows for a child's sustained participation for up to 6 years. Also unlike Head Start, a vast national program that typically has undergone evaluations characterized at best as spasmodic and controversial, the far more contained CPC program has been the subject of rigorous and sustained evaluation in the highly regarded, ongoing Chicago Longitudinal Study. This finely crafted volume reports new findings from that study, findings that should be widely heralded and, more important, heeded by policymakers throughout the nation.

While some thinkers continue to advocate against the involvement, any involvement, of government in the workings of family life, the CPC program quietly and tenaciously has done its work, holding fast to the proposition that an intervention program with a strong focus on parental involvement will prove valuable to children and families and will show the most far-reaching and durable benefits for all family members (Provence & Naylor, 1983; Seitz, 1990). Arthur Reynolds's investigation of the CPC program has demonstrated firmly the principles we have advanced for decades: the importance of intervening early in children's lives to foster scholastic and cognitive growth, as well as the critical importance in sustaining and reinforcing these gains through continued program participation by parent and child.

With the recent increase in our understanding of human brain development, findings like these become all the more compelling. Some scientists have suggested that in the case of brain function, we have a relatively small window of opportunity in which to stimulate a child's potential. With the help of technological advancements in brain imaging, neuroscientists are studying how a combination of good nurturing and stimulation during the first 3 years of life may actually lay down neural pathways in the growing child's brain. Thus programming that provides such stimulation, and that teaches parents the importance of providing it, is invaluable for ensuring a bright future for children.

Unfortunately, at the very time we learn about the importance of cognitive stimulation in early life, we as a nation see distressing trends that threaten to limit the amount and the quality of critical time many children are able to spend in the secure and nurturing company of a loving caregiver. Although child poverty at the national level has decreased slightly in the last few years, in 1996, about 20% of all children in the United States were poor; for Hispanic or black children the figure was over 40% (Children's Defense Fund, 1998; National Center for Children in Poverty, 1998). Poverty endangers children's life chances: children who are poor during the preschool years are more likely to have problems down the road in completing school. Children raised in low-income families are also likely to score lower on measures of health, cognitive development, school achievement, and emotional well-being than are children in higher-income families (Brooks-Gunn & Duncan, 1998).

Moreover, parents as a whole are suffering from unprecedented amounts of stress and a lack of leisurely, unstructured time with their children, the inevitable result when most parents must work long hours to support their families (Schor, 1992). The dual-parent family in which one parent stays at home while the other works is fading from memory, with only about 20%

of children growing up in such families in 1996. Among women with preschool-age children, the 1996 rate of participation in the out-of-home work force increased to about 62% (Annie E. Casey Foundation, 1998). Although we do not yet know precisely the social consequences of recent welfare reform legislation, it is clear that many children will be spending less time with their mothers as a result. Thus we as policymakers and researchers must find more effective ways to assist parents and children who are living under the deleterious conditions of poverty and the many forms of stress that poverty brings. As Arthur Reynolds amply demonstrates in this book, the CPC program has been providing such a way. Although he himself points out that this is not a perfect program, with the kind of insight his careful research has provided, we can devise better, more focused interventions.

The appearance of this monograph marks an important stage in the development of large-scale intervention programs. Although our understanding of the change agents at work within higher quality, more intensive programs has clearly increased over the years since Head Start's inception, we have continued to need further exploration of the avenues by which positive growth occurs. A good deal of such evidence is provided here. For example, we have grappled for years with the problem of "fade-out," in which early gains from participation in programs like Head Start seem to diminish over time. Reynolds has made the significant finding that these early gains can result in long-term positive effects even into adolescence when the program's major components are reinforced through the school years.

For some decades now, in fact since around the time that both Head Start and the Child-Parent Center programs were initiated, my colleagues and I have been saying that the obstacle faced by the nation in establishing broad-based, fully funded programs that better the life chances of low-income children is not that we as a people lack the scientific knowledge needed to bring this about; the problem is that we apparently lack the political will. With the publication of Reynolds's fine book, our state of knowledge has become so enhanced that even the most adamant naysayer regarding the efficacy of comprehensive intervention programs will have difficulty remaining at the podium. Moreover, this is finely nuanced knowledge, conveyed to us through the medium of the most sophisticated modes of statistical analysis. Although I must ally myself with the wise Don Campbell, who noted that program evaluation is a dangerous and slippery business, Reynolds, a talented and clearheaded methodologist, has done much to make the beleaguered craft of research sail a straighter course. He has done his colleagues and the future of childhood intervention programs a great service: This is a remarkably fine and important book.

Edward Zigler

References

Annie E. Casey Foundation (1998). KIDS COUNT databook. Baltimore: Author.

Brooks-Gunn, J., & Duncan, G. J. (Eds.) (1998). *Consequences of growing up poor.* New York: Russell Sage Foundation.

Children's Defense Fund (1998). *The state of America's children: Yearbook.* Washington DC: Author.

National Center for Children in Poverty (1998). *Young children in poverty: A statistical update* (March 1998 ed.). New York: Columbia University School of Public Health.

Provence, S., & Naylor, A. (1983). *Working with disadvantaged parents and their children: Scientific and practical issues.* New Haven, CT: Yale University Press.

Schor, J. B. (1992). *The overworked American.* New York: Basic Books.

Seitz, V. (1990). Intervention programs for impoverished children: A comparison of educational and family support models. *Annals of Child Development, 7,* 73–103.

Preface

Unlike most other social programs begun during the War on Poverty era, early childhood education today has widespread support from all levels of government and from the public at large. The nation's commitment to early childhood intervention is manifested by the substantial increases in funding for preschool programs at the state and local levels, by their high priority in school reforms, and by the sentiment embodied in the first national education goal that all children will start school ready to learn. Yet it is also true that the scientific evidence concerning the long-term effects of large-scale early interventions does not match the overwhelming support it engenders. After three decades of programs and opportunities for research, this limited evidence base is unfortunate.

This volume helps to correct that state of affairs. I report on the effects of participation in the Chicago Child-Parent Center (CPC) Program up to age 15 for over 1,100 low-income, mostly African-American children growing up in high-poverty central city neighborhoods. The CPC program is a federally and state-funded early childhood educational intervention for children in the Chicago Public Schools who are at risk for academic underachievement due to poverty and associated factors. Since 1967, the CPCs have provided educational and family support services from preschool to the early elementary grades for up to 6 years of continuous intervention. Little known outside of Chicago, the CPC program is the second oldest (after Project Head Start) federally funded early childhood intervention for economically disadvantaged children. It is the oldest extended early childhood intervention program and one of only a few such programs in the United States. I report on the progress of a 1986 cohort of children who graduated from all 20 of the centers with preschool and kindergarten. To gauge the effectiveness of the program, I also followed the progress of a natural comparison group of children who participated in an alternative government-funded kindergarten program in the Chicago Public Schools ("treatment as usual"); the socioeconomic characteristics of this second group matched those of the children from the CPCs.

The data reported in this monograph are from the Chicago Longitudinal Study. The primary purpose of the study is to investigate the effects of participation in the CPC program. Some history about the study may be helpful. The Chicago Longitudinal Study began in the spring of 1986 as a mandated evaluation of government-funded kindergarten programs in the Chicago Public Schools, including those associated with the ESEA Title I Child-Parent Centers and the Chicago Effective Schools Project, a school district program to assist schools in disadvantaged neighborhoods. The evaluation was carried out by Mavis Hagemann and Nancy Mavrogenes, who were early childhood specialists in the Bureau of Program Evaluation of the Board of Education's Department of Research and Evaluation. I was assigned to the evaluation as a data analyst in my capacity as a consultant in the Bureau of Program Evaluation. The focus of the evaluation was the kindergarten component, though coverage of the preschool years was included.

As former teachers of early childhood education in Chicago, Mavis and Nancy knew as much as anyone about early childhood programs—especially the Child-Parent Centers—and had completed many evaluations of early childhood programs. As part of the evaluation, Mavis and Nancy were planning a follow-up of the study sample of children. It was an opportune time because the evaluation included a representative sample of children who had graduated from the Child-Parent Centers in kindergarten in 1986. Moreover, there were few studies of the long-term effects of large-scale programs. To select a comparison group, over 300 children from six randomly selected schools were identified who enrolled in a compensatory all-day kindergarten program as part of the Chicago Effective Schools Project. In all, we began to follow over 1,500 children from these early childhood programs.

Having just moved to Chicago after earning my master's degree in psychology, I knew very little about early childhood education, let alone the

Child-Parent Centers and other early childhood programs. I hoped the project would give me valuable experience in evaluation research, my major professional interest at the time. Needless to say, I became very interested in this project, and Nancy and Mavis asked me to participate as a full partner in the follow-up project. In 1987, we completed the year 1 follow-up of the study sample by surveying first-grade teachers regarding children's classroom adjustment and transition to formal schooling. Over the next decade, we collected annual data on the study sample through a combination of school records, teacher surveys, parent surveys, student surveys, and classroom observations. After completing my doctoral dissertation using data from the first- and second-year follow-up, I became study director in 1990. In collaboration with Nancy, Mavis, and the Bureau of Program Evaluation, we began to investigate the factors contributing to children's early adjustment to school. Participation in early childhood intervention was one of these factors.

Although the Chicago Longitudinal Study is important because it is one of the only extensive longitudinal investigations of the schooling process of children throughout childhood, the fact that many children participated in the CPC program has special significance. Yet it was only since 1993 that the primary focus of the study was investigating the effects of the CPC program on children's development (largely displacing the focus on multiple influences). Indeed, the program is the only one of its kind in the country. Begun in 1967 in four west-side sites, the Child-Parent Center Program operates 24 centers today. The program offers a combined preschool, kindergarten, and school-age program for up to 6 years of intervention. The latter component is funded by the State of Illinois. From the beginning, the program was able to do what Head Start and Follow Through never accomplished: implement an extended early childhood intervention from preschool to third grade under a single administrative system. In an age of reforms intended to better coordinate services to children at risk and to promote parental participation in children's education, the CPC program is an early prototype of the concept of early childhood centers envisioned during the early 1960s.

The program has many innovative features that make it an ideal subject for a monograph. Besides offering early and extended childhood intervention, the program is implemented through a single administrative system—the Chicago Public Schools. In most centers the preschool and kindergarten program is combined. All centers provide transitional services for at least two of the first three school grades. The centers also are in close proximity to the elementary schools they serve, either as wings in the elementary schools or as separate buildings about a block away. Across the country, a typical arrangement for a child from a low-income family would include contact with two or three administrative systems, such as a preschool program run by a community action agency, a kindergarten program in or outside of a school system, and then an elementary school. Relative to other early childhood programs, the CPC program provides greater continuity of service provision. Another unique feature of the program is that each center is under the direction of a noninstructional head teacher and professional staff that serve only families in that center. This provides a lower staff–child ratio and thus a greater degree of intensity of program implementation.

Parent participation in the center is a defining feature of the program, and parents receive a large array of resources. A parent-resource room is located in each center under the direction of a parent-resource teacher. This noninstructional teacher coordinates parent activities both inside and outside the center. Parents are required to participate in the program with their children as well as for their own personal development.

Finally, the curriculum philosophy in all the centers emphasizes activities and experiences leading to the development of basic skills in language arts, reading, and math and to the promotion of good psychological and social development. Although the instructional materials vary across centers, the program as implemented was relatively structured, and all centers shared at least some curriculum materials. The program also offers a similar array of child, family, health, and nutritional services. In total, these program characteristics provide a good test of the effects of a child-development intervention integrating parental involvement and a relatively structured language-based instructional philosophy for up to 6 years of continuous intervention.

This monograph goes well beyond previous studies in the Chicago Longitudinal Study. First, I present findings for several youth outcomes at ages 14 and 15, including reading and math achievement, consumer skills, delinquency infractions, perceived school competence, and incidence of grade retention and special education placement. New findings for family outcomes of participation also are presented, including parent expectations for children's educational attainment, satisfaction with children's education at school, and parent involvement in school activities.

Second, I provide an extensive description of the CPC program, including its history and social context, organization of the curriculum and parent involvement components, implementation history, and a review of findings from previous studies. Because prior studies were reported in page-conscious scientific journals, coverage of these issues has never been complete or satisfactory. Yet these studies are critical to a full understanding of the effects and policy significance of the CPC program.

Finally, I investigate systematically which children benefit most from participation and the pathways through which participation in the program leads to youth development. Based on a confirmatory approach to program evaluation, I explore the extent to which long-term effects may be due to cognitive, family, school, and social psychological factors. These issues have never been fully investigated in prior research, let alone in a single study.

The monograph is organized as follows. In Chapter 1, I review the knowledge base on the effects of early childhood intervention and discuss emerging directions of research. Fifteen reviews of the effects of early childhood intervention are summarized to highlight the state of the field. In Chapter 2, I describe the Child-Parent Center Program, focusing on its history, organization and design, implementation history, and components of operation during 1983 to 1989 (the subject of the monograph). Outcome evaluations of the program leading up to the Chicago Longitudinal Study also are reviewed. I then describe the Chicago Longitudinal Study, including characteristics of the study sample and comparability of intervention and comparison groups. I also summarize previous studies of the program in the Chicago Longitudinal Study. Chapter 3 describes the study sample, research design, and measures used to investigate the effects. The analytic framework also is detailed. Study findings are reported in Chapter 4, including the effects of differential types and amounts of participation on youth and family outcomes, as well as effects for different groups of children. Chapter 5 reports the pathways through which program participation leads to long-term effects. This is key to an approach to evaluation I call *confirmatory program evaluation*. Chapter 6 discusses the significance of findings in the context of previous research and provides policy implications and lessons for the future in addressing the educational needs of children. In order to keep the technical details of the study to a minimum, I provide several appendixes describing the study sample, attrition, and complementary results. I turn first to the state of our knowledge about the effects of early childhood intervention.

Acknowledgments

I gratefully acknowledge funding support for the study from the National Institute of Child Health and Human Development (#R29HD34294), National Institute for the Education of At-Risk Students at the U.S. Department of Education (#R306Fg60055), Smith Richardson Foundation, Foundation for Child Development, and the Institute for Research on Poverty and the Graduate School of the University of Wisconsin–Madison. Given the rarity of extensive longitudinal studies of urban and low-income children, I am tremendously indebted to many individuals and institutions that have supported and encouraged the implementation of this study. The project would have been impossible to conduct without them.

As collaborators and co-investigators on the project, I thank Nikolaus Bezruczko, Judy Temple, and Mavis Hagemann for their innumerable contributions. I have benefited greatly from their sage and collegial advice on a wide range of topics over the years. Along with the late Nancy Mavrogenes, Mavis founded this project in 1985 and got me involved soon thereafter. None of us thought at the time that the project would continue to this day. Mavis and Nancy sparked my interest in child development and taught me many things. The photographs in Chapter 2 are courtesy of Nick, who also developed the Chicago Minimum Proficiency Skills Test. I also thank him for his contributions to the analysis of the test reported in this volume. Judy has made major contributions to the project that are represented in this volume, especially in methodology and data analysis. Finally, I thank all three for their feedback on earlier portions of this manuscript.

The Department of Research and Evaluation at the Board of Education of the Chicago Public Schools, the original sponsor of the project, has provided invaluable assistance in carrying out the project, especially during the early years, and has aided in data collection and management. Among the individuals who deserve special thanks for their help over the years are Geraldine Oberman, Fred Schuster, Carlos Rosa, William Rice, Ron Toles, John Easton, and Joe Hahn. Daisy Garcia has graciously provided assistance in data management and retrieval of student records for over a decade and for which I am very thankful. I also thank the Department of Early Childhood Education at the Board of Education, which has helped to further develop the Chicago Longitudinal Study in the past 3 years, especially the coverage of the Child-Parent Center Program. Velma Thomas, Linda Langhart, Pamela Stevens, Pat Haight, and Geneva Galloway have been most gracious with their time and have significantly deepened my understanding of education.

At the University of Wisconsin, a team of outstanding students and colleagues also has been critical to the success of the project. I'm especially grateful to the dedicated work of Heesuk Chang, who spent countless hours helping with data management and analysis. The special contributions of Wendy Miedel, Emily Mann, Paul Smokowski, Terri Branden, Suh-Ruu Ou, Leigh Rosenberg, and Edmund Hickey in conducting the Chicago Longitudinal Study also deserve note. They have greatly enhanced the success of the project.

I thank Lorraine Sullivan, the program founder, for sharing her insights on the history of the program and for generously making available to me key documents on the development of the program. Debora Gordon and Louise Owens also have been very helpful in this regard.

Thanks also go to Edward Zigler for encouraging me to submit this manuscript for publication. I am honored to have done so. My gratitude also goes out to Larry Schweinhart and Sheldon Rose for many valuable suggestions on earlier versions of this manuscript. The initial draft of this book presented at the 1997 biennial meeting of the Society for Research in Child Development also benefited from Steven Barnett's timely suggestions.

Finally, I thank the teachers, parents, and children who have participated in the Chicago project for their wonderful cooperation and for taking the time to help me and my colleagues better understand education. I also thank the Child-Parent Centers for their helpful cooperation. For all those who work on the project, I hope we are wiser.

The State of Early Intervention

Low-income children and families today face many challenges that place them at risk of educational, social, and economic difficulties. This is especially the case for children growing up in central-city neighborhoods in which institutional and economic resources are limited and poverty is more concentrated. Identifying the effects of interventions to counteract these challenges and to promote child and family development is a national priority and is increasingly the focus of social research. The 1997 White House Conferences on Early Childhood Development and Learning and on Child Care are representative of the high priority given to early intervention. In this volume, *early intervention* is defined as the provision of educational, family, or social services to children and families, beginning in the preschool years (0–5 years), who are at risk of poor developmental outcomes due to poverty and associated factors or environmental conditions.[1] I use the terms *intervention*, *program*, and *services* interchangeably throughout this book.

In recent years, early childhood interventions from birth to the primary grades have received renewed attention as one of the most desirable strategies for promoting optimal development throughout the childhood years (Carnegie Task Force, 1994; Phillips & Cabrera, 1996; Karoly et al., 1998; Zigler, 1994). Federal and state expenditures on early childhood programs are about $10 billion and are likely to continue to rise, given that only one-half of all young children enroll in preschool (National Science and Technology Council, 1997). The years from 3 to 10 have received special attention as crucial "intervention points" for healthy development (Carnegie

Task Force, 1996), thus renewing efforts begun in the early 1960s to promote children's continuity of development (also see Ramey & Ramey, 1998, and Zigler & Styfco, 1993).

In this monograph, I investigate the long-term effects of an established, large-scale, early childhood intervention for economically disadvantaged children—the Chicago Child-Parent Center Program—7 to 10 years after the end of program participation. The centers implement a comprehensive early childhood intervention in the public schools for children aged 3 to 9. Four major questions are addressed.

1. Are different measures of participation in early childhood intervention from ages 3 to 9 associated with youth social competence and family outcomes, including reading and math achievement, consumer skills, perceived school competence, grade retention and special education placement, delinquency, parent involvement in school, parent expectations of children's educational attainment, and parent satisfaction with their children's education?

2. Is participation in extended childhood intervention from preschool to second or third grade associated with better social competence and family outcomes relative to participation that is less extensive or that ceases in preschool or kindergarten?

3. Do particular subgroups of children benefit from program participation more than others? Across program outcomes, for example, do boys benefit more than girls, do children with greater levels of risk benefit more than those with lower levels of risk, and do program effects vary by instructional approach?

4. Which individual, family, and school-related factors and pathways account for the long-term effects of participation in early childhood intervention?

I report new findings from the Chicago Longitudinal Study (CLS), an ongoing investigation of the 1986 kindergarten cohort of graduates from the Child-Parent Centers and other government-funded programs in the Chicago Public Schools. The original study sample included 1,539 low-income children, most of them black, who participated in the Chicago Child-Parent Centers from ages 3 to 9 (0 to 6 years of participation). Based on a prospective matched control group design, several program and comparison groups were analyzed. Extensive process and child outcome data have been collected from children, parents, and school records for children up to age 15.

The study differs from previous investigations of the effects of early intervention in four significant ways. Unlike most previous evaluations, the study emphasizes the long-term effects of a large-scale, federally funded early childhood intervention. The sample size is large, and children participated in a program initiated by a school system. Findings are thus more likely to generalize to Head Start and other established large-scale programs. A second distinguishing characteristic of this study is the investigation of participation in extended childhood intervention in addition to participation in preschool and kindergarten intervention. As discussed below, very few studies have investigated the long-term effects of established large-scale programs. I report findings through middle adolescence. Third, I investigate effects for both youth and family outcomes. Early childhood programs like the Child-Parent Centers are expected to affect both child and family development. Most studies of large-scale programs do not investigate family outcomes of program participation primarily because of a reliance on administrative records. Although such family outcomes are under-investigated, I use them as secondary to child outcomes. Finally, the study probes the pathways through which the effects of program participation are transmitted to adolescent outcomes. Their identification provides important information for causal explanation, for program design and modification, and for the maintenance of program effects.

Assumptions of Early Childhood Intervention

Four assumptions guide early childhood interventions for children at risk. The first and most basic is that environmental conditions of poverty are insufficient to promote healthy development. Without this assumption, there would be little need for intervention. Poverty is associated with a wide range of childhood difficulties, including school underachievement, undernutrition, delinquency, and low educational attainment (Danziger & Danziger, 1993; Duncan & Brooks-Gunn, 1997; Hill & Sandfort, 1995; Sherman, 1994). The social contexts in which children from low-income families grow up are characterized by lack of adequate housing, lack of access to preventive health care, and poor-quality schools and employment opportunities (Comer, 1993; Dryfoos, 1990; McLoyd, 1998; Weissberg & Greenberg, 1998; Wilson, 1987). Exposure to violence and stress also are more likely in areas of concentrated poverty (Comer, 1993; Wilson, 1996). These disadvantages can lead to behavioral patterns that place children at risk of developmental problems.

The second assumption is that early childhood intervention, in the form of educational enrichment, can compensate for disadvantages brought about by poverty and associated circumstances. As a result of child development, family, and health services, children are expected to start school more ready to learn and to narrow the performance gap with their more economically advantaged peers (Ramey & Ramey, 1992; Zigler & Berman, 1983). Such programs are often designed to promote cognitive and language skills, social development, and psychological development (e.g., motivation). This assumption of compensation through educational enrichment was a foundation upon which many programs of the War on Poverty era were developed. Of course, early childhood interventions represent one of many approaches to compensating for environmental risk.

The third assumption of early childhood intervention is that it is more likely to lead to children's later educational success. As a central mechanism of occupational attainment, educational success is strongly linked to the cognitive and social advantages promoted by participation in early intervention (Ramey & Ramey, 1998; Schweinhart & Weikart, 1980; Zigler, 1994). Most program designers and researchers expect that success will occur in the short term and in the long term, and this is typically measured through language and literacy development, motivation to succeed, school achievement, and educational attainment. Other than being of practical importance, most program designers and scholars make no assumptions about the expected magnitude of the effects of intervention exposure. The early belief of some environmentalists that program participation for a relatively brief period of time could produce very large improvements in cognitive and social functioning was overestimated. Indeed, from an ecological perspective, observed effects are expected to vary as a function of child and family attributes, the quality of the program, and the quality of children's postprogram environments (Bronfenbrenner, 1975, 1979; Woodhead, 1988).

The fourth assumption of early childhood intervention, and one tested specifically in this book, is that longer-lasting effects can be achieved by extending intervention into the primary grades. Given that low-income children experience multiple risk factors and that many early childhood interventions are complex packages, a longer duration of implementation should provide greater opportunities for learning and thus enhance competence (National Head Start Association, 1990; Reynolds, 1994; Zigler & Styfco, 1993). Programs that extend into the elementary grades also are expected to promote greater continuity during a key transition point in children's lives—the adjustment to formal schooling (Alexander & Entwisle, 1988; Carnegie Task Force, 1996). Extra educational and family support during this time would be expected to enhance children's scholastic and social functioning. The planners of Head Start envisioned programs that extend into the primary grades (U.S. Department of Health and Human Services, 1994; Zigler & Muenchow, 1992).

Effects of Early Childhood Intervention: What Is Known
Since the founding of Project Head Start in 1965, our understanding of the effects of early childhood intervention for economically disadvantaged children has grown dramatically. From the hundreds of studies of demonstration programs and large-scale programs, there is overwhelming evidence that most programs of relatively good quality have definite and meaningful short-term effects on cognitive ability and school achievement (Guralnick, 1997; Haskins, 1989; McKey et al., 1985; White, 1985). There is increasing evidence that early intervention has mid- to long-term effects on school achievement, retention in grade and special education placement, juvenile delinquency, and high school graduation (Barnett, 1995, Consortium for Longitudinal Studies, 1983; Schweinhart, Barnes, & Weikart, 1993; Zigler, Taussig, & Black, 1992). Of course, these child cognitive and social benefits are in addition to the physical health, nutrition, and family benefits often associated with program participation (Haskins, 1989; Zigler, 1994; Zigler & Styfco, 1993).

The positive benefits of early childhood intervention may be best represented by considering the reviews of research. In a literature search of reviews of the effects of early childhood intervention, 15 published research reviews were identified for the years 1983–97. As shown in Table 1, they integrate the findings of hundreds of program evaluations since the middle 1960s. Two results are apparent. In contrast to a decade ago, there is substantial support for long-term effects of early childhood programs on children's development, especially for school competence outcomes (e.g., reduced grade retention and placement in special education). The vast

5

Table 1. Major Reviews of Early Childhood Intervention Programs, 1983–1997

Author/Year	Source	Type of review	No. studies reviewed
1. Barnett (1995)	*The Future of Children*	narrative	36
2. Barnett (1992)	*Journal of Human Resources*	narrative	22
3. Bryant & Maxwell (1997)	In *The Effectiveness of Early Intervention*	narrative	12
4. Farran (1990)	*Handbook of Early Childhood Intervention*	narrative	32
5. Goldring & Presbrey (1986)	*Education Evaluation and Policy Anaylsis*	selected meta-anaysis	8
6. Haskins (1989)	*American Psychologist*	narrative	16
7. Karweit (1994)	*Preventing Early School Failure* (Ch. 3)	narrative	6
8. Locurto (1991)	*Intelligence*	narrative essay	12
9. Royce et al. (1983)	In *As the Twig Is Bent: Lasting Effects of Preschool Programs*	meta-analysis narrative	11 (9 in meta-analysis)
10. Schweinhart et al. (1993)	In *Significant Benefits: The High/Scope Perry Preschool Study thru Age 27*	narrative	11
11. Seitz (1990)	*Annals of Child Development*	narrative	8
12. White (1985)	*Journal of Special Education*	meta-analysis	300
13. Woodhead (1988)	*American Psychologist*	narrative essay	5
14. Yoshikawa (1995)	*Future of Children*	narrative	40
15. Zigler et al. (1992)	*American Psychologist*	narrative essay	6

Note: Short-term: 1–3 years after program participation; long-term: 4 or more years after program participation. The last two columns reflect approximate calculations based on the individual study's definition of variables relating to short- and long-term effects. Haskins (1989) identifies seven Head Start Synthesis Programs and nine studies outlined in the Consortium. Locurto (1991) does not specify studies within the Consortium. White (1985) does not indentify individual studies. Woodhead (1988) does not specify studies within the Head Start Synthesis. Yoshikawa (1995) is for antisocial and delinquent behavior.

**Effects were either not indicated or not explicitly discussed by the author.

majority of studies reviewed in Table 1 support both short-term and long-term (i.e., beyond 3 years) effects. The most recent reviews (Barnett, 1995; Bryant & Maxwell, 1997; Karoly et al., 1998; Yoshikawa, 1995) confirm

No. large-scale & Head Start programs	No. model programs	Percentage of studies		
		reporting positive short-term effects	reporting positive long-term effects	investigating long-term effects
22	14	85	77	72
15	7	100	57	32
4	8	90	100	42
4	28	62	25	25
2	6	100	75	100
7	9	100	64	88
0	6	N/A	N/A	N/A
2	10	100	100	33
2	6	100	100	64
5	6	100	40	45
0	8	100	100	50
N/A	1	N/A	N/A	N/A
1	4	100	80	100
4	36	55	100	10
0	6	100	100	100

this state of affairs. Moreover, evidence is increasing that participation in programs that provide both center-based child development and family-support services can prevent delinquency and antisocial behavior (Reynolds, Chang, & Temple, 1998; Yoshikawa, 1995; Zigler et al., 1992).

Barnett's (1995) conclusion after reviewing 36 model and large-scale programs is representative of many others: "results indicate that early childhood programs can produce large short-term benefits for children on intelligence quotient (IQ) and sizable long-term effects on school achieve-

Table 2. Most Frequently Cited Early Childhood Programs from Research Reviews, (1983–1997)

Early childhood program	No. of citations
High/Scope Perry Preschool Project	13
Houston Parent Child Development Center	8
Carolina Abecedarian/Project CARE	8
Early Training Project	7
Syracuse Family Development Research Program	7
Consortium on Longitudinal Studies	6
Milwaukee Project	6
Philadelphia Project	6
Yale Child Welfare Research Program	6
Harlem Training Project	5
Experimental Variation of Head Start – Louisville	5
Chicago Child-Parent Centers*	4
New York State Experimental Pre-Kindergarten*	4
Head Start Synthesis Project*	3
Mother-Child Home Program	3
Gutelius Child Health Supervision Study	3
Curriculum Comparison Study	2
Gordon Parent Education Program	2
New Haven Follow Through Program	2
University of Rochester Nurse Home Visiting Program	2
Verbal Interaction Project	2

*Large-scale program.

ment, grade retention, placement in special education, and social adjustment." Such conclusions are at odds with the view outside of the field of early intervention that the effects of early childhood intervention fade out over time. Certainly, based on the total evidence, the effects of early interventions go well beyond cognitive development and school achievement and can be long lasting.

What is the magnitude of program effects reported in the reviews of research? Programs in the Consortium for Longitudinal Studies (1983) were associated with an average improvement of about 8 IQ points at the end of preschool, with about a 4-month gain in school achievement by age 9, and with significantly lower rates of special education placement and students dropping out of high school. In 36 programs reviewed by Barnett (1995), participation in early childhood intervention was associated with a 31% reduction in grade retention, a 50% reduction in special education placement, and a 32% reduction in high school dropout rates (this last result is for only four studies). Interestingly, the pattern of findings was similar for model and large-scale programs. The median reduction in rates of grade retention and special education placement over the comparison group were, respectively, 38% and 50% for model programs and 24% and 50% for large-scale programs. These are educationally meaningful long-term effects and appear to surpass the findings of most other social programs for children and families (Durlak & Wells, 1997; Lipsey & Wilson, 1993).

The second key finding of this research synthesis is that the vast majority of the empirical evidence comes from model demonstration programs rather than large-scale, government-initiated programs like Head Start. As shown in Table 2, 17 of the 21 (81%) most frequently cited programs from the reviews were model demonstration projects rather than large-scale public-service interventions. Moreover, 89% of the total citations (93 of 104) from the research reviews referenced model programs. No typical Head Start programs were frequently reviewed, although the Head Start Synthesis Project (McKey et al., 1985) was cited 3 times, largely in support of short-term effects. The reviews indicated only limited support for the effects of early childhood interventions that extend to the primary grades. The Abecedarian Project, the New Haven Follow Through Program, and the Chicago Child-Parent Center Program were the most frequently cited in this regard. More generally, analyses of Project Follow Through (Rhine, 1981; Doernberger & Zigler, 1993) and those of later interventions (Fuerst & Fuerst, 1993; Jordan, Grallo, Deutsch, & Deutsch, 1985; Reynolds, 1994) suggest that extended programs can be beneficial if they are comprehensive and well-coordinated, and if they alter the learning environment.

Although studies of model programs indicate how effective early interventions *can be*, policymakers and the public are most interested in knowing how effective different large-scale programs *are*. In a time of intensive fiscal accountability at all levels of government, research on the effects of large-scale programs is needed more than ever. This need was reinforced in a recent report on Head Start by the U.S. General Accounting Office (1997). In 1996, for example, Head Start expended only one third of 1% of its federal budget on research and evaluation activities. Other programs for children and youth provide the same low level of investment in research and evaluation (National Science and Technology Council, 1997).

Overall, these and related findings have served to place early childhood interventions for low-income families as a top funding priority at the state and national levels. Nevertheless, there are ongoing debates concerning the optimal program content, timing and duration, differential effectiveness of model and large-scale programs, and the pathways through which long-term effects are achieved. Certainly, greater investments in research on these and other issues are needed as well.

What Is Not Yet Known about the Effects of Early Intervention

As much as these studies demonstrate that a wide variety of programs can and are effective, it also is the case that several important questions have not been fully examined. These reviews as well as my own identify several questions that need to be further addressed (see also Guralnick, 1997; Karoly et al., 1998; Phillips & Cabrera, 1996; Reynolds, Mann, Miedel, & Smokowski, 1997).

LONG-TERM EFFECTS OF LARGE-SCALE PROGRAMS

The amount and quality of existing evidence concerning the long-term effects of large-scale government-funded programs do not adequately inform public policy. As repeated often but forgotten frequently, most of the evidence on long-term effects into high school comes from small-scale model programs that differ in significant ways from large-scale established programs like Head Start (Crum, 1993; Haskins, 1989; White, 1985; Woodhead, 1988; Zigler & Styfco, 1993). Compared to model programs, participants in large-scale programs are often more disadvantaged and experience a lower degree of intensity. Yet large-scale programs tend to be more comprehensive and have more extensive implementation histories. Of the 21 large-scale public programs reviewed by Barnett (1995), only 7 presented evidence through the elementary grades, and there were only 3 follow-ups into high school or beyond. In contrast, 8 of 15 studies of model programs reported follow-up analyses in grade 8 or beyond, and 5 of these went beyond high school. Methodological limitations exist in almost all studies, but they are particularly acute for large-scale programs. Certainly, programs may be heterogeneous in design and effectiveness.

A related issue is the scope of outcomes tested. Yoshikawa (1995) reported only 11 studies that investigated program effects on antisocial and delinquency behavior. Of the 4 programs showing reduced delinquency as a result of program participation, all provided both early education and family services mainly through home visitation. No evidence of delinquency effects has been reported for large-scale, government-initiated programs. Other social psychological outcomes (i.e., attitudes, competence perceptions) also have not been subjected to adequate or extensive longitudinal tests.

Family outcomes of program participation also have not been adequately tested in longitudinal studies. Early childhood interventions are designed, in part, to affect family development, and there is some empirical evidence that program participation affects later family socialization practices (Lazar, Darlington, Murray, & Snipper, 1982; Seitz, 1990). In the Consortium for Longitudinal Studies (Consortium, 1983; Lazar et al., 1982), parents of program participants reported greater satisfaction with children's school success than the parents of the no-preschool comparison group.

Again, most of this evidence comes from model programs. Notably, model and large-scale programs differ in several ways. Model programs are usually more expensive to operate than large-scale programs, have larger and better trained staffs, and are rarely implemented in inner-city communities. Studies of model programs often have more rigorous and comprehensive evaluations than studies of large-scale programs, but the small sample sizes often used in studies of model programs limit statistical power and generalizability. For example, the median sample size used in the studies of model programs is about one-quarter (140) of that used in studies of large-scale programs (660) (Barnett, 1995). This is a relatively small sample size when considering attrition rates of up to 50% in some studies. Likewise, studies of large-scale programs typically rely on retrospective designs and suffer from problems regarding noncomparability of groups, attrition, and limited postprogram and child outcome data (Barnett, 1992, 1995; Haskins, 1989). Such problems can make findings difficult to interpret.

OPTIMAL DURATION AND TIMING OF INTERVENTION EXPOSURE

A second major substantive issue is that research has not determined the optimal timing and duration of intervention exposure. Although there is some support for the principle that the earlier intervention occurs, the more likely it is to be effective (Ramey & Ramey, 1992, 1998; Wachs & Gruen, 1982), individual studies have rarely investigated this question in sufficient depth. Studies also have not investigated the relationship between length of intervention and child outcomes. It is now widely believed that a 1- or 2-year preschool program cannot immunize children from school failure and other associated problems (National Head Start Association, 1990; Zigler & Styfco, 1993). Yet the optimal length of intervention is not evident. Long-lasting and better coordinated programs seem particularly important within the context of the inner city, given the often extreme social and educational problems found there. In explaining why the cognitive effects of early interventions like Head Start fade with the passage of time, Wilson (1996) observed:

> [C]hildren of the inner-city ghetto have to contend with public schools plagued by unimaginative curricula, overcrowded classrooms, inadequate plant and facilities, and only a small proportion of teachers who have confidence in their students and expect them to learn. Inner-city ghetto children also grow up in neighborhoods with devastating rates of joblessness, which trigger a whole series of other problems that are not conducive to healthy child development or intellectual growth. Included among these are broken families, antisocial behavior, social networks that do not extend beyond the confines of the ghetto environment, and a lack of informal social control over the behavior and activities of children and adults in the neighborhood. (pp. xv-xvi)

Certainly, better and more extensive programs may help. Of particular interest in recent years are the effects of interventions that extend into the primary grades. In other words, do these programs yield more long-lasting effects than programs that stop in preschool or kindergarten? Most developmental theories would indicate that additional environmental support during the transition from preschool to kindergarten and the primary grades can be important. Studies of Project Follow Through (Meyer, 1984; Seitz, Apfel, Rosenbaum, & Zigler, 1983; Stallings, 1975) and other programs (Jordan et al., 1985; Madden, Slavin, Karweit, Dolan, & Wasik,

1993; Reynolds, 1994) suggest that school-age programs can be an effective add-on to earlier intervention rather than a replacement for earlier intervention if they provide relatively structured educational experiences and significantly alter the school environment (see also Entwisle, 1995). Thus, they may help prevent the fading cognitive effects of early intervention found in the literature.

Unfortunately, most studies confound the effects of timing and duration of intervention (e.g., Jordan et al., 1985; Seitz et al., 1983; Fuerst & Fuerst, 1993; Madden et al., 1993). One exception is the Abecedarian Project (Campbell & Ramey, 1994, 1995), which traced 93 children who participated to varying degrees in a model intervention in Chapel Hill, North Carolina, from birth to age 8. Investigators found that participation in the 5-year preschool program was positively associated with higher cognitive ability and school achievement, as well as lower rates of grade retention and special education placement up to age 15. The 3-year school-age program was found to have limited independent effect and was consistently associated just with reading achievement, but only marginally at age 15. In addition to its being a small-scale model program, the Abecedarian Project differs from most early childhood programs in that the preschool intervention began at 3 months of age, much like an infant day care. The school-age program was not as comprehensive as the preschool program. Moreover, children participated for either 0, 5, or 8 years, so the marginal effect of an additional year could not be determined.

Importantly, it is unclear how generalizable are the findings of the Abecedarian Project and those of other studies in addressing whether interventions of longer duration should have high funding priority in budget-constrained federal, state, or local governments. By definition, they provide additional educational resources to children that need them, thereby helping to maintain learning gains from earlier intervention (Zigler & Styfco, 1993; National Head Start Association, 1990). To the extent that such innovations enhance the transition to school and the quality of the postkindergarten learning environment, they would be expected to benefit children (Carnegie Task Force, 1996; Entwisle, 1995).

WHO BENEFITS MOST FROM INTERVENTION?

Because of the compensatory nature of early interventions, it is often believed that children and families at the greatest level of risk should benefit most from participation relative to those at lesser risk. Relatively few studies have systematically investigated interactions of program by child or family characteristics within participant populations. For the most part, there is little support for differential program effects across child and family characteristics (Lazar et al., 1982). Some studies of model programs report that program girls have higher achievement test scores than program boys but not by wide margins (Barnett, 1995). Olds's (1988) evaluation of a home-visiting program indicated that high-risk infants benefited from the program more than participants at lower risk. In the Brookline Early Childhood Program, Pierson (1988) found that children of college graduates benefited more than children of noncollege graduates. Reynolds (1998a) reported that rates of scholastic and social success at age 12 among program participants did not vary as a function of number of socioeconomic risk factors experienced.

While some studies have investigated the differential effects of program curricula on child and family outcomes, findings have been generally mixed, and the evidence has been primarily limited to children in poverty. Some studies provide support for child-centered or child-initiated curriculum approaches (Marcon, in press; Schweinhart & Weikart, 1997; Stipek, Daniels, Galluzzo, & Milburn, 1992). Others have failed to detect differential effects of program curricula (Lazar et al., 1982) and have emphasized that many instructional approaches can be successful for children provided the approaches are well implemented. Still other studies have reported that programs that are teacher directed or provide direct instruction lead to greater effects on academic achievement in the short term (Becker & Gersten, 1982; Meyer, 1984; Miller & Bizzell, 1983). Nevertheless, hardly any studies have examined whether program effects vary or are moderated by other program attributes (e.g., parent involvement) or by community and socioeconomic context (Barnett, 1995; Guralnick, 1997).

PATHWAYS OF PROGRAM EFFECTIVENESS

A final question that has not been addressed adequately regards the factors that mediate (account for) long-term effects of early intervention. Once a direct relationship is established between program participation and long-term outcome (main effect), the pathways that produce this effect must be identified (Ramey & Ramey, 1998; Reynolds, Mavrogenes, Bezruczko, & Hagemann, 1996; Wachs & Gruen, 1982). Woodhead (1988), for example, argued for the study of home, school, and related factors in the "search for processes that might account for transmission of long-term effects" (p. 447). A major assumption of studies of pathways of effectiveness is that long-term effects depend on the quality of the postprogram environment and the later experiences of participating children and families (Bronfenbrenner, 1979; Bronfenbrenner & Morris, 1998; Ramey & Ramey, 1992, 1998).

At least three hypotheses have been postulated as explanations of long-term effects. In the cognitive advantage hypothesis, the immediate positive effect of program participation on cognitive development at school entry initiates a positive cycle of scholastic development and commitment that culminates in improved developmental outcomes in adolescence and beyond (Berrueta-Clement, Schweinhart, Barnett, Epstein, & Weikart, 1984; Lazar et al., 1982; Reynolds, Mavrogenes, et al., 1996). In the family support hypothesis, the long-term effects of intervention occur to the extent that family functioning has been improved. Because early intervention programs often involve parents, it is believed that family processes must be impacted to produce long-term effects (Bronfenbrenner, 1975; Seitz, 1990). A third hypothesis is the school-support hypothesis, which indicates that the effects of early intervention will be maintained to the extent that the postprogram schools that children attend are of sufficient quality to meet their scholastic and developmental needs. This hypothesis has never been directly tested, but some studies provide indirect evidence (Berrueta-Clement et al., 1984; Carter, 1984; Lee & Loeb, 1995). Currie and Thomas (1998) provide a more recent treatment.

Research on the pathways of intervention effectiveness has significant implications for research and practice. It adds to basic theoretical knowledge of how early interventions exert their effects over time in conjunction with other influences. Also, the pathways that are identified can be used to help design and modify intervention programs for children and families. For example, all three hypotheses direct attention to a different ordering of intervention components. Cognitive and language stimulation would be emphasized under the cognitive advantage hypothesis, whereas family involvement and environmental maintenance, respectively, would be emphasized in the family support and school support hypotheses. Finally, investigation of the pathways of intervention effects helps identify factors that can be used to maintain and enhance the effects of earlier interventions. The present study is the first to investigate these and other hypotheses systematically.

A Confirmatory Approach to Evaluating Long-Term Effects

My approach to investigating the effects of intervention programs is called *confirmatory program evaluation*. Confirmatory program evaluation is a theory-driven methodology (Reynolds, 1998b). In contrast to method-driven approaches, in which causal inference derives from the research design, and model-driven approaches, in which causal inference is facilitated through statistical adjustment, theory-driven approaches emphasize the explication and testing of a priori program theories in determining the effects of programs. Confirmatory program evaluation is an impact assessment that examines the pattern of empirical findings against several causal criteria, including (a) temporality, (b) size, (c) gradient (dosage/response), (d) specificity, (e) consistency, and (f) coherence of relations. Special emphasis is given to testing causal mechanisms and pathways that produce program effectiveness over time.

Three sequential questions are addressed in this approach:

1. Do groups differ significantly on the outcome variables?
2. Do estimated program effects differ by subject characteristics and by outcome domain?
3. What are the developmental mechanisms or pathways that explain group differences, and are they consistent with the program theory?

To the extent that these questions are satisfactorily addressed, causal inferences are strengthened for both experimental and quasi-experimental approaches. Understandably, confirmatory program evaluations are most appropriate in longitudinal studies of program impact.

Conceptual Model for the Present Study

Figure 1 shows the key constructs and pathways through which early childhood intervention is hypothesized to affect social competence in adolescence. Social competence is the ascribed goal of early childhood interventions (National Head Start Association, 1990; Zigler & Berman, 1983) and in this study includes the indicators of school achievement, consumer skills, perceived school competence, incidence of grade retention and special education placement, and delinquency infractions. The family social-

Fig. 1. Pathways Model of Program Effectiveness

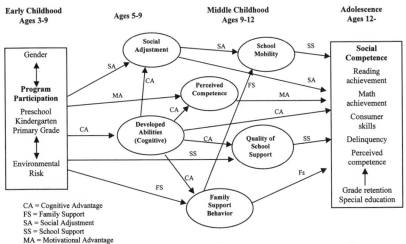

izaton outcomes of parent expectations for children's educational attainment, parent satisfaction with children's education, and parent participation in school were included as secondary program outcomes. The major intervening variables that were expected to transmit the effects of early intervention were (a) developed cognitive abilities in early childhood, (b) classroom social adjustment (SA), (c) family support behavior (FS), (d) children's motivation to succeed, or motivational advantage (MA), via perceived school competence, and (e) quality of school support (SS) as measured by school-level achievement and children's frequency of school mobility. Each pathway displayed denotes a particular hypothesis in support of the transmission of effects to adolescent outcomes.

Participation in early childhood intervention was expected to directly influence developed abilities, classroom adjustment, family support behavior, and motivation during the transition to formal schooling. Program participation may be during preschool, kindergarten, or the primary grades. Sex of child and risk status (the number of risk factors experienced) also may affect the process of early school adjustment and may vary with program participation. Developed abilities in early childhood (at school entry or at the end of the primary grades) and classroom adjustment may be further associated with family support behavior and children's perceived competence at the end of early childhood. These factors then may affect the quality of school support factors that children experience and the number of school moves.

The conceptual model for the present study is informed by ecological systems theory and resilience theory. Ecological systems theory (Bronfenbrenner, 1979, 1989) specifies that outcomes of development are substantially affected by the social contexts, both proximal and distal, in which children are embedded. The magnitude of program effects increases or is sustained as the relationships between the individual, family, and institutional systems are enhanced (i.e., parent-child, child-teacher, parent-teacher). From this perspective, the persistence of effects of participation in early childhood intervention may depend on the quality and continuity of the postprogram learning environment, primarily the family and school-related interactions that occur in the primary microsystems in early development (i.e., home and school). In Bronfenbrenner's more recent bioecological model (Bronfenbrenner & Morris, 1998), proximal processes of development are emphasized, particularly those activities that "occur on a regular basis over extended periods of time" (p. 698). This supports the role of relatively intense and extensive interventions for children at risk.

In resilience theory (Masten & Garmezy, 1985; Rutter, 1987), outcomes of development are a function of individual responses to risk factors, which are negatively associated with developmental functioning, and protective factors, which are positively associated with functioning and which interact with risk status. A primary focus of resilience theory is the identification of protective mechanisms or pathways that lead individuals to overcome adversity and exhibit successful adjustment. Applied to intervention research, protective mechanisms are conceptualized as intervening behaviors and experiences that mediate the effects of program participation on ultimate program outcomes. Thus, they are the active ingredients that promote long-term beneficial effects. The five sets of pathways in Figure 1 represent these ingredients.

Both ecological systems theory and resilience theory predict individual variation in response to risk experiences and to participation in early intervention. In ecological theory, program effects are expected to vary by characteristics of the person, by processes occurring within the immediate environment, by the social context, and over time. In resilience theory, person attributes are emphasized. Consequently, I investigated the dif-

18

ferential effects of program participation by the level of environmental risk experienced growing up.

Measures of family and school contexts are expected to be primary mediators of the effects of early intervention. Program outcomes include the penultimate experiences of grade retention and special education placement, which lead to (a) school achievement in reading and math, (b) consumer skills, and (c) social behavior as measured through school-reported delinquency infractions. As displayed in Figure 1, the pathways through which program participation was expected to influence adolescent development are defined by five hypotheses.

The *cognitive advantage hypothesis* indicates that the long-term effects of intervention are initiated by improvements in children's developed abilities in early childhood. The cognitive and language stimulation experienced in center-based education may directly affect children's cognitive functioning as well as their social and motivational behavior. A major focus of the activity-based educational component is the development of literacy skills through group reading and writing activities, play, and frequent field trips in the community to acquire knowledge and understanding of the world. These systematic educational experiences produce cognitive advantages that initiate a positive cycle of performance culminating in more successful adolescent adjustment. The cognitive advantage hypothesis is the most frequent explanation for the long-term effects of early intervention (Schweinhart & Weikart, 1980; Schweinhart et al., 1993; Consortium for Longitudinal Studies, 1983; Reynolds, Mavrogenes, et al., 1996). In this study, cognitive developed abilities are measured by cognitive readiness at school entry (age 5) and by school achievement test scores (age 9), both on the Iowa Tests of Basic Skills.

The *family support hypothesis* indicates that long-term effects of early intervention will occur to the extent that program participation enhances the capacities of parents to support children's learning and development. Parenting behavior may include those activities with or on behalf of children such as home support for learning or school support for learning through participation in school-related activities. A central goal of early childhood interventions is to promote family development, often through the provision of family education activities. The family support hypothesis was offered by Bronfenbrenner (1975) as an explanation for the observed dissipating cognitive effects of participation in Head Start. He noted, for example, that family functioning and parent-child relations must be impacted in order for long-term effects on child development to occur. The family-support hypothesis has been the central theory of family-based programs and educational interventions since the 1960s and 1970s (Seitz, 1990). Indeed, family involvement in children's early education was a linchpin of Project Head Start. In this study, the primary measure of family support is parent participation in school activities during elementary school.

In the *motivational advantage hypothesis*, the long-term effects of program participation are due to changes in children's motivational development rather than in their cognitive or language development per se. Motivation is broadly defined to include self-system attributes such as perceived competence, self-concept of ability, self-efficacy, task persistence, and effort. This hypothesis derives, in part, from Zigler and Butterfield's (1968) and Zigler, Abelson, Trickett, and Seitz's (1982) findings that changes in intelligence test scores among low-income children may have a substantial motivational component. Indeed, motivational development was one of the original goals of the Head Start program (Zigler & Muenchow, 1992). In one of the few studies of this hypothesis, Schweinhart et al. (1993) found that teacher-rated motivation contributed to the transmission of preschool effects only as a result of enhanced cognitive development. The measure of motivation used in this study is children's perceived school competence at age 9.

The *social adjustment hypothesis* indicates that improved social development is the major reason why participation in early intervention leads to long-term program effectiveness. Rather than directly changing children's cognitive status or motivation, participation may enhance children's internalization of social rules and norms as well as peer relations necessary for school adjustment and negotiating social situations. As a result of participation in the organized activities of early educational intervention, children are expected to learn self-regulating skills such as following directions, working with others, and inhibition of behavior. This hypothesis on the effects of early intervention has rarely, if ever, been directly tested. Social adjustment is measured through teacher ratings of classroom adjustment at age 9.

Finally, in the *school support hypothesis* the effects of program participation would persist to the extent that children attend schools of sufficient quality to maintain or enhance their achievement patterns. This hypothesis is the school-based version of the family support hypothesis. It has never been directly tested as an explanation of long-term effects, although there is evidence that postprogram enrollment in poor-quality schools may reduce the persistence of learning gains (Currie & Thomas, 1998; Lee & Loeb, 1995), and that school mobility and the consequent disruptions it causes also may affect this process (Reynolds, 1989, 1991, 1992a). In the current study, I measure school support as the number of years children attend elementary schools in which a relatively large proportion of students perform at or above national norms in achievement. As a secondary indicator, I also measure the number of different schools in which children enroll after the end of the program participation.

Note that while these hypotheses are independently associated with positive developmental outcomes, they also must be significantly and simultaneously associated with program participation, and must be independent of each other, to be valid mediators of the long-term effects of program participation. Of course, the hypotheses could work in combination. For example, program participation may affect adolescent social competence through early developed abilities and family support experiences or through a combination of early developed abilities, family support, and school support factors. These and other combinations are considered. However, the pathways that initiate the mediated effect (i.e., the effect is directly predicted by program participation) were emphasized. To the extent that long-term effects of program exposure (if detected) can be explained by these hypotheses, the inference that the program caused these changes is strengthened.

In summary, the long-term effects of participation in early childhood intervention are expected to depend, in large part, on five hypotheses of causal mediation involving cognitive, family, motivational, school, and social-psychological factors. This conceptual model provides a foundation for explaining group differences and is central to the confirmatory approach to evaluating the effects of the Child-Parent Center Program.

The Child–Parent Center Program and Stud

Unity

I dreamed I stood in a studio
And watched two sculptors there;
The clay they used was a young child's mind
And they fashioned it with care.
One was a teacher; the tools he used
Were books, music and art;
One was a parent, who worked with a guiding hand
And a gentle loving heart.
Day after day the teacher toiled,
With touch that was deft and sure,
While the parent labored by his side
And polished and smoothed it o'er.
And when at last the task was done,
They were proud of the work they had wrought
For the things they had moulded into the child
Could neither be sold nor bought.
And each agreed they would have failed
If he had worked alone.
For behind the teacher stood the school
And behind the parent, the home.

Cleo Victoria Swarat

Program Overview

The Child-Parent Center (CPC) Program is a center-based early intervention that provides comprehensive educational and family support services to economically disadvantaged children and their parents from preschool to early elementary school.[1] The CPC program was established in 1967 through funding from the landmark Elementary and Secondary Education Act of 1965 (ESEA). Title I of the act provided grants to local public school districts serving high concentrations of low-income children for a broad set of programs and projects and for personnel and instructional materials, including, among others, preschool training, enrichment programs for the elementary grades, training for teachers, supplemental health and food services, programmed instruction, additional teaching personnel to reduce class size, summer school, and remedial programs in reading and math. The act also emphasized the development of innovative programs that would encourage local school districts to "employ imaginative thinking and new approaches to meet the educational needs of poor children" (U.S. Senate, 1967, p. 1455). Establishment of the CPC program was based on this latter concept through implementation of comprehensive preschool education with a major emphasis on parent involvement.

Initially implemented in 4 sites and later expanded to 25, the CPC program was designed to serve families in high-poverty neighborhoods that were *not* being served by Head Start or other early childhood programs. The program has several distinctions. It is the second oldest (after Head Start) federally funded early childhood program in the United States and is the oldest extended early childhood program. In 1976, it was selected as an exemplary education program by the Joint Dissemination Review Panel of the U.S. Office of Education. In 1998, it received a similar honor as part of the Title I Distinguished Schools National Recognition Program.[2] The CPC program is unrelated to the Parent-Child Development Centers, a family-support program for children under the age of 3 years funded through the U.S. Department of Health and Human Services.

Currently, the CPC program operates in 24 centers throughout the Chicago public schools; 19 provide services in preschool (ages 3 or 4) and kindergarten, 5 provide services in preschool but not kindergarten, and 13 centers implemented the primary-grade program in 1997–98.[3] The preschool and kindergarten components of the program are funded through Title I of the Improving America's School Act (replacing ESEA). Since

1977, the primary-grade portion of the program (also called the Adaption/ Expansion program) has been funded by Chapter I through the State of Illinois. Eighteen centers are in separate buildings proximate to the elementary school, and 6 are in wings of the parent elementary school.

The major rationale of the program is that the foundation for school success is facilitated by the presence of a stable and enriched learning environment during the entire early childhood period (ages 3 to 9) and when parents are active participants in their children's education. Four program features are emphasized: early intervention, parent involvement, a structured language/basic skills learning approach, and program continuity between the preschool and early school-age years. The program theory is that children's readiness for school entry and beyond can be enriched through systematic language-learning activities and opportunities for family support experiences through direct parent involvement in the centers. This theory is embodied in the following goal statement: "The Child-Parent Education Centers are designed to reach the child and parent early, develop language skills and self-confidence, and to demonstrate that these children, if given a chance, can meet successfully all the demands of today's technological, urban society" (quoted in Naisbitt, 1968, p. A).

There are three conditions of eligibility. First, children must reside in school neighborhoods that receive federal Title I funds. Enrollment is reserved for children and families in most educational need as determined by a screening interview with center staff. Second, children must not be enrolled in another preschool program (e.g., Head Start). Third, parents must agree to participate in the program at least one-half day per week, though many parents do not often participate to this extent. To enroll children who are most in need and to reduce self-selection, the centers conduct extensive outreach activities such as distributing program descriptions in the community, visiting families door-to-door, and advertising locally. Several previous analyses have confirmed the substantial educational needs of program children and their parents (Chicago Public Schools, 1974, 1985, 1987; Schuster & Jennings, 1982).

Program History

The development of the Chicago Child-Parent Centers can be traced to the middle of 1966 when Benjamin Willis, general superintendent of the Chicago Public Schools (CPS), asked Lorraine M. Sullivan, superintendent of CPS District 8 and the program founder, to report on ways to improve student attendance and achievement in her district. District 8 was located in the center of the West Garfield Park community area (a term used in Chicago to designate a geographical area larger than a neighborhood) and had one of the highest concentrations of poverty in the city. It bordered North Lawndale, another high-poverty area. The residential population in West Garfield Park (and in North Lawndale and East Garfield Park) was nearly 100% minority; 30% of the residents had incomes below the federal poverty level. The district schools were also among the most overcrowded. During the preparation of the report, a door-to-door survey of families was conducted concerning attitudes toward education and the district schools.

In the report to the general superintendent, Sullivan recommended that the district address attendance and academic problems of students by focusing on the early childhood years when children and parents are most receptive to change. The major recommendations emphasized five elements: (a) parent involvement in the early years of school, (b) instructional approaches tailored to children's learning styles, (c) instruction designed to develop children's speaking and listening skills, (d) small class sizes to provide for individual attention, and (e) attention to health and nutritional services (Sullivan, 1970, 1971). These principles were implemented through the opening in May 1967 of four Child-Parent Education Centers (or Child-Parent Centers). Three were in District 8 and one site was just over the border in District 10 (serving North Lawndale) because of a lack of available land in District 8. Due to the lack of space in existing schools, these centers began as clusters of mobile units in close proximity to elementary schools. The units were composed of six rooms: four classrooms, a parent room, and an administrative office. Each center had an enrollment of 120 and offered a half-day (2.5 hours) preschool and kindergarten program for 40 weeks plus an 8-week summer program. In 1960 and 1970, these community areas were among the lowest in family income in the city. In addition, the area was described as having the "most serious educational needs in Chicago: last year, only 8% of the sixth grade students in District 8 were reading at or above grade level" (Naisbitt, 1968, p. A).

In early 1967, Sullivan hired four principals to run the new centers— Wayne Hoffman, Helen Brennan, Debora Gordon, and John McGovern.[4] They were given wide flexibility to hire their own staff and to develop their own instructional approaches. Among the curricula and materials the principals investigated were the High/Scope Perry Preschool Program, the Bereiter-Engleman Program, the Bank Street Program, the Gotkin Language Lotto, and several home-based parenting programs.

Originally, the centers were called clusters and were officially named within the next 2 years as Nathaniel Cole, Charles Dickens, Lorraine Hansberry, and Milton Olive Child-Parent Education Centers. Because the centers were located in the lowest income areas of the city, Title I funding was granted from the beginning after approval by the Chicago Board of Education. Although not in the original plan, extended intervention services were available in first grade beginning in the fall of 1968 for June 1968 kindergarten graduates, and these services were extended to third graders over the next several years. The Olive Center provided services up to the sixth grade for several years (see Fuerst & Fuerst, 1993).

Although the genesis of the CPC program was in response to the identified needs of children and families in District 8, the social conditions of the middle 1960s were ripe for innovation in early childhood education. Project Head Start had begun about a year earlier as the first federally funded preschool program for low-income children. Scientific support also was growing for the primacy of early experience (Bloom, 1964) and for the large effects that modifications in the social environment could have in shaping child development (Hunt, 1961). Other community action programs were being developed in response to the urgent social problems of poverty, school failure, and crime, which were disproportionately affecting inner-city minority children. Beginning in 1966, for example, the Model Cities Program began implementation in many large cities, including the North Lawndale, Woodlawn, Grand Boulevard, and Uptown neighborhoods of Chicago (Janowitz, 1967; Campbell, Marx, & Nystrand, 1969). Although these efforts provided financial resources to coordinate and improve housing and general economic conditions at the community level, these innovations, like those of the Child-Parent Education Centers, were also designed to empower families who were distrustful and alienated from social and educational institutions.

Sullivan (1971) described the philosophy of the Child-Parent Centers as a way to enhance the family-school relationship: "In a success-oriented environment in which young children can see themselves as important, they are 'turned on' for learning. Attitudes toward themselves and others,

26

interest in learning, increased activity, conversation, and enthusiasm are all evidences of the change. Parents are increasingly aware of the role of the home in preparing children for school and have renewed hope that education will develop the full potential of their children" (p. 70). To accomplish this, the centers offered a structured program of parent involvement and language enrichment. Although physical health and psychological development were important goals of the program, promoting the basic skills of written and spoken language as well as numeracy became the primary focus over time. As noted by Naisbitt (1968), "as the program has evolved, the objectives have become more specific in the direction of providing a highly structured, instruction oriented educational program for preschool children, with maximum emphasis on language and reading skills" (p. 1).[5]

PROGRAM EXPANSION

Largely due to the initial success of children in the original sites, program expansion began in 1969. The four original CPC sites were located in the West Garfield Park, East Garfield Park, and North Lawndale neighborhoods on the west side of the city. Two more were added in 1969: Miller CPC in East Garfield Park and Wheatley CPC in Riverdale. Together, these six sites are considered the original Child-Parent Centers. Five centers were added in 1970, seven in 1974, and six centers in 1975. The 25th and last CPC was founded in 1978. One center closed in 1987 (Oakenwald North), so there are currently 24 program sites.

From its inception until the spring of 1977, the CPC "activity" was administered completely in the centers for the duration of children's enrollment (up to 6 years). All funding was through ESEA Title I. In the fall of 1977, the funding and administrative structure of the program was divided. The primary-grade component (expansion program) was funded through Chapter I of the State of Illinois and was implemented in the affiliated elementary school serving the centers. The preschool and kindergarten components of the program continued to be implemented in the CPC sites. This is the current program configuration. Interestingly, the primary-grade component of the program was put in place in order to provide extra support to the original kindergarten graduates during their transition to first grade in 1968.

The extended early childhood program was most consistent with the vision of success in early intervention described by the Planning Committee

Fig. 2. Community Areas of the Child–Parent Centers

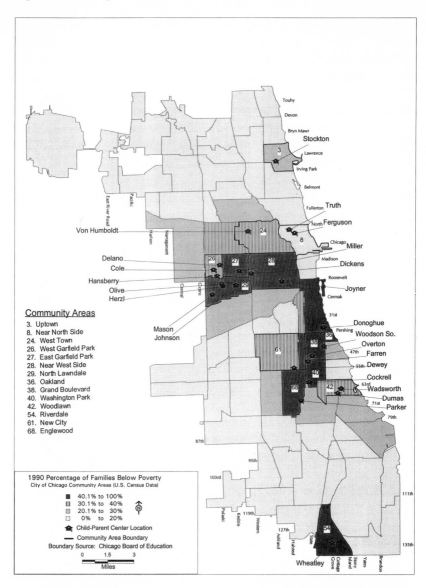

Stockton
3
Lawrence
Irving Park
Belmont

Touhy
Devon
Bryn Mawr

Fullerton Truth
North Ferguson
8
Chicago Miller
Madison Dickens
Roosevelt
Joyner
Cermak

Von Humboldt

Delano
Cole
Hansberry
Olive
Herzl

Mason
Johnson

31st

Donoghue
Pershing Woodson So.
Overton
47th Farren
55th Dewey
Cockrell
63rd Wadsworth
Dumas
71st Parker
79th

36
38
61
40
68
42
54

Community Areas

3. Uptown
8. Near North Side
24. West Town
26. West Garfield Park
27. East Garfield Park
28. Near West Side
29. North Lawndale
36. Oakland
38. Grand Boulevard
40. Washington Park
42. Woodlawn
54. Riverdale
61. New City
68. Englewood

24
26 27 28
29

87th

95th

103rd

111th

119th

127th

135th

Wheatley

1990 Percentage of Families Below Poverty
City of Chicago Community Areas (U.S. Census Data)

■ 40.1% to 100%
▥ 30.1% to 40%
▦ 20.1% to 30%
☐ 0%   to 20%
🏠 Child–Parent Center Location
── Community Area Boundary
Boundary Source: Chicago Board of Education

0   1.5   3
Miles

for Head Start in February 1965: "It is clear that successful programs of this type must be comprehensive, involving activities generally associated with the fields of health, social services and education. Similarly, it is clear that the program must focus on the problems of child and parent and that these activities need to be carefully integrated with programs for the school years" (quoted in Richmond, 1997, p. 122). These elements remain the touchstone goal for programs today. Thus, the CPC program was the earliest prototype of this concept of comprehensive and integrated early childhood intervention.

NEIGHBORHOOD CONTEXT

From the beginning, the Child-Parent Centers have served families from the most economically and educationally disadvantaged neighborhoods in Chicago. The surroundings were described at the time of the inception of the centers as including "dilapidated housing, boarded up buildings and vacant land, mixed industrial, retail, and residential use. The public schools are very large, some new and others very old and out-dated. Most are crowded, with playgrounds covered by mobile units. Broken windows are a common sight" (quoted in Naisbitt, 1968, p. 2).

Figure 2 shows the community areas in which the Child-Parent Centers are located. In 1990, 22 of the 24 centers were scattered through the 20 poorest neighborhoods (Chicago Department of Public Health, 1994). The two other centers (Ferguson and Truth) are adjacent to the Cabrini Green public housing project and are similarly disadvantaged. Five of the six poorest neighborhoods have at least one Child-Parent Center. Herzl, Stockton, Truth, Woodson South, and Cole Centers do not currently operate kindergartens (the first four are not included in findings reported in this book).

Table 3 reports the U.S. census poverty rates for the community areas in which the CPCs are located. From 1970 (near the beginning of the program) to 1990, the proportion of residents with family incomes below the federal poverty level was two to three times higher in CPC community areas than in areas without a CPC. The individual-level poverty rate for CPC community areas grew from 25.9% in 1970 to 40.5% in 1990, a 56% increase (Chicago Department of Public Health, 1994; Chicago Fact Book Consortium, 1995). Although the poverty rates for the non-CPC community areas were substantially below those of the CPC community areas, they also increased from 7.7% in 1970 to 16.9% in 1990, a 119% change. Of course, this large increase is partly due to the relatively low baseline rate in 1970.

A similar pattern of disadvantage occurred for unemployment. The un-

Table 3. Poverty Rates for Community Areas Serving the Child-Parent Centers

Area	No. of areas	No. of residents (1970)	No. of residents (1990)	% in poverty 1970	% in poverty 1980	% in poverty 1990	% change 1970–1990
Community areas with Child-Parent Centers	14	907,858	559,475	26	39	41	56
East Garfield Park		52,185	24,030	32	40	46	44
Englewood		89,713	48,434	24	36	40	67
Grand Boulevard		80,150	35,897	37	51	64	73
Near North Side		70,269	62,842	22	26	18	-18
Near West Side		78,703	46,197	35	49	52	49
New City		60,817	53,226	10	22	32	220
North Lawndale		94,772	47,296	30	40	44	47
Oakland		18,291	8,197	44	61	70	59
Riverdale		15,018	10,821	38	45	63	66
Uptown		74,838	63,839	16	23	28	75
Washington Park		46,024	19,425	28	43	57	104
West Garield Park		48,464	24,095	25	37	36	44
West Town		124,800	87,703	19	27	31	63
Woodlawn		53,814	27,473	28	32	32	14
Other community areas	63	2,459,099	2,224,251	8	15	17	119
Total	77	3,366,957	2,783,726	13	20	22	72

Note: 1980 is the baseline year for children in the CLS cohort. Community areas include an average of 40,000 residents. Proportions are for families based on the U.S. Census as reported in the Chicago Metroplitan Area *Local Community Fact Book* (Chicago Fact Book Consortium (1984, 1995). All percentages rounded to the nearest whole number. Totals for CPC community areas, other areas, and for Chicago are weighted by the resident population.

employment rates in the CPC community areas were, respectively, 7.3%, 16%, and 16.9% for the decades of 1970 to 1990, compared to 3.7%, 9.3%, and 10.7% for the non-CPC community areas (Chicago Department of Public Health, 1994; Chicago Fact Book Consortium, 1984, 1995). These averages do not reflect the fact that some subgroupings within these areas (i.e., census tracts) had unemployment rates approaching 50%. A major reason for the worsening socioeconomic conditions in the neighborhoods surrounding the CPCs is the large decline in the residential population. For example, the community areas housing a Child-Parent Center experienced a 38% decline in population from 1970 to 1990, compared to only 9% for other Chicago community areas. Because the families that left were more socioeconomically advantaged than those that remained, poverty and unemployment became more concentrated, and the employment sector diminished as well (Wilson, 1996).

The Chicago Fact Book Consortium (1995) starkly described the social and economic conditions of North Lawndale, one of the locations of the early Child-Parent Centers, during these changing times:

The newest residents of North Lawndale encountered a series of community catastrophes after 1960, which resulted in a stagnated economy and a deteriorating social fabric. First were the riots which came after the King assassination in 1968, during which substantial parts of the Roosevelt Road shopping strip were destroyed by fire. After that store owners moved when insurance companies either canceled their policies or prohibitively increased their premiums. Another severe blow fell when the International Harvester Company's tractor works closed in 1969, with the loss of an estimated 3,400 jobs.

The riots, coupled with the racial turnover in North Lawndale between 1950 and 1970, purportedly resulted in the loss of 75% of its business establishments and 25% of its jobs. The department store and other retail facilities burned out or closed on Roosevelt Road were never replaced.

In 1974, Sears, Roebuck moved its headquarters to Sears Tower downtown, leaving behind a reduced facility employing 3,000. During the 1970s, 80% of the area manufacturing jobs disappeared, as Zenith and Sunbeam electronics factories shut down, and a Copenhagen snuff plant was closed. The closing of an Alden's catalogue store was a signal event in a sequence that wiped out 44% of the retail and service jobs in North Lawndale.

The downturn continued through the 1980s when Western Electric started closing down, to disappear completely by 1985. Two years later, without warning, Sears, Roebuck closed the Homan Avenue complex, resulting in the dismissal of 1,800 employees. (p. 107)

A similar pattern of social upheaval and decline occurred in West Garfield Park:

Between 1960 and 1970, more than 40,000 new African-Americans were added to the population of 7,000. With 40,000 whites relocating outside the area. West Garfield Park became predominantly black during the 1970s, bringing the community to the most pivotal decade in its most recent history. All community indices relating to previous

31

vitality were reversed. Between 1970 and 1980, the population decreased significantly by 30%. . . . This change was accompanied by a drop in housing units of 28%. . . . Unemployment rose from 8 percent to nearly 21 percent. At the same time, the number of families living below the poverty line increased from 24 percent to 36 percent and female-headed households doubled to 58 percent. One major anomaly appeared as home ownership rose to 22 percent and subsequently continued to rise.

By 1980, the landscape was transformed dramatically as large empty lots, formerly occupied by small and medium-sized apartment buildings evidenced the loss of living space resulting from the withdrawal of investment, undermaintenance, and arson.

In 1980, 3 years before children's preschool participation in the Chicago Longitudinal Study, the poverty rate for residents in the 14 community areas served by the CPCs was 39%, compared to 15% for the non-CPC community areas. Alternatively, 66% of children in the school attendance areas served by the CPCs resided in low-income families at the time of kindergarten entry in 1985. The average rate for the Chicago public schools was 42% (Chicago Public Schools, 1992).[6] Thus, children and families served by the Child-Parent Centers are at high risk of experiencing educational and social difficulties, and few U.S. children are probably at higher risk (see Appendix G).

There are 16 Child-Parent Centers currently located in the following 7 community areas: North Lawndale (4), West Garfield Park (3), Washington Park (2), Woodlawn (2), Grand Boulevard (2), Near North Side (2), and East Garfield Park (1). These areas typically have the highest concentration of poverty and unemployment in the city (Chicago Fact Book Consortium, 1984, 1995).

Child–Parent Centers and Head Start

Like Project Head Start, the CPCs provide comprehensive services, expect parent participation, and implement child-centered approaches to social and cognitive development for economically disadvantaged children. There are three distinguishing features of the Child-Parent Centers. As part of the school system, the CPCs are administrative centers housed in separate buildings or in wings of the affiliated elementary schools. They also staff a parent-resource room. Head Start programs typically contract

Fig. 3. Child-Parent Center Program

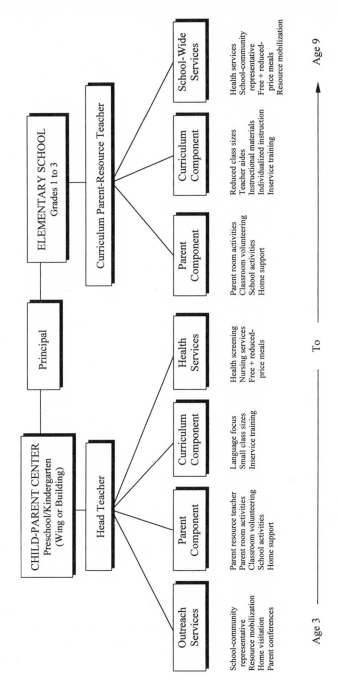

Table 4. Major Features of CPC Program Components

Preschool and Kindergarten	Primary grades
Staffing	
Head teacher	Curriculum parent resource teacher
Parent-resource teacher	School community representative (serves whole school)
School community representative	Classroom teachers & aides
Classroom teachers & aides	Clerk
Clerk	
Instruction and organization	
Located in separate building or wing of elementary school; serves ages 3 to 6	Located in elementary school; serves ages 6 to 9
Supervision & coordination by head teacher	Supervision & coordination by curriculum parent resource teacher
Child:teacher ratios of 17:2 & 25:2 in preschool & kindergarten	Child:teacher ratio of 25:2; individualized instruction
Emphasis on language development & pre-reading skills; Chicago EARLY materials	Instruction in basic skills; Chicago Reading Program
Extra instructional materials & supplies	Extra instructional materials & supplies
Parent involvement	
Participation required	Participation expected
Staffed parent room & provision of materials/supplies	Staffed parent room & provision of materials/supplies
Organized activities	Organized activities
Staff development	
Centralized inservices for head teachers & principals	Centralized inservices for curriculum parent resource teachers & principals
Inservices for classroom teachers & aides	Inservices for classroom teachers & aides
Health & nutrition	
Health screening & referral	Schoolwide health screening/referral
Special services for speech	Special services for learning problems
Free breakfast & lunch	Free breakfast & lunch for eligible students
Expenditures	
Average annual per-pupil expenditure 1996 dollars: $4,350	Average annual per-pupil expenditure 1996 dollars: $1,500

with social service or community agencies, not with school systems, and usually do not have staffed parent rooms in addition to classrooms, although they do provide extensive health screening and services on site (which the CPCs do not do). Second, eligibility for the CPCs is based pri-

Dickens Child-Parent Center

Wheatley Child-Parent Center

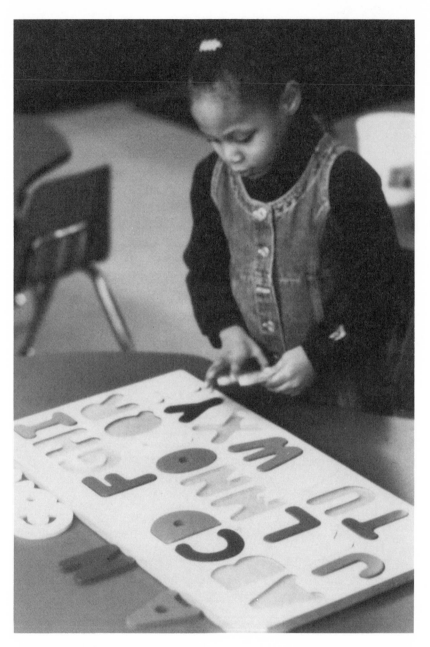

Child using letter board at Dumas CPC

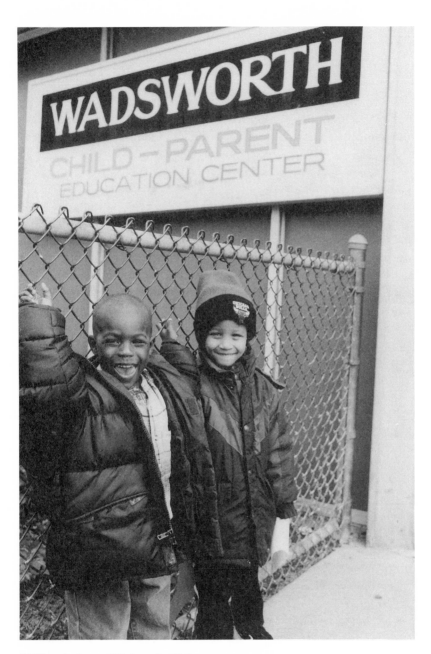

Children in front of Wadsworth CPC

Parent–resource room in Truth CPC

marily on neighborhood poverty; for Head Start it is primarily family-level poverty. Since both programs give preference to children in most educational need, this distinction is more illusory than real in practice. A third and most important difference is that the CPCs have historically provided up to 6 years of intervention services for children from ages 3 to 9, whereas Head Start is a preschool program. Thus, the CPC program provides the opportunity for a school-stable environment (i.e., minimal school transfer) during preschool and the early primary-grade years.

The two major CPC program components are described below for the years of program implementation experienced by the children in the Chicago Longitudinal Study. Figure 3 displays the organizational features of the CPCs for the 1983–89 implementation. Photographs of two current Child-Parent Centers and some participating children and parents are provided as well.[7] See Appendix F for a complete list of centers.

Preschool and Kindergarten Component (1983–1986)

The preschool and kindergarten component in each Child-Parent Center is administered under the supervision of the head teacher, who is responsible for all aspects of program delivery. The program is implemented in a separate building in close proximity to the affiliated elementary school or in a wing. Each center has its own budget and administrative operations. The major services coordinated by the head teacher are the child education program in the classroom, parent involvement, community outreach, and health and nutrition. The head teacher reports directly to the principal of the affiliated elementary school, which is the location of the primary-grade component (CPC expansion program). I describe the components in the following areas: staffing, structure of operations, curriculum philosophy and activities, parent involvement, health and nutrition, inservice training, and costs. Table 4 summarizes the key program features.

STAFFING

The head teacher is the program coordinator with overall responsibility for organizing and implementing program services. This primarily involves teaming with and supervising other primary staff, including the parent-resource teacher, the school-community representative, classroom teachers, and teacher aides (one for each classroom). Administrative support staff including a clerk and janitor are funded as part of the program. Several speech therapists and school nurses also serve the centers but service several centers at a time.

STRUCTURE OF OPERATIONS

Centers offer a half-day preschool program in the morning and afternoon (for 3 hours each) and a half-day (for 2.5 hours) or all-day (for 6 hours) kindergarten program at most sites (20 of 25 sites during 1983–86). The centers operate on the regular 9-month school year calendar. An 8-week summer program also is provided. Children enter preschool as 3-year-olds (i.e., 2 years, 9 months or older) in separate classrooms. The kindergartners typically are 5-year-olds and also have separate classrooms. Although the centers vary in the number of children served (from 130 to 210), they typically house four to six classrooms plus a parent room and office for the head teacher or staff.

In preschool, class sizes were set at a maximum of 17 children. With a classroom teacher and a teacher aide for each class, the child-to-staff ratio averaged 17 to 2 (or about 8 to 1). In kindergarten, class sizes could be no larger than 25 children. With the teacher and teacher aide, the child-to-staff ratio averaged 25 to 2 (about 12 to 1). Of course, parent volunteers further lowered these ratios, and they often were in the classroom. The relatively small class sizes and the presence of several adults enable a relatively intensive child-centered approach to early childhood education.

CURRICULUM PHILOSOPHY, MATERIALS, AND ACTIVITIES

The philosophy of the Child-Parent Centers has consistently emphasized the acquisition of basic knowledge and skills in language arts and math through a relatively structured but diverse set of learning experiences (e.g., whole class, small groups, individualized activities, field trips). While not ignoring the importance of psychological development and self-confidence, these affective learning outcomes were built into the reading and language-based instructional activities. For example, teachers provided frequent feedback and positive reinforcement and emphasized task accomplishment. The foundational skills of recognizing letters and numbers, oral communication, listening, and an appreciation for reading and drawing were of primary importance.

Although teachers had wide flexibility in selecting instructional materials for use in their classrooms, in the early 1980s they began using the cur-

Fig. 4.A. Instructional Activity in the Chicago EARLY Guide—Critical Thinking
(Reprinted by permission, Chicago Public Schools)

CRITICAL THINKING   Language J2
Categorical Association   Shopping Game
Naming

Objective: When shown visual stimuli which represents the same category, the child
             will verbally explain the categorical relationship.

Materials: Pictures that illustrate a variety of objets from three different categories,
             such as toys, clothing, and furniture.
             Three Boxes.

Procedures:
1.   Put three boxes on the table.
2.   Paste a picture on each box that represents each categorical group and label them:
      "toy store," and "food store." Keep the rest of the pictures face down in the
      middle of the table.
3.   Say, "Today we are going to play a shopping game. Each one of these boxes will
      be a store." Point to the picture on each box and have the child name it. For each
      one, tell the child the category name.
4.   Have the child pick up one of the pictures on the table and name it (e.g., a milk
      carton). Ask appropriate questions such as, "Where do we buy milk? Do we buy
      milk at the grocery store or at the toy store?" etc. If necessary, model an
      appropriate response for the child, for instance, "we buy food at the food/grocery
      store." Have the child put the picture in the box that is the "food store."
5.   Follow the same procedure until all the pictures have been identified and sorted
      into the appropriate boxes. Encourage each child to name other items that could
      be bought at each store.
6.   Have each child explain why the different sets of pictures were placed in the
      different boxes or categories (e.g. , "milk, oranges, and meats are all foods; you
      can eat them. You can't buy them at the toy store; you buy them at the
      food/grocery store.")

Criterion:
The child will verbally explain categorical relationships.

riculum program called the Chicago Early Assessment and Remediation
Laboratory, or EARLY (Chicago Board of Education, 1988), developed
by the Board of Education's Department of Research and Evaluation
(Naron & Perlman, 1981). The EARLY program contains a comprehensive set of instructional activities for preschool children and was designed
to supplement other instructional materials. Because all centers used the
program on a fairly regular basis, it is representative of the types of instructional activities in the preschool and to a lesser extent in kindergarten. The
cognitive domains of the activities are summarized below.

Fig. 4.B. Instructional Activity in the Chicago EARLY Guide—Arithmetic/Art
(Reprinted by permission, Chicago Public Schools)

ARITHMETIC/ART   Arithmetic A3
One-to-One Correspondence   The Bunny Hole Game
Reproducing Equal Sets -
    Drawing

Objective: The child will draw a set of objects equal in number to a standard set which contains
          from one to five objects, when given the appropriate demonstration and materials.

Materials: -Circles of many colors - use large buttons, color chips, covered bottle caps, or circles
          cut from felt or construction paper.
          -Worksheet with five circles the same size as the color circles.

          -Crayons the same colors as the circles

Procedure:
1. Use one copy of the worksheet as your model. Tell the children that each circle on the page
   is really a hole that leads to a bunny rabbit's home underground. When it's hot outside the
   bunnies like to have doors on their holes. The children are to cover the same number of holes
   as you do.
2. Give each child a worksheet and a crayon. Tell them the bunnies are hot and want lots of
   open holes. Cover one hole on your worksheet with a circle. Tell the children to cover the
   same number of holes by coloring them. Check each child's work by holding his/her
   worksheet directly below the model.
3. Give each child a new worksheet and follow the same procedure with a different number of
   holes to be covered.

Caution: If a child has difficulty, have him/her place circles on the holes as you do, instead of
        coloring the holes. After he/she can do this, then have the child color the appropriate
        hole(s).

Extension:

If it is available, use a puppet, particularly one of a rabbit, to liven up this activity. The puppet
can tell the children how many holes to cover up and can check the children's responses.

Criterion:
The child will draw equivalent sets with from one to five objects.

A. Body Image and Gross Motor Skills
    1. Discrimination of body parts
    2. Nonlocomotor movement
    3. Locomotor movement
    4. Kinesthetics
    5. Spatial integration

B. *Perceptual-Motor and Arithmetic Skills*
1. Discrimination of colors, shapes, sizes, and familiar objects
2. Arithmetic such as one-on-one correspondence, sequencing, counting, and number symbols

C. *Language*
1. Auditory discrimination such as sound recognition
2. Sentence building with nouns, verbs, and adjectives
3. Critical thinking such as story comprehension, functional association, and verbal problem solving

Most of the activities were for use in small groups of four or five children. Each of the activities included seven operational components: objective, materials, procedure, cautions, suggestions for extension, the criterion, and the item measuring mastery of activity. Figures 4.A and 4.B show two example activities. Among other frequently used curriculum materials were Peabody Language Development Kits, Alpha Time, Bank Street Readers, Math Their Way, Language Lotto, and a variety of basal readers, but the latter were primarily for use in kindergarten. None of the instructional materials were used exclusively but rather in combination. Indeed, the centers had substantial funds to purchase instructional supplies and materials.

In kindergarten, classrooms largely followed the school system's Comprehensive Reading Program, or CRP (Chicago Public Schools, 1985). The EARLY program was used less often in kindergarten. The CRP, a mastery learning approach to instruction, was designed to facilitate the development of basic skills in language arts and math. Kindergarten classrooms allotted approximately 45 minutes per day in specific prereading and reading instruction. Social studies, science, and music and art activities also were included. Activities often centered around learning outcomes associated with the areas of word attack, comprehension, study skills, and literature with increasing complexity throughout the year. In addition, a variety of basal reading materials were used (e.g., Ginn, Houghton-Mifflin, and Open Court readers).

As with preschool, children learned to read and write through a broad spectrum of experiences both in and outside the classroom. Field trips had special significance in the program and were frequent during both preschool and kindergarten. Parent volunteers almost always went on these outings. For example, classes went to places such as the Museum of Science and Industry, the Lincoln Park or Brookfield Zoo, public libraries, the Art Institute, Union Station railroad depot, and local businesses. Upon return, events and observations from the trip served as a basis for classroom and small group discussion (see Chicago Public Schools, 1987).

Based on teacher reports of instructional materials and classroom activities in the centers and on previous evaluations (Chicago Public Schools, 1985, 1987), I classified each of the 20 centers into one of three within-study instructional categories: (a) those that were relatively teacher oriented (or initiated) in their classroom activities, (b) those that were developmental, and (c) those that were undifferentiated (mixed) in that equal emphasis was given to teacher-oriented and developmental activities.[8] Centers classified as teacher oriented were those that emphasized large-group activities, academic skills, and a structured set of instruction materials (e.g., workbooks, basal readers). Prereading instruction was more frequent as well. Centers classified as developmental emphasized child-initiated activities in small-group settings, interest centers, and the use of materials such as the Peabody Language Kits and Bank Street Readers as well as the EARLY. Less emphasis was devoted to prereading activities and more to social development. Centers classified as undifferentiated had no distinct focus or were mixed, so that teacher-directed and developmental activities were used equally.

Seven of the 20 centers were classified as primarily teacher oriented, 10 were considered developmental, and 3 were classified as undifferentiated. These designations provide an overall within-study descriptor of implemented instructional approaches. Because all centers used a diversity of instructional activities, the categories are best viewed along a continuum from teacher-oriented to developmental activities. Most of the centers were in the middle range. Implementation occurred within the context of low adult-child ratios and extensive parent participation. Moreover, this classification best describes the preschool program. In kindergarten, most of the centers were relatively structured and oriented toward the development of academic skills.

PARENT INVOLVEMENT

As the program's title indicates, a central operating principle of the program is that parent involvement is the critical socializing force in children's development. Direct parent involvement in the program is expected to en-

Table 5. Types of Parent Involvement in the Child-Parent Centers

Parent involvement examples	Relative focus
Volunteer in the classroom	Medium
Read to small groups	
Assist with field trips	
Supervise play activities	
Play games with small groups	
Participate in parent room activities	High
Participate in parent reading groups	
Complete craft projects	
Inservices in child development, financial management, cooking, and home economics	
Participate in school activities	High
Attend meetings and programs	
Attend parent-teacher conferences	
Attend social events	
Enroll in educational courses	Low
Enroll in parent education courses	
Complete high school coursework	
Home support activities	High
Receive home visits	
Interact with child through reading and playing	
Go to library with child	

Note: Ratings are based on teacher interviews, classroom observations, and the program theory.

hance parent-child interactions, parent and child attachment to school, and social support among parents, and consequently to promote children's school readiness and social adjustment. The centers make substantial efforts to involve parents in the education of their children, so much so that it is hard to overestimate. At least one-half day per week of parent involvement in the program is required.[9] The unique feature of the parent program is the parent room, which is located adjacent to the classrooms. The full-time parent-resource teacher organizes the parent room in order to implement parent educational activities, initiate interactions among parents, and foster parent-child interactions. There are funds for materials, supplies, and speakers for the parent room, and areas of training include consumer education, nutrition, personal development, health and safety, and homemaking arts. Parents may also attend GED classes at the centers. Parent also serve on the School Advisory Council, which assists staff in educational planning and implementation.

As shown in Table 5, a wide range of activities is encouraged in the program, including parent-room activities (e.g., arts & craft projects), classroom volunteering, participating in school activities, taking part in class field trips, helping to prepare breakfasts and lunches, and engaging in education and training activities. The diversity of activities is designed to accommodate parents' daily schedules and different needs. Such activities help parents (a) understand themselves, (b) understand the importance of teaching their children at home, (c) feel comfortable in the role of volunteer, and (d) learn more about child development (Chicago Public Schools, 1983). Among the commercial programs used were Exploring Parenting, Parent Effectiveness Training, and Parents as Partners in Reading.

Examples of parent activities in the classroom are provided below (see Bureau of Early Childhood Programs, n.d.):

Reading stories to small groups of children

Changing the bulletin board

Finishing activities begun by the teacher (e.g., a reading lesson)

Arranging games for children who finish assignments early

Listening to children describe their experiences

Assisting in the planning of field experiments

Conducting science experiments with small groups

Working on craft projects with children in the interest center

Practicing math activities one-on-one or in small groups.

SCHOOL-COMMUNITY OUTREACH SERVICES

In each center, the full-time school-community representative, who usually has grown up in the neighborhood, provides outreach services to families in three related areas. First, they identify families in the neighborhood who are in most need of the educational services provided by the CPC. They make door-to-door visits to likely participants in the program, distribute program brochures and advertisements, and communicate with prospective families both formally and informally. Second, the school-community representative conducts a home or school visit with all enrolling families. One visit upon enrollment in the program is required. Additional visits occur on a most-in-need basis. Moreover, informal conferences are held between the parent and the school-community representative. Finally, this representative mobilizes resources by referring families to community and social service agencies such as employment training and education, mental health services, and welfare services. The school-community representative also organizes transportation and related services for families.

PHYSICAL HEALTH AND MEDICAL SERVICES

Upon entry into the program, children undergo a health screening from a registered nurse on-site. Tests are given for vision and hearing. Enrolling parents are expected to provide records of their child's medical and immunization history. All children are required to have a physical and dental examination. Children in need of preventive services are referred to appropriate service agencies. Special medical and educational services such as speech therapy also are available. All children in the morning and all-day programs receive free breakfasts and lunches as part of the national programs offered by the U.S. Department of Agriculture. Children in afternoon programs receive free lunches.

INSERVICE TRAINING

The CPC program also provides funds and time for staff development for the head teachers, classroom teachers and aides, the parent-resource teacher, and the school-community representative. The head teacher typically provides inservice training to teachers and instructional staff and often invites outside speakers to present information on salient topics. Staff from the school system's Department of Early Childhood Programs also sponsor training activities for head teachers and other instructional staff on a regular basis.

COSTS

Expenditures for the CPC program (in 1996 dollars) were estimated at $4,350 yearly per child in the half-day preschool program and the half-day kindergarten program. These amounts do not include expenditures for the free breakfast and lunch program (funded by the U.S. Department of Agriculture) or for implementing full-day kindergarten programs in 14 centers (funded by Title II of ESEA).

Primary-Grade Component (Follow-on Program)

Beginning in the fall of 1977, the primary-grade component was implemented in the elementary schools serving the Child-Parent Centers. This follow-on to earlier intervention is implemented as a vertical expansion of the preschool and kindergarten component. Previously, all program operations were implemented in the centers and were administered by the principals (now head teachers) in their respective sites as part of the federally funded program. Thus, one major difference between the preschool/kindergarten and primary-grade components is that the latter is implemented in the affiliated elementary school rather than in the center. In addition, all children are eligible for and participate in the primary-grade program regardless of whether they participated in preschool and kindergarten. Moreover, program coordination is streamlined. The head teacher and the parent-resource teacher are combined into one position (curriculum parent-resource teacher). The school-community representative serves the whole school instead of just of the center. The six schools serving the original CPCs (opened in 1967–69) provided 3 years of service (first to third grade); the remaining centers provided 2 years of service (first and second grade). This one less year of the program was due to the lack of available funding.

STAFFING

The curriculum parent-resource teachers in each school supervises all program operations in the elementary school and coordinates the teachers and teacher aides in the program classrooms. They also work directly with the school-community representative and other auxiliary staff in the school. The curriculum parent-resource teacher's responsibilities are to (a) coordinate the primary level classroom program in the school, (b) order materials and supplies, (c) conduct on-going parent programs, including coordinating parent classroom involvement, (d) assist teachers in implementing individualized instructional activities, and (e) provide and organize inservice training. The teacher reports directly to the principal and also cooperates with the head teacher in the affiliated preschool/kindergarten component.

STRUCTURE OF OPERATIONS

Program schools offered an all-day program in 24 sites during the 1986–89 implementation (one school closed in 1987). Children entered first grade

44

as 6-year-olds. Although all first and second graders (and third graders in selected schools) participated in the program, it was the policy that at least half of each classroom included children from the CPC preschool/ kindergarten component. The number of rooms per school devoted to the program varied from 4 to 18 and included from 90 to 420 students.

The program was designed to enrich the primary-grade classroom experience. The main innovation was a modification in organization. In each grade, class sizes were reduced to a maximum of 25 children, and each teacher was provided with a teacher aide. The child-to-staff ratio averaged 25 to 2 (or about 12 to 1). These reduced class sizes and ratios required the additional funding each year of approximately 40 full-time teachers and 220 teacher aides across schools. Parent volunteers further lowered these ratios. The reduced class sizes in the program contrasted significantly with classrooms in other schools, which typically had 30 or more students per class and usually lacked teacher aides.

CURRICULUM PHILOSOPHY, APPROACH, AND MATERIALS

The instructional philosophy of the CPC program emphasized the development of basic skills in language arts, math, and social studies in first and second grade, with greater attention to science beginning in third grade. All schools implemented the CRP, and reading comprehension was the explicit objective of the curriculum. The instructional approaches in the classroom did not differ markedly between CPC and non-CPC schools. Because CPC classrooms had fewer students, more adults, and a wider array of instructional supplies and materials, CPC program children experienced a more intensive, individualized education than their comparison-group counterparts.

CRP was a directed reading program organized to include developmental reading (basal readers), corrective reading, remedial reading, recreational reading, and enrichment reading. A five-step directed reading lesson included the following components: (a) preparation, (b) reading, (c) interpretation, (d) development of skills, and (e) extension of experiences. In each of the grades, an hour in developmental reading with a basal reader was offered and 30 minutes for skill emphasis. As part of the skill emphasis, Chicago Mastery Learning materials or other supplementary materials were used. One day per week, an hour of recreational enrichment reading was provided. In the program sites, a variety of basal reading programs

45

were used including Ginn (seven sites), Houghton-Mifflin (six), Holt, Rinehart, & Winston (5), Harcourt Brace (3), and Open Court (3).

Learning goals were as follows. By the end of first grade, students were expected to successfully complete activities designed to identify the main ideas of written stories and pictures and to draw conclusions from them, identify short vowel sounds in words, recognize plural forms of words, compound words, and contractions, and identify parts of books. In grade 2, students engaged in activities to identify synonyms, antonyms, and homonyms; to recognize cause and effect relationships; and to identify character traits, settings, and plots in written stories. At the end of grade 3, students were expected to identify word meanings, obtain information from graphs and charts, make predictions, use a dictionary, and identify facts and opinions.

PARENT INVOLVEMENT

The main difference between the parent programs within the two program components is that parent involvement is strongly encouraged but not required in the primary grades. Aside from that difference, the elementary school curriculum parent-resource teacher implements activities in the parent-resource room in a similar fashion to the preschool/kindergarten component. For example, each teacher has a budget for supplies, materials, and equipment to conduct parent education and training activities, encourages home support for learning, and organizes and participates in field trips.

SCHOOL–COMMUNITY OUTREACH

The school-community representative serves the primary-grade program by conducting home visits, meeting with parents and children at school about educational activities, providing referrals to social service agencies, monitoring student attendance, and assisting the curriculum parent-resource teacher and the head teacher in the Child-Parent Center. Because the school-community representative serves all children in the school, the intensity of service delivery to program participants is lower than in preschool and kindergarten.

HEALTH AND NUTRITION

A schoolwide nurse is available to assist children with identified health problems. The curriculum parent-resource teacher also monitors children's needs and refers them to schoolwide services or to community agencies. Speech therapists, school psychologists, and social workers also are available as part of the schoolwide coverage. Children receive free breakfasts and lunches if they are eligible.

STAFF DEVELOPMENT

Like the head teacher, the curriculum parent-resource teacher provides inservice training to classroom teachers and aides in the expansion classrooms. Staff from the Department of Early Childhood Programs provide inservices to the curriculum parent-resource teachers and have orientation meetings with principals of the elementary schools.

EXPENDITURES

Expenditures for the primary-grade program were approximately $1,500 annually per child above and beyond the regular school program (1996 dollars). This translates to $3,000 per child for 2 years and $4,500 for 3 years of participation. The largest portion of this expenditure was to reduce class sizes and to provide teacher aides for each class. These amounts do not include expenditures for the free breakfast and lunch program (funded by the U.S. Department of Agriculture) that is provided to eligible students.

The CPC program was designed to serve children during the formative early childhood years, ages 3 to 9. Because of differences in age of entry and exit, substantial variation in exposure to intervention occurs. This is due to administrative selection, family self-selection, and mobility. Children enrolling in the six original centers at age 3 can remain in the program up to 6 years, whereas those entering at age 4 remain up to 5 years. Children entering a later CPC at ages 3 or 4 can participate for up to 4 or 5 years. Because any child can enroll in the follow-on (expansion program) in grades 1 to 3, this opportunity contributed to variation in program participation.

Implementation History

Over the years, the implementation of the CPC program has been investigated extensively. The Educational Testing Service (Marco & Landes, 1971) completed the first process evaluation of the CPC program for the 1969–70 implementation period. Based on surveys and interviews of staff and school administrators, the CPC program earned the highest overall quality rating of the 24 Title I Chicago programs. The program was rated

high on general quality, administrative desirability, and social consequences and moderately high on efficiency. Especially high were ratings
on the items "fostering pupil interest" and in "stimulating good relations
among the school, home, and community."

Results of later evaluations have confirmed that the program has consistently served the intended target population and successfully provided the
expected educational and family support services. Specifically, these evaluations have found that (a) the population of at-risk families served
matched the intended target population (Chicago Public Schools, 1974),
(b) rates of child attendance regularly exceeded 92%, which is 4 to 6 percentage points higher than other Title I programs (Institute for the Development of Educational Auditing [IDEA], 1973, 1974; Schuster & Jennings, 1982), (c) centers implemented their programs similarly in their
attention to a basic skills approach and a focus on child development and
parent involvement, and (d) the distinctive elements of the program were
observed and were present to a greater degree than in instructional programs at non-CPC sites (Chicago Public Schools, 1985, 1987; Conrad &
Eash, 1983; IDEA, 1974).

Conrad and Eash (1983), for example, found that CPC classrooms were
rated by observers as significantly higher than non-CPC classrooms in
child-centeredness (i.e., small class size, individual and small-group work)
and in basic skills and evaluation orientation. CPC classrooms also were
judged to have somewhat but not significantly more enriched material environments and greater parent classroom participation. Relative to non-
CPC parents, CPC parents displayed better control over their children at
home and greater support for their children. In the IDEA study, parental
program involvement significantly discriminated between CPC participation and nonparticipation and also led to changes in children's school
achievement. Schuster and Jennings (1982) found that over 80% of CPC
parents indicated in surveys that they visited the center or had been involved in the instructional program. A review of records for the parent-
resource rooms at selected sites revealed that over 50% of parents were ac-
tively involved in their children's center for at least two days per month.

Program implementation during the early to middle 1980s, the years of
operation covered by the study sample, indicated a similar pattern of successful service delivery (see Chicago Public Schools, 1985, 1987; Reynolds, 1994), thus reinforcing the basic program elements of early parent

48

involvement and a basic skills approach to early education and language development. In assessing kindergarten programs in the Child-Parent Centers, an evaluation by Nancy Mavrogenes (Chicago Public Schools, 1987) indicated that reading activities (e.g., decoding) comprised 50% of all activities observed and writing activities comprised 23%. Field trips were common and usually involved extensive preparation and discussion during class. Parents of CPC children also were found to be more involved in the center than other parents. Their involvement frequently included engaging in activities in the parent-resource room, going on class field trips, tutoring students, and performing clerical tasks.[10]

Finally, parents, staff, and school administrators have indicated strong support for early intervention and program continuity exemplified in the 6-year duration of the program. Reports of the CPC program also have identified two major areas for improvement. Because the centers select their own instructional materials, use of a uniform curriculum has been recommended (Schuster & Jennings, 1982). To address this recommendation, the centers began using the EARLY materials in the early 1980s. The second recommendation was to increase parent participation in the program. Both program staff and parents have commented over the years that a greater proportion of parents should participate in the program (Chicago Public Schools, 1987; IDEA, 1974). One advantage of requiring parent involvement is that more parents participate, but this stated policy leads to the expectation that all parents will participate. It has been observed that although all parents do not fully participate in the program, participation is high relative both to programs that do require participation and to those that do not (Chicago Public Schools, 1987; Schuster & Jennings, 1982).

Early Studies of Program Impact

Although there have been many reports documenting the success of the CPC program in promoting children's school achievement, controlled studies have been rare. The initial outcome evaluations were mandated monitoring studies and performance audits by contractors at the Institute for the Development of Educational Auditing (IDEA) during 1971–72 and 1972–73 (IDEA, 1973, 1974; Stenner & Mueller, 1973). Among the major findings were that CPC participants scored at or above the national average in language and math tests in kindergarten and that the vast majority of participants scored in the range of "ready for first grade" on the Metropolitan Readiness Test. Children who remained in the Child–Parent Centers in first to third grades maintained their level of performance relative to the national average and increased their performance advantage relative to Chicago students generally as well as students in other Title I programs. Postkindergarten academic performance was reported only for students who continued their participation in the program. The fourth and fifth grade scores of CPC students with extensive program participation were substantially higher than the Chicago average and Title I students, but they scored, on average, 6 to 8 months lower than the national average.

Nevertheless, the findings that programs for educationally disadvantaged children in the poorest inner-city neighborhoods can effect substantial performance gains led to further on-site observation and analysis that resulted in the program's selection in 1974 as one of 12 outstanding reading programs by the Right to Read Office of the U.S. Office of Education. In 1976, the CPC program was selected as one of 33 exemplary programs by the Joint Dissemination Review Panel of the U.S. Office of Education.

Two controlled studies of the full program (preschool/kindergarten and primary-grade components) were completed after the mid 1970s. Investigating the long-term effects of extensive participation in the six original CPCs for 684 students, Fuerst and Fuerst (1993) found that those who participated in the CPCs for 4 or more years during 1967 to 1977 scored, on average, 7 to 8 months higher in eighth-grade reading achievement and 4 to 5 months higher in math achievement than students who did not participate in the program but who attended schools serving a similar composition of students. A significantly higher proportion of CPC students (62%) graduated from high school, compared to 49% for the no-treatment comparison group. Only program girls, however, had a significantly higher graduation rate than their same-sex peers (74% versus 57%), although the direction of influence for boys favored participants (49% versus 40%). The effects of the full program relative to participation in only the preschool and kindergarten component or in the follow-on component were not investigated.

Conrad and Eash (1983) investigated the effects of participation in both the preschool/kindergarten and CPC expansion programs in four sites from 1977 to 1982 under the reconfigured program structure (with the primary component transferred to the elementary school). Relative to a non-CPC comparison group matched on family and school demographic characteristics, 227 children who participated in the CPC program in preschool or kindergarten had significantly higher scores on several indicators of kindergarten achievement. Similar to Fuerst and Fuerst's (1993) findings, participation in the CPC expansion program after preschool and kindergarten was associated with significantly higher scores in reading and math achievement at age 8 and with higher scores on locus of control. Nevertheless, these later analyses included only 54 students. The kindergarten findings were similar to comparative outcome evaluations of later implementations (Chicago Public Schools, 1985, 1987).

Overall, these later comparative evaluations largely supported the findings of the early monitoring reports that participation in the CPC program was associated with significantly higher scores on achievement tests and ratings of social psychological development. By the end of kindergarten, CPC children have consistently been at or above the national average in reading readiness, language development, and math achievement and appear to maintain their scholastic advantages to a greater degree than children participating in most other early childhood interventions, presumably because of participation in follow-on programs as well as the focus on parent involvement and language skills. None of the earlier evaluations, however, investigated the effectiveness of the program at all centers nor the differential effects of timing and duration of intervention exposure. These earlier studies also did not include a comprehensive set of child outcome variables that are common in contemporary evaluations of early childhood intervention. Moreover, sample attrition after kindergarten was not taken into account in analyses. Ongoing, prospective longitudinal studies are usually recommended for evaluating the effects of prevention programs and of programs that receive substantial priority in funding. They offer many advantages over retrospective studies that rely on administrative records as well as time-limited studies that provide snapshots of program effectiveness.

Chicago Longitudinal Study of the Child–Parent Centers

The Chicago Longitudinal Study (Reynolds, 1989, 1991; Reynolds, Bezruczko, Mavrogenes, & Hagemann, 1996) was designed as a prospective investigation of the scholastic development of 1,539 children who graduated from government-funded kindergarten programs in the Chicago public schools in 1986. The study includes all children ($n = 1,150$)

who enrolled in the 20 CPCs with preschool and kindergarten programs beginning in the fall of 1983 and who were kindergarten graduates. Children enrolled at age 3 or 4 and could continue their participation up to age 9 in the spring of 1989 (end of third grade). Some children received services from the CPCs in kindergarten (but not in preschool) and participated in the primary-grade component. Most of these children were classified as CPC participants (because of participation in the primary grades). Six of the 20 centers offered the intervention through third grade while the other centers offered it through second grade. Consequently, the relationship between duration of participation and school adjustment can be investigated.

The original comparison group included 389 children who graduated in 1986 from government-funded all-day kindergarten programs in seven schools participating in the Chicago Effective Schools Project (CESP). Five kindergartens were randomly selected, and the other two were located in the CPCs or their affiliated elementary school (Donoghue and Wadsworth). The schools participated in the CESP, a school system program to meet the needs of high-risk children. The five randomly selected sites were located in the East Garfield Park, Woodlawn, Austin, Humboldt Park, and Lower West Side community areas. Children served by these schools matched the poverty characteristics of the CPCs, and like CPC participants, they were eligible for and participated in government-funded programs. This non–CPC comparison group had no systematic intervention experiences from preschool to third grade, although some were enrolled in Head Start or the primary-grade component. Thus, children in the comparison group had intervention experiences that were fairly representative of low-income families in Chicago in the middle 1980s and probably more extensive than many low-income families in other cities.

PATTERNS OF ENROLLMENT

Table 6 displays the program characteristics of the study sample in kindergarten and in the follow-on period at age 14.[11] Program group 1 includes children in the six original CPCs, who participated for up to 6 years (preschool to third grade). All original centers have all-day kindergarten programs; five are located in wings of the affiliated elementary school. Program group 2 includes children in the newer CPCs, in which follow-on participation is limited to 2 years (second grade). A majority of these cen-

Table 6. 1985–1986 Kindergarten Cohort in the Chicago Longitudinal Study

Program group	Kind. grade 8	Sample size	No. sites	Prog. start date	Years/Extent of intervention exposure Pre-K	Kind.	Schl. age	Range of yrs
1. Original Child- Parent Centers	1986 1994	325 238	6	1967– 1969	1 or 2	Fday	3	2–6
2. Later Child- Parent Centers	1986 1994	649 524	14	1970– 1978	1 or 2	Fday Hday	2	2–5
3. No-preschool CPC comparison 1	1986 1994	176 116	6	—	None	Fday	3	0–3
4. Non-CPC compari- son 2	1986 1994	389 286	7	—	Mostly none	Fday	Mostly none	0–4
Total	1986 1994	1539 1164	25	—	—	—	—

Note: School-age (expansion) component included first, second, and third grades. The total number of different sites was 25 because groups 1 and 3 enrolled in the same sites and groups 2 and 4 overlapped by two sites. Groups 3 and 4 were eligible for participation in the school-age (primary-grade) component. Group means of study sample for years of CPC participation were, respectively, 4.69, 3.78, 1.99, and 0.24.

ters have all-day kindergartens and are in separate buildings near the affiliated elementary school.

Program groups 3 and 4 did not participate in the CPC preschool program and together served as the preschool comparison group. However, group 3 did participate in kindergarten programs in the six original Child-Parent Centers or affiliated elementary schools, and these children received a similar pattern of services as children who began in preschool. Group 4 constituted the CESP (non-CPC) comparison group and included 389 children who did not participate in the CPCs in preschool or kindergarten.[12] Because all children who attended program schools were eligible for the primary-grade component, some children in the non-CPC comparison group did participate in the CPC follow-on program. Thus, there was significant variation in participation in preschool, kindergarten, and the primary-grade components of the CPC program. This variation enabled comparisons of the timing and duration of intervention exposure (see Appendix A for the characteristics of the study sample over time).

Table 7 shows the distribution of program and comparison-group children across the 25 sites at the beginning of the study in 1985–86. The centers and their affiliated elementary schools are listed by year of implementation. The 6 centers that opened in 1967–69 provide up to 6 years of inter-

Table 7. Program and Sample Characteristics for the Chicago Longitudinal Study

Child-Parent Center/ elementary school	Original sample	Prog. start date	Center location	Percentage low income in 1980	Max. yrs. of exposure			
					Pre-K	K	Foll	Total
Cole/Melody	70	1967	Wing	56.1	2	Fday	3	6
Hansberry/Webster	76	1967	Wing	55.0	2	Fday	3	6
Dickens/King	70	1967	Wing	68.0	2	Fday	3	6
Olive/Henson	53	1967	Wing	59.8	2	Fday	3	6
Miller/Jensen	76	1969	Wing	61.8	2	Fday	3	6
Wheatley/Carver Primary	155	1969	Bldg.	72.1	2	Fday	3	6
Ferguson/Manierre	61	1970	Bldg.	49.1	2	Fday	2	5
Donoghue	124	1970	Bldg.	74.3	2	Fday	2	5
Mason	41	1970	Wing	61.8	2	Hday	2	5
Wadsworth	44	1970	Bldg.	61.3	2	Fday	2	5
Dumas	27	1974	Bldg.	60.1	2	Hday	2	5
Overton	42	1974	Bldg.	65.2	2	Hday	2	5
Johnson	25	1974	Bldg.	86.3	2	Hday	2	5
Joyner/Smith	54	1975	Bldg.	77.8	2	Fday	2	5
Cockrell/Ross	44	1975	Bldg.	77.1	2	Hday	2	5
Farren/Beasley	64	1975	Bldg.	77.8	2	Hday	2	5
Delano	38	1975	Bldg.	64.1	2	Hday	2	5
Dewey	50	1975	Bldg.	66.6	2	Hday	2	5
Parker	21	1975	Bldg.	58.9	2	Fday	2	5
Von Humboldt	66	1978	Bldg.	63.9	2	Hday	2	5
Beidler*	70	—	Elem sch	67.4	-	Fday	-	-
Howe*	60	—	Elem sch	52.8	-	Fday	-	-
Komensky*	28	—	Elem sch	44.8	-	Fday	-	-
Ryerson*	66	—	Elem sch	70.0	-	Fday	-	-
Dulles*	114	—	Elem sch	81.7	-	Fday	-	-
Donoghue*	34	—	Elem sch	74.3	-	Fday		
Wadsworth* (in Child-Parent Center)	17	—	Bldg.	61.3	-	Fday	-	-

Note: Percentage low income is for children residing in the school attendance area. Low-income status is defined as eligibility for the federal free lunch program. Foll = school-age grades 1 to 3.
*CESP comparison group site.

vention services; those that opened in 1970 and later provide up to 5 years of service.

DEFINING THE EXPERIENCES OF THE NON–CPC COMPARISON GROUP

The non-CPC comparison group included children who enrolled in seven randomly selected schools participating in the all-day kindergarten program of the CESP. Two of the schools were elementary schools into which children from the Child-Parent Centers progressed, and five were not. In contrast to children in the CPCs, children in the CESP schools did not receive systematic intervention services from preschool to the primary grades. They matched the racial and socioeconomic composition of children from the CPCs and were eligible for and received early childhood intervention services. About one fifth of the non-CPC comparison group did enroll in Head Start, however. Consequently, all comparison groups in this study received alternative intervention (i.e., treatment "as usual") rather than no intervention.

Begun in 1981 and administered by the Office of Equality of Educational Opportunity, the CESP was designed to improve the achievement patterns of educationally disadvantaged students in racially isolated schools. The 27 schools in the project were selected primarily because they enroll a large proportion of low-achieving students as determined by scores on the Iowa Tests of Basic Skills. Other criteria included student mobility, attendance rates, socioeconomic status, and percentage of minority students enrolled (Chicago Board of Education, 1984). Generally, the CESP was designed to target key areas of school improvement as informed by research on effective schools. These areas included school leadership, instruction, school climate, staff development, parental involvement, and assessment of school progress. Implementation of an all-day kindergarten program, which began in 1984, was a manifestation of these principles in that the program provided reduced class sizes with teacher aides, extra funds for instructional materials ($650 per room), and staff inservice training. Parents also were encouraged to participate in children's schooling but without the resources of a staffed parent-resource room.

GROUP COMPARABILITY

Table 8 shows the sample characteristics of the original CPC program and comparison groups prior to children's participation in the follow-on pro-

Table 8. Original Sample Characteristics of CPC Program and Comparison Groups

Characteristic	Program group (n = 1,150)	Comparison group (n = 389)	F	p
Percent girls	50.0	50.5	0.03	.870
Percent black	93.1	92.2	0.32	.571
Age in Kindergarten	63.3 (3.7)	63.8 (4.0)	3.08	.079
Percent of parents who are high school graduates	59.7	50.9	5.36	.021
Percent who are eligible for a free lunch subsidy	84.2	82.1	0.58	.447
School poverty (% of low-income children in attendance area)	66.5 (8.7)	67.5 (11.6)	3.29	.070
Number of children in family	2.4 (1.6)	2.7 (1.8)	4.13	.043
Years of CPC participation	3.68 (1.32)	0.22 (0.66)	—	—

Note: Sex of child, race/ethnicity, age, and school poverty measured at school entry. High school graduation, free lunch, number of children, and program participation were measured after kindergarten. Total n ranges from 947 to 1,539.

gram. The CPC program group includes children with any participation in the program from preschool to grade 3. At the beginning of the study, the groups were similar on several characteristics including school poverty, sex, race, and socioeconomic status as determined by eligibility for free lunch. CPC participants, on average, had fewer brothers and sisters (2.4 versus 2.7), and their parents had a higher rate of high school graduation (60% versus 51%). These differences are taken into account in estimating program effects.

Of the original sample of 1,539 children, 1,164 (76.5%) were active in the Chicago public schools at age 14 (77% of the program group and 72% of the comparison group); 1,070 (70%) were active in Chicago schools at age 15. Although CPC participants were more likely to be active in the study sample, the differences were not significant for the most part (see Appendix B), and no selective attrition has occurred on youth outcomes in this study (see Appendix B) or in previous ones (Reynolds, 1994, 1995; Reynolds & Temple, 1995). The lone exception was that selective attrition did occur for measured family outcomes. Program participants (in preschool) whose parents provided family outcome data had higher word analysis scores in kindergarten than those whose parents did not provide data (attrition sample; see Appendix B for details).

Children in the comparison group of this quasi-experimental study did not enroll in the CPCs primarily because they did not live in a neighborhood containing such a center. Thus, geographic location rather than family motivation or other self-selection factors determined nonparticipation. Reynolds and Temple (1995) found that preschool participation can be predicted with 86% accuracy from child, family, and school-level information. Program site characteristics were the best predictors of program participation, and effects persisted when they were included in the model. As shown in Table 8, some children from the original comparison group did participate in the CPC follow-on program, and they were counted as participants.[13]

Why did children who enrolled in the CPCs leave before the end of the program? Some parents preferred to send their children to regular school programs. They enrolled their children in preschool and kindergarten with the intention of moving to other schools afterward. Other parents moved out of the school neighborhood due to professional (e.g., job change) or personal reasons. Some children participated for 6 years instead of 5 years because of administrative selection, since 6 years were offered only in six schools while the remaining schools offered a maximum of 5 years. Thus, for the most part, children did not leave the program after kindergarten because of poor performance or because of superior performance.

Summary of Evidence in the Chicago Longitudinal Study

For the past decade, the Chicago Longitudinal Study has investigated the effects of different levels of program participation. A brief summary of previous findings is provided below. Table 9 reports some of the major findings for school achievement, grade retention, and special education placement.

PRESCHOOL INTERVENTION

Studies of the effects of preschool participation on school competence outcomes indicate that children who participated for 1 or 2 years in the CPC

Table 9. Summary of Effects of CPC Preschool, Kindergarten and Primary-Grade Participation in Chicago Longitudinal Study (Effect Sizes Are Standard Deviation Units x 100)

Study	Total sample size	Group sample size	Years of follow-up	Analysis method	No. of covariates
Preschool/Kindergarten					
R 1991*	1,539	1011 P 528 C	3	CORR	0
RB 1993	1,255	798 P 382 C	1	OLS	7
R 1995	887	757 P 130 C	1–7	OLS/LV	6
RMT 1995	887	757 P 130 C	7	OLS	8
				OLS	27
				TS-SEL	9
RT 1995	806	566 P 240 C	1–7	OLS	7
				TS-SEL	8
				IV	7
				LV-COV	8
				LV-MEAN	7
RMBH 1996	360	240 P 120 C	7	OLS	6
Extended program, primary grades					
R 1994	1106	542 P 207 C	1–3	OLS	9
RT 1998	559	426 P 133 C	4–5	ML-SEL	9

Note: Preschool/Kindergarten values > 20 are educationally significant.

R = Reynolds, B = Bezruczko, T = Temple, M = Mehana, H = Hagemann. OLS = ordinary least squares, IV = instrumental variables, TS-SEL = two stage least squares with selection, LV = latent variables (mean or covariances). For effect sizes, R = reading, M = math,

	Effect sizes estimates at									
Age 5 EK ready	Age 6 Kind.		Age 8 Gr. 2		Age 9 Gr. 3		Age 12 Gr. 6		% Reduction in	% Reduction in
	R	M	R	M	R	M	R	M	% GR	% SP
56	46	46	42	36						
50										
77	35	46	35	35	09	13	36	32	24	12
									34	22
							36	33	26	
							38	35	30	
							37	36	13	
63	58				18		26			
61	58				08		30			
60	58				08		28			
46	57				04		28			
46	42				21		27			
							37	30	20	
									30	

Age 9 Gr. 3				Age 11 Gr. 5				Age 13 Gr. 7			
R	M	% GR	% SP	R	M	% GR	% SP	R	M	% GR	% SP
55	48	11	7	29	22	19	8				
		26	4			32	11				
48	35	—	—					43	28	15	10
										30	16

%GR = grade retention, %SP = special education placement, ML-SEL = maximum likelihood estimation with selection equation.

Extended program/primary grades total and group sample sizes may differ.

*For study R 1991, Child-Parent Center and Head Start groups are combined.

preschool had higher reading and math achievement test scores and lower rates of grade retention and special education placement up to age 12 (end of sixth grade) (Reynolds, 1995; Reynolds & Temple, 1995; Reynolds, Mehana, & Temple, 1995). Consistently significant differences in favor of preschool participants also have been found for parent participation in school (Reynolds, 1995) but less so for classroom adjustment (Reynolds, 1995) and children's perceived competence (Reynolds et al., 1995).

Although both 1 and 2 years of participation were found to be significantly associated with positive adjustment, the estimated effects of the second year of preschool were mixed. They were significant and educationally meaningful only for kindergarten entry and exit achievement and for special education placement in the early elementary grades (Reynolds, 1995).

PRIMARY–GRADE INTERVENTION ALONE

Reynolds (1994) found some support for the short-term effectiveness of intervention beginning in kindergarten and continuing to third grade, compared to kindergarten-only intervention. The 76 children who participated in the program from kindergarten to third grade scored higher than the 191 children in the no-treatment comparison group in reading and math achievement and had a lower rate of grade retention at the end of the program (third grade). This advantage persisted at the 1-year follow-up for reading achievement (Ms = 102.6 versus 99.6) and for grade retention (M rate = 18.7% versus 25.9%). No significant differences were detected at the 2-year follow-up for any measure.

EXTENDED INTERVENTION TO SECOND AND THIRD GRADE

Recent analyses of children up to age 12 indicate that although preschool intervention contributes significantly to positive adjustment over time, extended intervention appears to add significantly to the effect of preschool and kindergarten intervention (Reynolds, 1994). At the end of the program in third grade and at the 2-year follow-up, duration of program participation was significantly associated with higher reading achievement, higher math achievement, and a lower rate of grade retention. Relative to program participation ceasing in kindergarten, participation that extends to second or third grade was associated with higher reading and math achievement and with lower rates of grade retention and special education placement at the 4-year follow-up. Notably, the estimated effect of participating in 3 years of the follow-on component was higher than participation in 2 years. Recent findings at age 13 support these results (Reynolds & Temple, 1998; see also Reynolds, 1998d).

Two studies have specifically addressed the mediators, or pathways, through which program participation influences later performance. Based on a subsample of children in the six original CPCs, Reynolds (1992a) found that cognitive readiness at school entry (measured by the Iowa Tests of Basic Skills) was the primary mediator of the effects of preschool participation on grade 3 achievement for children in the six original CPCs. Parent participation in school, school mobility, and teacher ratings of classroom adjustment did not directly mediate the effects of program participation. Parent participation in school mediated preschool effectiveness indirectly through school mobility.

A follow-up study of the sample in sixth grade (Reynolds, Mavrogenes, et al., 1996) used a confirmatory structural modeling approach and found that both cognitive readiness at school entry and parent participation in school (teacher and parent ratings) independently mediated the effects of preschool participation on reading and math achievement. Teacher ratings of classroom adjustment in first grade and avoidance of school mobility and grade retention also contributed to the transmission of preschool effects. In support of the mediating role of parent participation in school, Reynolds (1994) found that parent participation in school significantly explained differential performance in reading and math achievement among children who participated in the CPC program for different lengths of time from preschool to second and third grade.

Evidence supporting the social adjustment and school support hypotheses of program effectiveness is limited. In previous studies (Reynolds, 1992a; Reynolds, Mavrogenes, et al., 1996), teacher ratings of classroom adjustment were influenced by preschool participation only through cognitive readiness at school entry. School mobility (an indicator of school support) also did not directly mediate the effects of program participation on school achievement. The motivational advantage hypothesis has not been investigated. Alternative hypotheses explaining the effects of extended early intervention also have not been investigated.

MODERATORS OF EFFECTS

Previous studies have not extensively investigated program effects by subgroup. Several studies (Reynolds, 1995, 1994; Reynolds, Mavrogenes, et al., 1996) reported no gender differences in the effect of preschool or extended participation on school achievement and school adjustment—girls and boys benefited equally. Children experiencing a higher number of environmental risk factors (e.g., growing up in a high-poverty neighborhood, with a mother with limited education, and with large family sizes) were as likely to benefit from the program as children experiencing relatively few environmental risks (Reynolds, 1998a). More refined analyses involving parent education, school attributes, and program characteristics have not been completed.

The present study extends these earlier analyses by systematically investigating the effects of timing and duration of intervention exposure, the pathways of program effectiveness, and the moderators of program effectiveness for the age 14 and 15 follow-up sample. No prior studies in the CLS sample have done this, and I am aware of no studies of large-scale programs that have done so.

Summary of Methodological Issues

The present study reports new outcome data for the active Chicago sample. The methodological issues inherent in this longitudinal project have been addressed extensively. The principal threats to the validity of findings are selection bias into the program and nonrandom attrition from the sample. Selection bias due to the quasi-experimental design of the study has been extensively investigated. Selection bias into the preschool intervention appears to be small and does not affect estimates of program impact (Reynolds & Temple, 1995; Reynolds, Mavrogenes, et al. 1996).[14]

As shown in Table 9, the estimated effects of preschool participation have been found to be educationally meaningful (values ≥ .20 standard deviations or increases in the rate of success of 20% or more) regardless of sample size, analytic method, comparison group, and adjustments for selection bias and measurement error. Concerning selection bias associated with participation in the follow-on intervention, Reynolds and Temple (1998) found that although children who participated in the follow-on program had higher achievement test scores prior to the follow-on program than the group that did not participate in the follow-on program, preprogram growth rates in achievement from the beginning to the end of kindergarten were equivalent between groups. This finding renders the selection-maturation explanation of observed effects unlikely. Program effects persisted up to seventh grade, even after taking into account differences in kindergarten pretest scores, kindergarten growth rates, and family demographics.

Sample attrition also has had minimal effects on the findings of the Chicago Longitudinal Study. Most of the original study sample was active in the Chicago public schools at age 14 (eighth grade), and no selective attrition among groups was found, although program participants were more likely than comparison-group participants to be active in the study sample after controlling for differences in child and family factors (see Appendix B). Reynolds and Temple (1998) found that taking into account sample selection due to attrition increased rather than decreased the size of the effects of extended intervention.

Compared to many other studies, the generalizability of the findings of the Chicago Longitudinal Study is high. This large sample of children participated in an established, government-funded program for different lengths of time. Consequently, generalizability extends to low-income children in many public programs in central cities. As indicated in the introduction, research on the long-term effects of such programs is quite limited. That the program and comparison groups are well matched on several background characteristics and equally eligible for early childhood programs further strengthens the interpretability of findings and thus increases their significance for public policy.

In summary, the CPC program is a center-based early intervention that provides comprehensive educational-support and family-support services to children and families in the poorest neighborhoods in Chicago during ages 3 to 9. As one of the earliest educational innovations of the 1965 Title I Act, the program has a long history of successful program implementation. In the past decade, the Chicago Longitudinal Study has investigated the effects of program participation for a 1983 to 1989 cohort and the conditions under which long-term effects may be achieved. Previous studies using a variety of analytic approaches have consistently found that program participation is significantly associated with greater school achievement and fewer problem behaviors. Long-term effects across a wide range of youth and family development are yet to be determined. This is the goal of the rest of the volume.

3

Study Methods and Measures

This chapter describes the characteristics of the CPC program and comparison groups, defines the outcome and explanatory measures used to investigate program impact, and describes the statistical methods used to address the major research questions. As reviewed in Chapter 2, the Chicago Longitudinal Study (CLS) began with a cohort of 1,539 children who graduated from the CPCs and other public early childhood kindergarten programs in 1986. By early adolescence, over 1,100 youth remained active in Chicago. Because the CLS is primarily a study of children's experiences in the Chicago public schools, this group (and the age 15 sample of 1,070) is the main study sample for the rest of the volume. The significance of the Child-Parent Center Program and its successful history of implementation make it a most appropriate subject for the analytic methods described in this chapter.

In the analysis that follows, program impact is investigated for seven youth outcomes at ages 14 and 15 and for three family socialization outcomes at age 12. These outcomes, shown in Table 10 for each of the four major study questions, are formally investigated in Chapters 4 and 5. Comprehensive programs like the Child-Parent Centers are expected to impact multiple outcomes for both children and parents. These outcomes index social competence, which is defined generally as everyday effectiveness in meeting individual, family, and school responsibilities. It is the ascribed goal of Head Start (National Head Start Association, 1990) and most other early childhood programs (Phillips & Cabrera, 1996; Reynolds et al., 1997; Zigler & Berman, 1983). Key components of social compe-

Table 10. Study Questions and Youth and Family Outcomes

Major study questions	Social competence outcomes

Question 1. Are measures of CPC participation associated with youth and family outcomes? (Chapter 4)
    Participation measures
        Any (preschool or follow-on)
        Preschool
        Follow-on
        Extended (preschool plus follow-on)
        Total number of years
    Controlling for
        Sex of child
        Risk status

Question 2. Is extended program participation to second or third grade associated with youth and family outcomes relative to less extensive participation? (Chapter 4)
    Participation measures
    Extended for 4, 5, or 6 years of education
    Additional control factor
        Kindergarten achievement

Question 3. Do subgroups of children benefit more from program participation than other subgroups? (Chapter 4)
    Subgroup indicators
        Girls vs. boys
        Educational status of parent/guardian
        Risk status
        School poverty during preschool/kindergarten
        Parent participation in school
        Instructional emphasis in preschool

Question 4. Which individual, family, and school-related factors mediate the long-term effects of program participation? (Chapter 5)
    Factors/processes
        Cognitive advantage hypothesis
        Family support hypothesis
        Social adjustment hypothesis
        Motivational advantage hypothesis
        School support hypothesis

Social competence outcomes:

Youth at ages 14–15
Reading achievement
Math achievement
Consumer skills
Grade retention
Special education placement
Delinquency infractions
Perceived school competence

Family socialization at age 12
Parent participation in school
Expectations for child's educational attainment
Satisfaction with child's education

Table 11. Outcome and Intervening Measures Used to Investigate Program Effects

Study variable	Collected at age	Mean	Min	Max	Sample N
Youth Outcomes					
Reading achievement (standard scores)	14–15				
Age 14 ITBS (levels 14/13)		145.1 (22.4)	77	212	1158
Age 15 TAP or ITBS (levels 15/14)		149.9 (23.5)	68	220	1042
Mathematics total achievement	14–15				
Age 14 ITBS (levels 14/13)		147.4 (18.7)	82	225	1158
Age 15 TAP or ITBS (levels 15/14)		152.2 (19.5)	77	220	1042
Consumer skills (Chicago MPST)	14–15				
Raw score (63 items)		40.0 (10.6)	10	63	1159
Percentage passing		0.60	0	1	1159
Grade retention (cumulative)	6–15				
Age 14 (up to grade 8)		0.27	0	1	1164
Age 15 (up to grade 9)		0.29	0	1	1070
Special education placement (cumulative)	6–15				
Age 14 incidence		0.17	0	1	1164
Age 14 years receiving services		0.65 (1.7)	0	8	1164
Age 15 incidence		0.17	0	1	1070
Age 15 years receiving services		0.79 (2.0)	0	9	1070
Delinquency behavior (school reports)	13–15				
Age 13/14 incidence		0.13	0	1	1164
Age 13–15 incidence		0.23	0	1	1070
Perceived school competence (12-item scale)	12	37.4 (4.7)	15	48	788
Family socialization outcomes					
Parent educational expectations for child's education (some h.s. to beyond bachelor's degree)	10–12	3.3 (1.13)	1	5	756
Parent satisfaction with child's education (very satisfied to very unsatisfied)	10–12	3.9 (1.07)	1	5	756
Parent participation in school (freq. of ratings of ave./above; teacher & parent ratings)*	8–12	1.8 (1.4)	0	5	1164
Intervening measures					
Cognitive readiness at kind. entry (ITBS composite)	5	47.6 (10.3)	28	83	840
Early school achievement (ITBS)	9				
Reading achievement (level 9/8)		96.9 (16.9)	48	145	1081
Math total achievement (level 9/8)		100.7 (13.3)	54	133	1082
Perceived school competence (10-item scale)	9	23.6 (3.3)	10	30	914
Teacher ratings of classrm adjust. (6-item scale)	9	19.0 (5.4)	6	30	981
School mobility (no. school moves from grades 4–7)	10–13	0.98 (1.1)	0	4	1164
School quality (no. yrs. in school where 25% of students score at/above nat'l ave.)	10–13	0.83 (1.49)	0	4	1164

Note: Except where noted, sample sizes are for age 14 sample. *This measure also was used as an intervening variable.

tence during childhood and early adolescence include school performance, cognitive achievement, and social adjustment. In this study, the indicators include reading and math achievement, consumer skills, grade retention, special education placement, delinquency infractions, and perceived school competence. For family outcomes, I measure parent involvement in school, expectations for children's educational attainment, and satisfaction with children's education at school.[1] These outcomes are not only consistent with the CPC program theory described in Chapter 2 but also are commonly used measures of program impact in the literature (Barnett, 1995; Guralnick, 1997; Karoly et al., 1998).

Descriptions of the explanatory and outcome measures used to investigate the study questions are located in Table 11. They include the youth and family outcomes, intervening variables relevant for determining pathways of effects, program measures, and the child background factors of sex of child and risk status. They are discussed below after the description of the sample.

Study Sample

The study sample included the 1,164 youth who were active in the Chicago public schools at age 14, their eighth-grade school year (1993–94). A slight majority of the study sample were girls (51%), and 93% were African American. Findings also were reported for the 1,070 youth who were active in the Chicago public schools at age 15, their ninth-grade year (1994–95). As indicated in Chapter 2, all families were eligible for educational intervention based on economic or educational need. The number of years of enrollment in the CPC program ranged from 0 to 6.

Table 12 reports the reasons for attrition from the study sample at ages 14 and 15 for both the CPC program and comparison groups. As discussed in Chapter 2, the comparison group matched the program group in eligibility for intervention, neighborhood and family economic disadvantage, and race/ethnicity, and the children in this group participated in another early intervention in kindergarten. For both groups, relocation out of Chicago after third grade (11% of original sample) was the most frequent reason for sample attrition by age 14. Moving from Chicago or to a Chicago nonpublic school (7.3%), becoming a dropout or lost (2.8%), attendance in a nonpublic school in Chicago (2.7%), institutional care (0.3%), and mortality (0.3%) were additional reasons. The pattern of reasons for leaving was similar between groups. The age 15 patterns also were similar.

Measures of CPC Program Participation

Table 13 displays the sample sizes for six measures of program participa-

Table 12. Reasons for Attrition from Study Sample at Ages 14 and 15

Reason for leaving	Program group N	%	Comparison group N	%	Total N	%
Age 14 (1994)						
Moved from Chicago or to nonpublic school by third grade	77	6.7	36	9.4	113	7.3
Moved from Chicago after third grade	122	10.6	47	12.2	169	11.0
Chicago nonpublic school	32	2.8	10	2.6	42	2.7
Residential or correctional institution	4	0.3	0	0.0	4	0.3
Deceased	3	0.3	1	0.3	4	0.3
Dropped out or lost	28	2.4	15	3.9	43	2.8
Total attrition	266	23.0	109	28.4	375	24.4
Total active	889	77.0	275	71.6	1164	75.6
Age 15 (1995)						
Moved from Chicago or to nonpublic school by third grade	73	6.3	36	9.4	109	7.1
Moved from Chicago after third grade	149	12.9	52	13.5	201	13.1
Chicago nonpublic school	53	4.6	18	4.7	71	4.6
Residential or correctional institution	5	0.4	0	0.0	5	0.3
Deceased	4	0.3	2	0.5	6	0.4
Dropped out or lost	54	4.7	23	6.0	77	5.0
Total attrition	338	29.3	131	34.1	469	29.5
Total active	817	70.7	253	65.9	1070	69.5

Note: Percentages reflect proportions of the total program and comparison groups.
Moved from Chicago = relocation to a suburb, another Illinois city, or out of state. Lost = truant officer cannot locate; usually denotes dropout.

tion used in the study. The measures index the timing and duration of participation in the CPC program. The ratio of program participants to sample size was similar for the study sample and the original sample. The program indicators described below overlap each other to some extent but provide conceptually distinct information. Any program participation, for example, is a general indicator of exposure without regard to timing of participation. Participation in follow-on (primary-grade) intervention is required for extended program participation, but some children participated in follow-on intervention without participating in earlier intervention (see Chapter 2). This explains variation in years of program participation as well. To distinguish the differential effects of preschool and follow-on intervention, both indicators were always entered simultaneously. Data

Table 13. Sample Sizes for Different Measures of Program Participation

CPC group	Program group (N)	Comparison group (N)	Study sample in program (%)	Original sample in program (%)
Any particip.	889	275	76.4	75
Any preschool	772	392	66.3	64.3
Yrs. of preschool	772	392		
1 yr	341		29.3	29.6
2 yr	431		37	34.7
Any follow-on	669	495	57.5	55.2
Yrs. of follow-on	669	495		
1 yr	109		9.4	10.9
2 yr	355		30.5	27.9
3 yr	205		17.6	16.4
Yrs. of CPC	889	275		
1 yr	21		1.8	2.8
2 yr	104		12	12.5
3 yr	223		19.5	19.7
4 yr	168		14.4	14.2
5 yr	265		22.8	20.3
6 yr	72		6.2	5.5
Extended particip.	461	703	39.6	35.9

Note: Study sample included 1,164 youth at age 14 (age 15 had 94 fewer cases). Original sample included 1,539. Follow-on = school-age, primary-grade component.

came from centralized school records as reported by each center. In some cases, participation was verified with center personnel.

Any program participation was coded 1 for children who received any CPC services from preschool to third grade and 0 for children who never enrolled in the CPCs from preschool to third grade. This measure provides a most conservative indicator of the effect of the program. Children in the original comparison group who later enrolled in the follow-on (primary-grade) program ($n = 29$) were coded as program participants.

Any preschool participation was coded 1 for children who participated in the CPC preschool component for 1 or 2 years and 0 for children who did not participate. All children who participated in CPC preschool also enrolled in CPC kindergarten. Non-CPC preschool participants enrolled in all-day kindergarten programs at age 5 (either a CESP program or the kindergarten program in the centers). I used years of preschool only to investigate pathways of program effectiveness because a previous study (Reynolds, 1995) indicated that years of preschool (0 to 2 years) affected cognitive school readiness but hardly any other child outcome after age 6, including school achievement, grade retention, and parent involvement in school.

Any follow-on participation was coded 1 for children who participated in the CPC primary-grade intervention component during grades 1 to 3 (in 1986–89) and 0 for children who did not participate but were enrolled in a regular school program. Follow-on participation was open to all children who enrolled in the elementary schools where the CPC program was located. Consequently, children who enrolled in a kindergarten program in the CPCs or in the CESP comparison sites were eligible for follow-on participation. Seventy-two (72) percent of CPC preschool and kindergarten participants (a similar proportion for the original sample) enrolled in the follow-on program in grades 1 to 3.

Years of follow-on participation was the number of years of participation in the CPC primary-grade program during grades 1 to 3. Values ranged from 0 to 3. Again, participation could include children who were originally in the CESP comparison group. For the total sample, the mean number of years of follow-on intervention was 1.2. In previous studies (Reynolds, 1994; Reynolds & Bezruczko, 1993), years of follow-on participation were significantly associated with school achievement and performance.

Years of program participation was the total number of years of participation in the CPC program from ages 3 to 9. Values ranged from 0 to 6 and included 0 to 2 years of preschool, 1 year of kindergarten, and 0 to 3 years of primary-grade intervention. For the total study sample, the mean number of years of intervention was 2.9, or 4.1 for those beginning as preschoolers.

Extended program participation was coded 1 for children who participated in each component of the CPC program from preschool to second or third grade (4 to 6 years). Children with less extensive participation in the CPC program (4 or fewer years) were coded 0. Those having 4 years of participation but only one year of follow-on intervention (i.e., program entry at age 3) were not considered extended program participants (coded 0). In previous studies (Reynolds, 1994; Reynolds & Bezruczko, 1993; Reynolds & Temple, 1998), this indicator of program participation has shown the strongest associations with social competence outcomes.

Child and Family Background Variables

The estimated effects of different measures of program participation take into account differences in sex of child and an index of risk status. Kindergarten achievement test scores also were used as pretest covariates in addressing the effects of extended intervention versus less extensive intervention as well as follow-on intervention.

SEX OF CHILD

Girls were coded 1 and boys were coded 0 as indicated by school records at the time of preschool or kindergarten entry.

RISK STATUS

A composite variable of the number of risk factors children have experienced was used to index environmental risk. Eight dichotomously coded variables were included that are likely to be associated with school performance or program participation:

low parent educational attainment

eligibility for free lunch (a proxy for socioeconomic status)

four or more children in the family

attending a kindergarten program in a school in which 60% or more of children in the attendance area reside in low-income families (neighborhood poverty)

unemployed parent (not working full- or part-time)

single-parent family status

missing data on family background (parent education or eligibility for free lunch)

minority status

Because children were minority (93% black, 7% Hispanic), the latter indicator was a constant. Children with missing data on the indicators were given estimates based on the number of indicators that were missing.[2] The range of the risk index was from 1 to 8. Neighborhood poverty and minority status were obtained from school records. The five family measures came from parent reports on surveys or in telephone interviews when children were ages 8 to 12.

These risk indicators were chosen because they were the most plausible correlates of both program participation and measured outcomes as judged from earlier studies with these data (Reynolds, 1994, 1995). The risk index may be a more reliable indicator of preexisting differences between program and comparison groups than any single indicator or a few indicators.

71

Table 14. Risk Indicators for CPC Program and Comparison Groups

Risk indicators	% of program group (n = 889)	% of comparison group (n = 275)	Significance (p)	Correlation with age 14 reading
1. Parent/guardian has < high school degree	41	49	.053	-.19*
2. Eligible for free lunch subsidy	84	82	.584	-.15*
3. Family has ≥ 4 children	14	18	.076	-.01
4. In a school area where ≥ 60% of students are low income (Kind.)	77	74	.306	-.03
5. Parent/guardian not employed full-time or part-time	56	57	.911	.01
6. Living in single-parent family	76	66	.024*	-.05
7. Missing on family background (education or lunch)	32	38	.060	-.15*
8. Minority status	100	100	—	—
Risk index (mean)	4.96	5.11	.107	-.19*

Note: N for parent education, lunch status, unemployment, and single-parent status were, respectively, 810, 818, 556, and 556. All others were 1,164.
* $p < .05$.

As predicted by resilience theory, cumulative or multiple risk has been found to be substantially associated with developmental functioning (Bendersky & Lewis, 1994; Rutter, 1987), and this is better captured with a risk index than with several indicator variables entered as main effects. Moreover, because several of the risk indicators were measured in different years (some during or after program participation), the risk index was used to proxy risk status at the time of program entry. This measure has the advantage of providing estimates of program effects that are conservative. To the extent that program participation affects these later measures (e.g., parent education, employment status), estimated program effects will be smaller than would otherwise be expected.

As shown in Table 14, the CPC program group, who had any program participation, experienced the same number of risk factors (M = 5.0) as the comparison group (M = 5.1). The largest differences were that the program group had a greater percentage of single parents and a smaller percentage of parents without a high school degree. These differences are taken into account in the analyses through the inclusion of the risk status index. Only parent education met the criteria of a confounding variable; it was significantly correlated with both program participation and age 14 reading achievement (other outcomes showed a similar pattern).

KINDERGARTEN ACHIEVEMENT

In analyses of the effects of extended program participation, I included age 5/6 (end of kindergarten) scores on the group-administered word analysis and math subtests of the Iowa Tests of Basic Skills (ITBS; Early Primary Battery, Form 7 Level 5; Hieronymus, Lindquist, & Hoover, 1980a). The test was administered orally by staff other than the classroom teacher. The word analysis subtest contained 35 items assessing prereading skills, including letter-sound recognition and rhyming. The math subtest included 33 items measuring numbering, classification, and quantification. The reliability of the word analysis (KR-20 coeff. = .87) and math (KR-20 coeff. = .82) subtests is the highest of the ITBS measures at this age. Developmental standard scores were used in the analysis. They have equal-interval scale points and index continuous development over the grade years such that the national average for kindergarten, third grade, and eighth grade are, respectively, 60, 108, and 168.

Comparability among Intervention Groups

Although the quasi-experimental design of the study would be expected to reduce the extent to which group differences are interpreted as program effects, the descriptive statistics in Table 14 indicate that program and comparison groups experienced similar levels of social disadvantage. Several other study features increase the likelihood that groups are comparable and that estimated effects are due to differential program participation.

All children were eligible for Title I program services due to economic and educational disadvantage and participated in at least one year of an early childhood program (CPC or other program).

Kindergarten achievement scores prior to the beginning of the primary-grade program were available as control variables and for determining cognitive growth over time (see Reynolds & Temple, 1998).

The variation in exposure to intervention provided several contrasts among groups with similar educational needs and degrees of self-selection. Self-selection is unlikely to be a significant factor in adjustment differences among the 3 groups with participation in preschool plus kindergarten, preschool through second grade, and preschool through third grade because all three groups enrolled in the CPC program beginning in preschool. Data on the variation in duration or strength of treatment enhances the capacity to determine program effectiveness (Rossi & Freeman, 1993; Yeaton & Sechrest, 1981).

Previous studies with this sample indicate that the effects of self-selection are relatively small and can be explained by variables that were measured in the study (Reynolds & Temple, 1995, 1998; see also Table 9). Nevertheless, the potential effects of self-selection continue to be investigated.

Differential exposure to the intervention was due to many factors, including administrative requirements, short-term parent interests, and residential or school mobility. Enrollment in the primary-grade component of the intervention for 3 years rather than for 2 years was the result of administrative requirements—many centers restrict enrollment to only 2 years while other centers provide 3 years of services. Thus, school differences rather than individual or family differences determined this variation in exposure. The non-CPC comparison group did not enroll in the CPCs because they did not live in a neighborhood in which a center was located, yet the characteristics of their neighborhoods matched those of the CPCs.

Youth Social Competence

Several indicators of social competence were utilized to investigate the effects of program participation. As indicated in the beginning of the chapter, social competence is the ascribed goal of most early childhood programs for low-income and special needs children. Although there are many components, social competence often includes cognitive ability, school achievement and progress, psychological development, and physical health as well as family development (see also Zigler & Trickett, 1978). In this study, I defined social competence by reading and math achievement, consumer skills, cumulative grade retention, cumulative special education placement, delinquency infractions, perceived school competence, and family socialization. The latter is considered in a separate section. These social competence outcomes were measured up to age 15. Reading and math achievement and life skills index the construct of developed cognitive abilities; grade retention and special education placement index school competence, and perceived school competence and delinquency are indicators of social-psychological behavior. These indicators have been

74

Table 15. Correlations among Social Competence Outcomes at
Ages 12–15

Competence Indicator	1	2	3	4	5	6	7
1. Reading achiev.	—	.78	.73	-.48	-.37	-.13	.40
2. Math achiev.		—	.75	-.53	-.42	-.13	.38
3. Consumer skills			—	-.31	-.33	-.10	.37
4. Grade retention			.	—	.25	.04	-.22
5. Years in special ed.					—	.06	-.18
6. School delinquency						—	-.08
7. Perceived competence							—

Note: School delinquency is measured at ages 13–14. Grade retention and delinquency are dichotomous indicators. Values were based on pairwise-present cases.

used frequently in previous studies and are among the strongest predictors of later socioeconomic status. Table 15 displays the correlations among the youth outcomes.

SCHOOL ACHIEVEMENT IN READING AND MATHEMATICS

School achievement was measured by standardized test scores in reading comprehension and mathematics total achievement on the Iowa Tests of Basic Skills (ITBS) and the Tests of Achievement and Proficiency at ages 14 and 15. Both are nationally normed tests and are administered each spring as part of the citywide testing program. The tests are group-administered by noninstructional personnel and include yearly audit testing. All reported scores are based on the 1988 normative sample. Developmental standard scores were the primary metric for the analysis. These scores are equated with a mean of 100 in the fall of third grade and a mean of 160 in the fall of eighth grade.

Age 14 scores (seventh or eighth grade) were from the Multilevel Battery of the ITBS (Level 13 / 14; Hieronymus & Hoover, 1990). The reading comprehension subtest has 58 items (Level 13 has 57 items) and emphasizes understanding of text passages. The reliability coefficient (KR-20) was .92. The mean raw score for the national sample was 30.7. The mathematics total achievement scale has 117 items (Level 13 has 113 items) measuring the domains of concepts, computation, and problem solving. The reliability coefficient (KR-20) was .95. The mean raw score for the national sample was 65.2.

Age 15 scores (eighth or ninth grade) were based on the Tests of Achievement and Proficiency (TAP; Level 15; Scannell, Haugh, Schild, & Ulmer, 1990) or Level 14 of the ITBS described above. The TAP is the high-school equivalent of the Iowa Tests of Basic Skills, and reading and math subtest scores are vertically equated across tests. The TAP reading comprehension subtest has 57 items with a reliability coefficient of .90. The mean raw score for the 1988 normative sample was 29.8. The mathematics subtest included 48 items and has a reliability (KR-20) coefficient of .91 (mean raw score = 21.3, normative sample).

The psychometric characteristics of both the ITBS and TAP are among the best of all standardized achievement tests (Linn, 1989). Although developmental standard scores were the primary metric for the analysis, grade equivalents also were used to facilitate interpretation.

CONSUMER SKILLS

The proficiency of youth in basic consumer skills in their communities was based on scores from the Chicago Minimum Proficiency Skills Test (MPST). The MPST is administered to all eighth graders in the Chicago public schools, and they must obtain a passing score (greater than 60%, or 38 items correct) to graduate from high school. For the analysis, I analyzed raw scores and the percentage of students who earned a passing score (1 = pass, 0 = fail). The MPST is a 63-item multiple-choice test first published by the Chicago Public Schools in 1977. It is administered annually to establish a minimum level of competency on community-related tasks that students must show before receiving a high school degree. This minimum level of competency represents the socioeconomic capacity to function independently in the community. MPST items test the cognitive domains of language arts, computation, and problem solving with item content from seven community-related areas of performance: personal finance, health, community resources, transportation, occupation, communication, and government.

To diminish the influence of reading on test scores, the vocabulary and sentence structure of the items is constrained not to exceed a third-grade reading level.[3] A typical item testing competency with personal finance is "Concert tickets cost 9 dollars per person. What is the total cost for you and four friends?" An item testing knowledge of community resources reads "To whom should you complain about a store that sells defective vacuum cleaners?" One of the items testing competency in the occupation area presents students with a job application, while communication would be tested with an item like the following: "Mary wishes to buy a new car and needs a loan from the bank to buy the car. What is a loan?" Consequently, the test measures a broad range of community-related performance, and consumer competency represents a major portion. Internal consistency reliability for the test commonly exceeds .85, and in the present study was .90 (see also Bezruczko & Reynolds, 1987; and Reynolds & Bezruczko, 1989).

RETENTION IN GRADE

Grade retention status was measured cumulatively up to eighth grade and up to ninth grade. Any child on record as repeating a grade from kindergarten to eighth or ninth grade was coded 1; all others were coded 0. A child was coded as retained if he or she had identical grade codes in consecutive school years according to centralized school records. Avoiding grade retention is a measure of basic school competency. Although at the time of the study sample's enrollment in elementary school, the Chicago Board of Education's policy (since toughened) stated that a "student shall not be promoted from one grade to the next if the student has not met the minimum levels of performance from the assigned grade levels," it also stated that grade retention should be used as a last resort or "only if all other intervention strategies have failed." (Chicago Public Schools, 1985, p. 2).

SPECIAL EDUCATION PLACEMENT

Placement in special education (self-contained or mainstreamed) was measured in two ways: (a) the number of years a student was placed in special education during elementary school (first grade onward), and (b) any placement during elementary school (up to ages 14 and 15). Data came from centralized school records. For these records, schools note the type of placement. Both self-contained and mainstream special education were included. The major placement categories (based on federal definitions) were specific learning disability, behavioral disorder, and speech and language impairments. Placement in special education means that children were receiving special education services, after appropriate referral by school personnel or parents and after review by a multidisciplinary team, which provides for an individual education plan for students judged in need of services.

DELINQUENCY INFRACTIONS

The cumulative incidence of delinquency infractions was measured during ages 13 and 14 and during ages 13 to 15 (1993–95) from school records. Delinquency reports are records of problem, illicit, or illegal behavior occurring in or outside of school. For each year, the frequency and severity of infractions are reported by school personnel (e.g., school counselors or truant officers). The degree of severity of behavioral infractions ranges from 1 to 5: Level 1 behavior refers to frequent tardiness, leaving class without permission, and disruptive behavior. Level 2 infractions include the use of profane language, smoking, alcohol use, or loitering. Level 3 behaviors include theft and fighting. Level 4 infractions include drug use, engaging false alarms, and use of weapons. Level 5 behaviors include arson, aggravated assault, sex assault, and gang activity. Although these records are primarily for acts that occur in the vicinity of school grounds, they include a wide range of acts of juvenile delinquency. Because the range of values was restricted for both frequency (most were 1 or 2) and severity (most were Levels 1 to 3), binary-coded delinquency status (1 = any infraction, 0 = no infractions) was the primary measure.

PERCEIVED SCHOOL COMPETENCE AT AGE 12

This 12-item scale measured school self-concept including task persistence. It was administered in children's sixth-grade year as part of a larger survey of school experiences. The items were rated from strongly agree (4) to strongly disagree (1). Statements included the following:

I get good grades in school.
My classmates like me.
I get in trouble at school (reverse coded).
I get along well with others.
I do my homework.
I answer questions in class.
I give up when school work gets hard (reverse coded).
When I get bad grades I try even harder.
I try hard in school.
My teacher thinks I will go far in school.
I am smart.
I do better in school than my classmates.[4]

Table 16. Correlations between Family Outcomes and Youth Outcomes

Youth outcome	Family outcome		
	Educational expectations	Satisfaction with education	Participation in school
1. Reading achiev.	.33	.18	.32
2. Math achiev.	.35	.19	.32
3. Consumer skills	.26	.20	.28
4. Grade retention	-.31	-.08	-.27
5. Years in special ed.	-.11	-.08	-.11
6. School delinquency	-.03	-.13	-.13
7. Perceived competence	.17	.19	.24

Note: Values are based on pairwise-present cases.

The reliability coefficient was .75. Previous studies in the Chicago study have indicated that perceived school competence is a predictor of school achievement and is associated with program participation (Reynolds et al., 1995). As a supplemental measure, I used child reports of their expectations for educational attainment (How far in school do you think you will get?) at age 10.

Family Socialization Outcomes

Three indicators of family socialization were used to measure the family effects of program participation: parent expectations, satisfaction with children's education, and parent involvement in school. These outcomes highlight attitudes and behaviors with or on behalf of children that are directly linked to the program theory described in Chapter 2. Because the major focus of the CPC parent program was involvement in children's educational development, these school-related indicators were emphasized. Parent involvement in children's education is one of the eight national educational goals (National Education Goals Panel, 1995) and is a frequent correlate of children's school progress and achievement (Haynes, Comer, & Hamilton-Lee, 1988; Reynolds, 1992b; Steinberg, Lamborn, Dornbusch, & Darling, 1992). The indicators were measured between second and sixth grades (up to 3 years after the primary-grade program). One of the measures, parent involvement in school, also was used as an intervening variable between program participation and youth social competence outcomes. Parent expectations was significantly but modestly associated with satisfaction with children's education ($r = .11$) and parent involvement in school ($r = .20$). The correlation between satisfaction with children's education and parent involvement also was low ($r = .12$). Correlations between family and youth outcomes are reported in Table 16.

PARENT EXPECTATIONS FOR CHILDREN'S EDUCATIONAL ATTAINMENT
As part of a questionnaire on family educational experiences, parents reported their expectations for children's educational attainment: "How far in school do you expect your child to get?" Approximately 90% of respondents were mothers. Responses were coded from 1 (less than high school graduation) to 5 (go beyond the baccalaureate). Other categories were high school graduation, some college, and 4-year college degree. Educational expectations were reported during grades 4 to 6 (children aged 10 to 12) through both survey questionnaires and telephone interviews. This item is the educational equivalent of the measure of occupational aspirations by Lazar et al. (1982).

PARENT SATISFACTION WITH CHILDREN'S EDUCATION
On the same survey, parents also responded to the question "How satisfied were you with the education your child has received at school?" Responses were coded on a 5-point scale, ranging from very satisfied (5) to very unsatisfied (1). The middle categories included satisfied, not sure, and unsatisfied. Presumably, parent participation in the program may foster good relationships with teachers and other parents, which may increase satisfaction with children's education. Using a similar measure, Lazar et al. (1982) found that program mothers were more satisfied than comparison mothers with how their children have done in school.

PARENT PARTICIPATION IN SCHOOL
Parental school participation was operationalized for parents of children from ages 8 to 12 (1988–92) as the frequency of participation that was rated in the middle range or higher by teachers or parents. Classroom teachers responded to the item asking them to rate for each child the "parents' participation in school activities" for four consecutive years (1989–92). Responses were coded dichotomously (1 = average/satisfactory or higher, 0 = otherwise). The sum of these four dichotomous items was added to the sum of two parent-reported ratings on school participation when children were between ages 8 to 12 (i.e., "How often do you participate in school ac-

Table 17. Correlations among Intervening Variables

Indicator	1	2	3	4	5	6	7	8
1. Cognitive school readiness at age 5	—	.19	.28	.25	.44	.45	-.17	.27
2. Parent participation in school		—	.35	.21	.29	.28	-.30	.08
3. Teacher ratings of class-room adjustment at age 9			—	.48	.57	.57	-.13	.07
4. Self-perceptions of school competence at age 9				—	.33	.36	-.11	.04
5. Reading achiev. at age 9					—	.80	-.15	.25
6. Math achiev. at age 9						—	-.11	.21
7. School mobility							—	-.19
8. School quality								—

Note: Values are based on pairwise-present cases.

tivities?"). Responses were coded dichotomously (1 = sometimes or often, or 1 = more than monthly; 0 = otherwise).[5]

For the analysis, I used the frequency of "average" or better ratings (Min. = 0, Max. = 5). Both teacher and parent ratings of school involvement complement each other and provide a more comprehensive measure than ratings from a single source (Reynolds, Mavrogenes, et al., 1996). Although teacher ratings of parent participation were available in first and second grade, I emphasized postprogram parent participation.

Intervening Variables

As part of the conceptual model in Figure 1, five additional factors were tested as mediators (pathways) of the effects of program participation on adolescent social competence. They were measured from grades 1 to 7. In previous studies, they have been found to be significantly associated with scholastic adjustment both directly and indirectly (Reynolds, 1991; Reynolds & Bezruczko, 1993; Reynolds, Mavrogenes, et al., 1996). Table 17 displays the correlations among the intervening variables. The intervening measure of parent participation in school is described above. The intervening variables are investigated in Chapter 5 as pathways of program effectiveness.

COGNITIVE DEVELOPED ABILITY AT AGE 5

To investigate the cognitive advantage hypothesis of the effects of program participation (see Chapter 1), two measures of cognitive (scholastic) development were used. Cognitive developed ability at entry into kindergarten or "developmental preparedness" was measured by the basic-composite scale of the ITBS Early Primary Battery in the fall of 1985 (Form 7, Level 5; Hieronymus, Lindquist, & Hoover, 1980a). The test measures listening skills, word analysis, language, vocabulary, and mathematics. The items were orally presented to children by a nonclassroom teacher over a one-week period. The composite battery has high reliability (coefficient = .94) and predictive validity (see Reynolds, Mavrogenes, et al., 1996). Developmental standard scores (based on 1988 norms) were analyzed. The national average was 51 (based on the 1988 normative sample).

Age 9 ITBS reading comprehension and mathematics total achievement scores (Levels 8 or 9; Hieronymus, Lindquist, & Hoover, 1980b) were used as measures of developed abilities in investigating the cognitive advantage hypothesis for duration of program participation and extended program participation. Children were in second or third grade. Reading comprehension was assessed through 47 items. The math total scale included 88 items on computation, concepts, and problem solving. Test reliabilities were greater than .90 (Hieronymus et al., 1980b). As with the kindergarten scores, developmental standard scores were used in the analysis.[6]

SOCIAL ADJUSTMENT

Teacher ratings of children's classroom adjustment at age 9 (third grade) were used to index social adjustment, including the capacity for self-regulatory behavior. The six-item scale had response categories from 1 (poor/not at all) to 3 (average/satisfactory) to 5 (excellent/much) and included the following items:

concentrates on work
follows directions
is self-confident
participates in group discussions
gets along well with others
takes responsibility for actions

The reliability coefficient for the scale was .94. The scale's moderate correlations with school performance (rs = .40-.50) indicate construct distinction.

PERCEIVED SCHOOL COMPETENCE AT AGE 9

Self-reported school competence perceptions were measured at age 9 (third grade) through a 10-item scale from a larger survey of children's early school experiences. Like the age 12 measure, items tap school self-concept and include: "I am smart," "I like school," "School is important," "I get along well with others," "I get good grades in school," "I like myself," "I try hard in school," "I do better in school than my classmates," "I answer questions in class,"and "I give up when school work gets hard" (reverse coded). Item responses ranged from 1 (not much) to 3 (a lot). Internal consistency of the scale was .76. The measure correlates moderately with school achievement and teacher ratings of social adjustment (Reynolds, 1998a; Reynolds & Bezruczko, 1993). It was used as the indicator of the motivational advantage hypothesis.

SCHOOL MOBILITY

School mobility was measured as the number of times children changed schools from fourth to seventh grade. This included both normative and nonnormative school transfers and was measured through centralized school records. Although the causes of mobility may vary, school transitions affect continuity in instructional environments and have been found to be negatively associated with school achievement both in prior analyses of the Chicago study (Reynolds, 1991, 1992a; Temple & Reynolds, in press) and in many other studies (Mehana, 1997). I interpreted the avoidance of school mobility as an indicator of school support. Based on the theory of the CPC program, extensive program participation would be expected to reduce the likelihood of school transitions because of increased commitment to and satisfaction with school.

SCHOOL QUALITY

School quality was defined as the number of years from fourth grade to seventh grade that children attended schools in which 25% of the student body performed at or above the national average in reading and math achievement (ITBS scores). This measure was derived from the State of Illinois Report Card on elementary schools, and scores were aggregated across grades 1 to 8. Values were based on the 1990–91 school year. Children were given the score for the school in which they were enrolled during the spring of each year. Although only one indicator of school quality, school-level achievement is relatively objective and is a widely used indicator of school-level performance by both families and policy analysts. Note that the threshold of 25% is a relative one. About two-thirds of the study sample never attended an elementary school in which 25% of the student body scored at or above the national average in reading and math achievement.

Analytic Methods

I reported mean differences on program outcomes between CPC participants and their respective comparison group in raw form (unadjusted) and adjusted for covariates. I used multiple linear regression to estimate the effects of different measures of program participation on youth and family outcomes, adjusted for at least the sex of child and risk status. Logit regression analysis was used for the dichotomous outcomes (e.g., grade retention, any special education, delinquency infractions). The basic model specification was

$$Y = constant + programB_1 + sexB_2 + riskB_3 \text{ (1)}$$

where Y = program outcomes measured at ages 12 to 15 (up to 6 years following primary-grade participation and 10 years following preschool participation). Program participation, the main variable of interest, was measured dichotomously (1 = CPC participation, 0 = comparison group) or in years of participation (e.g., 0 to 6 years). When estimating the effects of preschool/kindergarten and primary-grade intervention separately, these two measures were entered simultaneously. Thus, the estimated effect of preschool participation always controls for participation in primary-grade intervention, and the estimated effect of primary-grade intervention always controls for preschool/kindergarten participation.

Estimates of the basic model were compared to two others. The first was the unadjusted model—that is, the raw group mean difference (i.e., Y = constant + programB$_1$). This estimate, combined with the adjusted mean difference, defines the direction and magnitude of potential selection bias. If the regression-adjusted program effect is smaller than the unadjusted effect, positive program selection is suggested (i.e., "creaming"). If it is larger, negative selection bias is suggested ("decreaming"). The size of the

84

difference between the two program effect estimates is an indication of the magnitude of selection bias. A large difference indicates that the program estimates are sensitive to model specification. The adjusted effect size in this case may be more subject to change. A small difference indicates robustness of program estimates owing primarily to intergroup equivalence, at least on measured variables. To the extent the estimates of the adjusted and unadjusted effects are consistent with each other, the effect of omitted variables may be small (see Reynolds & Temple, 1995).

The second alternative model is an expanded model specification in which other control variables are added to the basic model specification. To estimate the effects of extended childhood intervention and participation in primary-grade intervention, scores on the ITBS word analysis or math subtests at the end of kindergarten were entered. The model was specified as

$$Y = \text{constant} + \text{program}B_1 + \text{sex}B_2 + \text{risk}B_3 + \text{K-achiev}B_4 \ (2)$$

The inclusion of kindergarten achievement test scores (K-achievB_4) addresses the question, Does participation in the primary-grade intervention after preschool and kindergarten yield greater effects than participation that ceases in kindergarten?

To further probe the relation between program participation and outcomes, parent participation in school activities (as rated by first-grade teachers) was added to the basic model specification. Findings from this model provide conservative estimates of the effects of program participation because they denote the mean group difference above and beyond that attributable to differential parent involvement (which in theory should be affected by program participation). Findings in favor of the program group would increase confidence that group differences are due to program participation and not family characteristics or selection bias. To further probe the robustness of estimates, site participation variables (24 dichotomous indicators for 25 sites) also were included in the model. These indicators represent site-specific influences associated with youth outcomes that are distinct from program participation. Their inclusion could either reduce or increase the size of the estimated program effects.

INTERPRETATION OF EFFECTS

The interpretation of the contrast between the program and comparison groups is relative and deserves explanation. Estimates of impact denote the extent to which the average performance of the program group (those who participated in the CPC program) exceeds that of the comparison group (those who participated in a less systematic intervention). All children participated in at least an all-day kindergarten program. For preschool, the contrast is between children who participated in the CPC program in preschool and kindergarten and children who participated in the CPC or another government-funded program in kindergarten without CPC preschool experience.[7] In other words, the comparison is between children who begin organized schooling at ages 3 or 4 versus those who start at age 5. I interpret any difference as an effect of preschool.

Similarly, the estimated effect of the follow-on program is relative to enrollment in the regular school program in the Chicago public schools. Thus, observance of a significant positive coefficient for follow-on intervention indicates that CPC children are performing, on average, above and beyond children in the regular school program. For this reason, it is difficult to compare the effect of follow-on with that of preschool. The estimated effect of follow-on participation would be expected to yield more conservative estimates because the comparison group, unlike during preschool, is enrolled in full-time schooling.

ASSUMPTIONS

The capacity of the regression technique to yield valid estimates of the effect of program participation depends on three major assumptions: (a) the slopes of the regression lines for program and comparison groups are parallel, (b) the variables in the model are reliably measured, especially program participation and the covariates, and (c) no confounding variables are omitted from the model that, if entered, would significantly change the interpretation of the findings.

The assumption of parallel slopes is the key operational requirement of regression analysis (or ANCOVA) and is empirically testable. In prior analyses in the CLS (Reynolds, 1994, 1995; Reynolds et al., 1995), this assumption has been satisfied in that the relation between covariates and program outcomes is similar for program and comparison groups.

The assumption of reliable measures also appears satisfied in this study since model indicators are relatively definable and stable attributes. Measurement of risk status as a composite indicator of social disadvantage was, in part, to enhance reliability and conceptual meaningfulness. The measured indicators are well defined, frequently measured, and relevant for assessing program impact. Among the outcome measures, both the consumer skills and ITBS scores have demonstrated high reliability (Reynolds & Bezruczko, 1989; Hieronymus & Hoover, 1990). Reading and math subtest scores on the ITBS are among the highest of all standardized tests (Linn, 1989). Only measurement error in the explanatory variables, however, can bias estimates of program impact. Unreliability in outcome variables reduces statistical power.

The third assumption, no confounding variables, is often referred to as omitted-variables (third-variable) bias. In evaluation, a confounding variable is one that is correlated with both program participation and program outcomes above and beyond the variables in the model (Anderson et al., 1980). A truly confounding variable, if entered in the analysis, would alter the interpretation of findings. Although quasi-experimental studies such as the present one are susceptible to selection bias, some forms of bias can be empirically tested. As reported in Table 9, previous studies with this data set have demonstrated that selection bias due to measured and unmeasured factors is small and accounts for only 10 to 15% of the observed group differences. Reynolds and Temple (1995) found that ordinary least-squares (OLS) regression analysis can detect most this bias, especially as the length of the postprogram follow-up increases.

For example, the correlation between the error term predicting program participation in preschool and the error term predicting school achievement in sixth grade was practically 0 using two-stage least squares and latent-covariance maximum likelihood analysis. Consequently, I used alternative specifications of OLS regression analysis to investigate the effects of the CPC program. Given the extensive evidence that selection bias into the program is minimal, attrition bias (selection out of the study sample) seems more plausible.

MODERATORS AND MEDIATORS

To investigate the question of who benefits most from program participation, several interaction terms were added to the basic model specification: sex of child by program, risk status by program, parent education by program, parent involvement in school by program, school low income by program, and instructional approach by program. Each program measure was tested against each outcome. I interpreted coefficients that were significant at the .05 level or beyond.

To investigate the hypothesized pathways through which program participation impacted program outcomes, I used structural equation modeling (e.g., path analysis) as implemented through LISREL (Joreskog & Sorbom, 1993a). In this approach, a series of equations is estimated simultaneously by maximum likelihood (one for each intervening and outcome variable), as shown in Figure 1. The resulting structural coefficients (standardized regression coefficients) are used to denote direct and indirect effects. An indirect effect is the extent to which the influence of an explanatory variable (i.e., program participation) on a outcome variable depends on an intervening variable (i.e., hypotheses denoted in Figure 1). The main focus of the analyses was the indirect (or mediated) effects of measures of program participation and the intervening variables that contribute to these effects. Both manifest and latent variables were specified, and estimates of measurement error were included in the model to increase accuracy.[8]

Finally, missing data for the model variables were relatively limited (see Table 7). The structural equation models were based on pairwise-present cases, which yielded conservative values of statistical significance. Sample sizes for the tests of main effects were based on the number of cases for each respective outcome variable (Ns = 756 to 1,164). There were only small amounts of missing data for the covariates. The smallest sample sizes were for the family outcomes (N = 756) and perceived school competence (N = 788). Statistical power and generalizability of findings were relatively limited for these latter measures.[9]

In summary, and following the confirmatory approach to evaluating effects, confidence is increased that observed group differences are due to program participation if the following pattern of results occurs:

1. adjusted and unadjusted estimates of program impact are of similar magnitude and are consistently in the same direction;
2. estimates of program effects for grade retention, school achievement, special education placement, and parent involvement in school are greater than for other outcomes;
3. estimates of program impact are similar for different types and subgroups of children;
4. pathways of program effectiveness converge with those predicted by the program theory, especially the causal hypotheses involving cognitive advantage, family support, and school support shown in Figure 1.

88

4

Program Participation and Social Competence

In this chapter, I report findings for the first three study questions discussed in Chapter 1:

1. Are measures of CPC participation associated with youth and family outcomes up to age 15? The program measures include any participation, preschool participation, follow-on participation, duration of participation, and extended participation.
2. Does extended program participation lead to better youth and family outcomes than less extended participation or participation that ceases in kindergarten, even after controlling for kindergarten achievement?
3. Do the effects of measures of program participation vary by child, family, and program characteristics?

A fourth question concerning the pathways through which program participation affects social competence is addressed in Chapter 5. This chapter is organized in three sections corresponding to the study questions above. Each section is organized by domain of outcomes. The estimated effects of each measure of program participation are considered separately for school achievement, consumer skills, grade retention and special education placement, delinquency behavior, perceived school competence, and family socialization. The full set of youth outcomes are presented first and then family outcomes.

As indicated in Chapter 3, I report program coefficients in two forms. Unadjusted coefficients denote performance differences between groups in raw scores or prevalence rates without adjustments for sex and risk status. The column labeled "adj. mean diff" in the tables to come provides estimates of program effects adjusted for group differences in risk status and sex of child (see Appendix C for all model coefficients).[1] Earlier or later program participation also was included. Except where noted, only coefficients at the .05 level of significance are interpreted as meaningful. Coefficients at the .10 level of significance, however, are identified for description. In the second section, kindergarten achievement was included as a covariate in estimating the effect of extended program participation relative to less extensive participation. Estimated effects for the dichotomous outcomes (grade retention, any special education, passing score on consumer life skills test, and delinquency infractions) were based on logit regression analysis. In the third section, I report on whether the effects of program participation favor particular subgroups of children on demographic, risk, and program characteristics. To highlight key findings, group means are displayed in charts for several outcomes. A summary of findings is provided in the concluding section.

Main Effects of Participation on Youth and Family Outcomes

YOUTH OUTCOMES

School Achievement in Reading and Mathematics

I used standard scores on reading comprehension and mathematics-total subtests of the Iowa Tests of Basic Skills. Youth who were ninth graders at age 15 took the Tests of Achievement and Proficiency, which are equated with the ITBS. Each point on the standard-score scale is equivalent to about one month of performance. The test-score performance of the total study sample is reported in Table 18 along with corresponding summary statistics for the Chicago public schools and national averages. In eighth and ninth grades, the average achievement of the study sample, without regard to intervention exposure, was 6 to 7 points lower in reading (5 to 6 months behind) and 2 to 4 points lower in math (2 to 3 months behind) than those of the student population in the Chicago public schools. These findings are not surprising given that the typical student in the study sample is substantially more disadvantaged than the typical student in the Chicago schools. Not surprisingly, the average performance of the total study

Table 18. Descriptive Statistics in Reading and Math Achievement for the Study Sample, Students in Chicago, and Students Nationally

Sample group	Standard score	Grade equiv.	Percentile rank	Percentage at/above nat'l ave.
Reading achievement				
Grade 8				
1. Study sample	148	7.2	25	21
2. Chicago average	154	7.7	33	29
3. National average	166	8.8	50	50
Grade 9				
1. Study sample	153	7.6	23	17
2. Chicago average	160	8.1	30	21
3. National average	174	9.7	49	50
Math achievement				
Grade 8				
1. Study sample	151	7.4	24	15
2. Chicago average	155	7.7	30	23
3. National average	176	8.8	52	50
Grade 9				
1. Study sample	155	7.7	22	18
2. Chicago average	157	7.9	25	23
3. National average	172	9.9	49	50

Note: For comparability with Chicago and national averages, values for the study sample include students who were ages 14–15 in grade 8 and 15–16 in grade 9. Chicago public school average for grade equivalents was the median value.

sample (program and comparison groups) and Chicago students in eighth and ninth grades was substantially below the average performance of students nationally, about 1.5 to 2 years behind for the study sample and 1 to 1.5 years behind for all Chicago students.

Table 18 also shows that the percentage of study sample youth who scored at or above the national average ranged from 15% (eighth-grade math) to 21% (eighth-grade reading). These were somewhat below the values for Chicago students and substantially below those for students nationally. These descriptive findings provide a context in which to interpret the group differences reported below. Given their observed patterns of

Fig. 5. Years of Program Participation and Social Competence at Age 14, Adjusted for Sex of Child and Risk Status

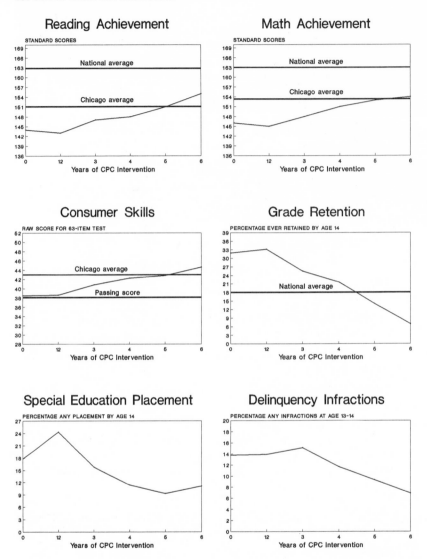

achievement, for example, most CPC participants would not be expected to reach national achievement norms in adolescence. This would not indicate that the program was ineffective, only the cumulative advantages of growing up in families with relatively high socioeconomic status and in neighborhoods with high-quality schools and more resources (see Figure 5

Table 19. Estimated Program Effects for School Achievement

Intervention group	Age 14		Age 15	
	Unadj. mean diff.	Adj. mean diff.	Unadj. mean diff.	Adj. mean diff.
Reading achievement				
1. Any CPC vs. none	4.6**	4.1**	3.8**	3.5**
2. Any preschool vs. none	5.9**	5.5**	4.7**	4.2**
3. Any follow-on vs. none	2.5t	1.6	2.4	2.0
4. Years of intervention	1.9**	1.6**	1.5**	1.3**
5. Extended vs. less extended	7.8**	6.5**	6.6**	5.9**
Math achievement				
1. Any CPC vs. none	4.0**	3.6**	3.6*	3.3*
2. Any preschool vs. none	4.7**	4.4**	3.5*	3.3*
3. Any follow-on vs. none	2.8*	2.0t	2.1	1.7
4. Years of intervention	1.7**	1.4**	1.2**	1.0**
5. Extended vs. less extended	7.2**	6.2**	4.9**	4.4**

Note: Unadj. = Unadjusted, Adj. = Adjusted for sex and risk status.
$t = p < .10$, $* p < .05$, $** p < .01$.

for further information on national comparisons). Performance relative to comparison groups is the key gauge of effectiveness.

ANY PROGRAM PARTICIPATION

To obtain conservative estimates of the impact of the CPC program, the performance of CPC participants was compared to nonparticipants without regard to the extent of program exposure. Participation was defined as enrollment in the CPCs in preschool, kindergarten, or in the primary grades. At the end of the program in third grade (one-year postprogram for second-grade graduates), I previously found that CPC graduates surpassed their comparison group counterparts by 4 to 6 points in reading and math achievement (Reynolds, 1994).

As shown in Table 19, these significant differences remained stable up to age 15, though the magnitude of effects declined somewhat over time. Any program participation from preschool to third grade was significantly associated with a 4.1 point increase in reading achievement at age 14 and a

3.4 point increase at age 15. This represents about a 3-month advantage over the comparison group, a modest improvement.

Regarding math achievement, program participation was significantly associated with a 3.6 and 3.3 point advantage over the non-CPC preschool group in math achievement at ages 14 and 15, respectively. This translates to about a 3-month advantage in performance. These are modest effects but are notable given the relative lack of evidence about the very long-term effects of large-scale early childhood programs on school achievement. Also note that in these and other analyses reported below, inclusion of the control variables reduced the size of the program effects only modestly (i.e., by 10–15%). This pattern suggests the relative stability of effects under different model specifications.

PRESCHOOL PARTICIPATION

Table 19 also shows the estimated effects of preschool participation. One or two years of CPC preschool participation was significantly associated with advantages of 5.5 and 4.2 points in standard scores, respectively, in reading achievement at ages 14 and 15. This corresponds to about a 4- to 5-month change.[2]

Likewise, preschool participation was significantly associated with a 4.4-point increase in standard scores in math achievement at age 14 and a 3.3-point advantage at age 15, above and beyond gender, environmental risk, and participation in follow-on intervention. This translates to a 3- to 4-month performance advantage over the comparison group. Again, although these coefficients are not large, the fact that observed effects persist up to 10 years postprogram is unique among early interventions and almost all social programs.

FOLLOW-ON PARTICIPATION

Any participation in CPC follow-on (primary-grade) intervention was not associated with higher reading achievement at ages 14 or 15. Mean group differences favored the program participants by only 2 standard-score points in reading achievement at age 15 and by 1.7 points in math achievement. Nevertheless, years of participation in the follow-on intervention were significantly associated with higher reading and math achievement at ages 14 and 15 above and beyond sex, risk status, and preschool participation.[3]

94

Because children participated in the program up to 6 years, I investigated the relation between years of participation and school achievement. If a dosage-response relationship is established between years of participation and program outcomes, then the likelihood is increased that program participation causes better school performance. As shown in Table 18, years of program participation were significantly associated with higher reading achievement at age 14 and 15. Indeed, this measure of participation had the most consistently positive associations with achievement. If the sex of the child and environmental risk are controlled for, each year of participation was associated with an increase of 1.3 to 1.6 points in the standard score for reading. A similar pattern of findings occurred for math achievement, though the size of the coefficients was smaller.

Figure 5 charts the relation between the number of years of participation and school achievement at age 14 and for other outcomes. Age 15 findings showed a similar pattern and are not shown. The value of zero is for the non-CPC comparison group. The means are adjusted for differences in sex of child and risk status. School performance increased noticeably after 4 years of intervention. Five or six years of participation yielded the best performance, and these two groups were at or above the Chicago averages in reading and math.

The total study sample, however, was performing well below the national average in reading and math achievement. In grade-equivalent scores, whereby the national average is 8.8 years, reading achievement was as follows: 6 years of intervention = 7.8 years, 5 years = 7.5, 4 years = 7.0, 3 years = 7.0, 2 or 1 year = 6.7, and 0 years = 6.8. Thus, full participation in the program for 6 years was associated with a 1-year gain in reading performance over the non-CPC comparison group. However, even 6 years of participation did not elevate the performance of the maximum intervention group to the national average. Note that these means are conservative because children who were retained are included in these averages.[4] Participation for 4, 5, or 6 years yielded significantly higher math achievement as well.

EXTENDED PARTICIPATION

The above analyses show the consistently positive relation between measures of program participation and school achievement up to age 15. The pattern of findings in Figure 5, however, suggests a threshold effect of pro-

Table 20. Estimated Program Effects for Consumer Skills

	Raw score		Percentage passing	
	Unadj.	Adj.	Unadj.	Adj.
Intervention group	mean diff.	mean diff.	mean diff.	mean diff.
1. Any CPC vs. none	3.3**	3.0**	0.129**	0.126**
2. Any preschool vs. none	2.9**	2.9**	0.107**	0.110**
3. Any follow-on vs. none	2.0**	1.5*	0.086**	0.069*
4. Years of intervention	1.1**	1.0**	0.042**	0.039**
5. Extended vs. less extended	4.2**	3.6**	0.170**	0.154**

Note: Unadj. = Unadjusted, Adj. = Adjusted for sex and risk status.
* $p < .05$, ** $p < .01$.

gram participation such that extensive participation is associated with higher school achievement relative to less extensive participation. As reported in Table 19, relative to participation up to 4 years, CPC participation in the preschool/kindergarten and at least 2 years of the follow-on component (4–6 years of participation) was significantly associated with a 6.5-point advantage in reading at age 14 and with a 5.9 point advantage at age 15.

For math achievement, extended intervention was associated with a 6.2-point increase at age 14 and with a 4.4-point increase at age 15 over less extended intervention (see Table 19). These findings indicate that the relation between years of participation and school achievement is not strictly linear but that greater advantages accrue as the length of intervention increases.

Consumer Skills

The 63-item Chicago Minimum Proficiency Skills Test measures basic consumer skills deemed necessary for everyday functioning. A passing score of 38 items correct is required for high school graduation. Findings are reported below in both raw scores and in the percentage of students earning a passing score on the test. Table 20 presents the contrasts for the total score and percent passing by level of participation. In general, these comparisons show that children who participated in both the preschool/kindergarten and follow-on components had the best performance.

ANY PROGRAM PARTICIPATION

For the total test, children with any CPC participation during preschool to third grade answered, on average, three more items correctly than did the non-CPC comparison group (40.7 to 37.7). A greater proportion of pro-

Fig. 6. Consumer Skills for 3 Program Comparisons

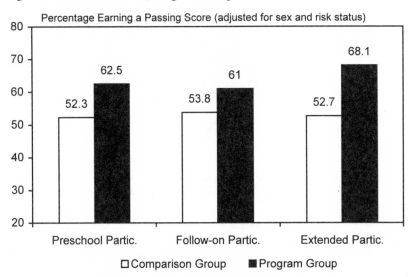

Percentage Earning a Passing Score (adjusted for sex and risk status)

gram participants also exceeded the passing criterion (62% versus 50%), indicating a passing rate 24% higher than the comparison group (see Figure 6).

ANY PRESCHOOL PARTICIPATION

Children with any CPC preschool experience answered correctly about 3 more MPST items, on average, than the comparison group, and their passing rate was 11 percentage points higher than children without any preschool experience (63% versus 52%). These findings are consistent with those for school achievement, if not slightly better, and indicate that the scholastic benefits of early intervention are not limited to traditional indicators of school achievement.

ANY FOLLOW-ON PARTICIPATION

Children with any participation in the follow-on program during the primary grades (regardless of earlier participation) answered correctly, on average, 2 more items than the comparison group, and their passing rate was 9 percentage points higher than children not participating in follow-on intervention. These effects are adjusted for sex of child, environmental risk, and preschool enrollment. The adjusted mean difference was similar to the unadjusted or raw mean difference. Years of follow-on participation also were significantly associated with better performance in consumer skills (see endnote 3).

YEARS OF INTERVENTION

As shown in Table 20, a significant dosage-response relation between years of intervention and consumer life skills was found. Each year of intervention was associated with a 1-point increase in the mean score. Given a maximum of 6 years of participation, full participation in the CPC program was associated with, on average, a 6-point (item) increase in test performance.

In regard to the percentage of students with a passing score, each year of participation was significantly associated with an increase of about 4 points in the rate of passing. This estimate is a substantial effect, in that 5-year participants experienced a 20-point increase and 6-year participants experienced a 24-point increase.

These patterns of performance are shown in Figure 5. As with school achievement, the relationship between years of participation and consumer skills was monotonic. The relation is closer to linear than for school achievement, however.

EXTENDED VERSUS LESS EXTENDED INTERVENTION

The CPC program is 1 or 1 years of preschool, one year of kindergarten, and 2 or 3 years of the follow-on component. Extended program participation was associated with an average improvement of about 4 points over less extended participation. This translates into an adjusted rate of passing that was 15.4 percentage points higher than the rate for children with less extended participation (68.1% to 52.7%).

I also compared groups on the three subscales of the consumer life skills test (language arts, computation, and problem solving) as well as across the content domains of personal finance, health, transportation, occupation, communication, government, and community resources. For the subscales, extended participation (preschool through second or third grade) showed the greatest difference from the comparison group, passing 1.2, 1.1, and 0.80 more items, respectively (all significant at the .01 level). Differences for the other groups were comparable though smaller in magnitude.

Table 21 presents group comparisons on the seven content domains of consumer life skills. In general, children in the extended program had

98

Table 21. Adjusted Mean Differences for Content Areas of Consumer Skills Test

| | Content area of consumer skills | | | | | | |
Program group	Health	Communi-cation	Finance	Trans-porta.	Gov.	Community resources	Occup.
Any CPC vs. none	.52**	.32*	.42**	.22	.32**	.31**	.42**
Any preschool vs. none	.42*	.35*	.36**	.13	.17	.26*	.29*
Any follow-on vs. none	.35*	.15	.24*	.23t	.28**	.15t	.30**
Years of intervention	.17**	.11**	.12**	.09**	.11**	.10**	.13**
Extended vs. less ext.	.62**	.46**	.45**	.38**	.40**	.33*	.45**
Sample mean	9.21	6.93	5.08	5.61	4.44	4.10	5.54
SD	2.65	2.22	1.74	1.98	1.56	1.52	1.86
No. of items	14	10	8	9	7	6	9

Note: N = 1,045. Group differences were adjusted for sex of child, risk status, follow-on or preschool participation. Gov. = Government, Occup. = Occupation.
$t = p < .10$, * $p < .05$, ** $p < .01$.

greater advantages across the content domains. An examination of specific domains shows that any program participation, preschool participation, and follow-on participation were significantly associated with better performance in the health, finance, and occupation domains. Follow-on intervention was not associated with communication and community resources. Preschool participation was not associated with transportation and government domains.

Grade Retention and Special Education Placement
I next turn to findings for two well-known indicators of school competence—grade retention and special education placement. Grade retention was measured cumulatively from kindergarten to the ninth-grade year (age 15), and special education placement was measured from the first grade to ninth-grade year and included both incidence and years of placement. Coefficients for the dichotomous indicators were transformed to represent percentage-point differences between groups. I emphasize the age 15 findings unless they diverge from those at age 14.

ANY PROGRAM PARTICIPATION
As reported in Table 22, CPC participants were significantly less likely than the non-CPC comparison group to be retained in grade by ages 14 and

Table 22. Estimated Program Effects on Grade Retention and Special Education Placement

Intervention group	Unadj. mean diff.	Adj. mean diff.	Unadj. mean diff.	Adj. mean diff.
	Age 14		**Age 15**	
	Ever retained in grade			
1. Any CPC vs. none	-0.107**	-0.103**	-0.122**	-0.122**
2. Any preschool vs. none	-0.082**	-0.069*	-0.087**	-0.078*
3. Any follow-on vs. none	-0.091**	-0.087**	-0.094**	-0.101**
4. Years of intervention	-0.043**	-0.042**	-0.045**	-0.044**
5. Extended vs. less extended	-0.173**	-0.162**	-0.166**	-0.164**
	Ever placed in Special Education			
1. Any CPC vs. none	-0.036	-0.033	-0.035	-0.034
2. Any preschool vs. none	-0.059*	-0.052*	-0.059*	-0.053*
3. Any follow-on vs. none	-0.029	-0.030	-0.024	-0.028
4. Years of intervention	-0.020**	-0.019**	-0.019**	-0.019**
5. Extended vs. less extended	-0.111**	-0.106**	-0.102**	-0.101**
	Years placed in Special Education			
1. Any CPC vs. none	-0.300**	-0.295*	-0.401**	-0.402**
2. Any preschool vs. none	-0.400**	-0.372**	-0.442**	-0.413**
3. Any follow-on vs. none	-0.128	-0.124	-0.210	-0.214
4. Years of intervention	-0.118**	-0.110**	-0.145**	-0.139**
5. Extended vs. less extended	-0.522**	-0.490**	-0.619**	-0.599**

Note: Values are percentage points. Negative values favor the program group.
Unadj. = Unadjusted, Adj. = Adjusted for sex and risk status. Values for "ever placed" are percentage points.
* $p < .05$, ** $p < .01$.

15. Rates of grade retention were 10 to 12 percentage points lower for program participants, which translates to a 31% lower rate of grade retention (24% versus 35%) than the comparison group.

As shown in Table 22, program participation was not associated with a significantly lower rate of special education placement by ages 14 and 15. Lower rates favored the program group but only by about 3 percentage points (i.e., 16% versus 19.4% at age 15). On the continuous outcome measure of years of placement, however, program participation was associated with significantly fewer years receiving special education services. Partici-

Fig. 7.A. Grade Retention by Age 15 for 3 Program Comparisons

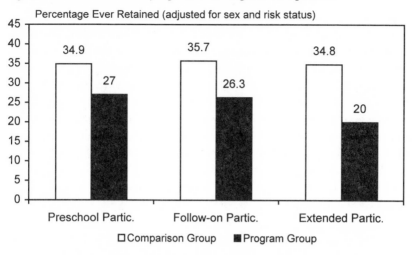

Percentage Ever Retained (adjusted for sex and risk status)

□ Comparison Group   ■ Program Group

Fig. 7.B. Special Education by Age 15 for 3 Program Comparisons

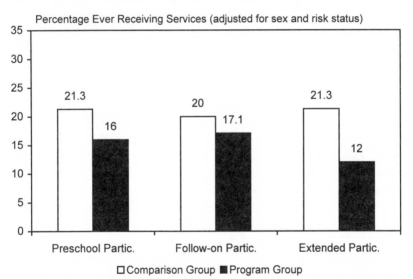

Percentage Ever Receiving Services (adjusted for sex and risk status)

□ Comparison Group   ■ Program Group

pants spent 0.30 fewer years in special education than the comparison group by age 14 and 0.40 by age 15.

PRESCHOOL PARTICIPATION

Preschool participation also was associated with a significantly lower rate of grade retention up to ages 14 and 15. After accounting for differences in sex, environmental risk, and later primary-grade participation, preschool participants had an 8-point lower rate of grade retention by age 15. This translates into a 23% reduction in grade retention (see Figures 7.A and 7.B).

For special education placement, preschool participation was associated with both a significantly lower rate of placement at ages 14 and 15 as well as fewer years receiving services. Preschool participants spent, on average, about 4 fewer months in special education than the comparison group.

FOLLOW-ON PARTICIPATION

Any participation in the primary-grade component of the CPC program was associated with a 9 to 10-point reduction in grade retention by age 15, a significant and sizeable change. Years of follow-on participation also were associated with significantly lower rates of grade retention.[5]

Follow-on participation was associated with a lower rate of special education placement and with fewer years receiving services only at the .10 level. By age 15, for example, 22% of follow-on participants were retained in grade compared to 30% for non-follow-on participants. Years of follow-on participation were more associated with reductions in special education placement (see endnote 3).

YEARS OF INTERVENTION

As shown in Table 22, each year of CPC participation was associated with about a 4-point reduction in grade retention through age 15. In other words, 5 years of participation was associated with a 51% reduction in grade retention over the non-CPC comparison group (16.6% versus 34.7%). By extrapolation, 6 years of CPC participation were associated with an 80% reduction in grade retention (35% to 7%). The overall pattern of findings is illustrated in Figure 5. Most impressively, the cumulative rate of grade retention for the 5-year and 6-year groups was below the national average of 18%. Some of the reduction in grade retention may be due to school characteristics and the CPC program policy discouraging grade retention.

A similar pattern of findings occurred for the two measures of special education placement. Each additional year of participation was associated with a 2-point reduction in the rate of special education placement at ages 14 and 15 and a 0.11- to 0.14-year reduction in years of placement. Figure 5 shows a similar pattern of grade retention.

Youth who participated in the CPCs from preschool to second or third grade were much less likely than other children to be retained in grade. The 16-point difference translates into about a 50% reduction in grade retention for the extended program group over the less extended program group.

For special education placement, youth with extended program participation had a 10-point reduction in special education placement by age 15 and spent, on average, 0.6 fewer years in special education. These differences occurred after accounting for the covariates and remained even after kindergarten achievement was included.

Interestingly, the magnitude of the estimated effects on grade retention and special education placement increased over time. Reynolds (1994) reported a 27% lower rate of grade retention between groups in third grade (19.2% versus 26.2%) and no significant differences for special education placement.

Delinquency Infractions

As an indicator of social behavior, delinquency infractions were reported by school personnel and included a variety of problem behaviors. This measure has hardly ever been used to investigate the effects of large-scale early intervention programs. Unlike grade retention and special education placement, delinquency infractions were measured only at ages 13 or 14 and at ages 13 to 15. Overall, 13% of youth had infractions at ages 13 or 14 while 23% had infractions over the 3-year period from ages 13 to 15. Most of the infractions were relatively minor or moderate in severity and included persistent truancy, fighting, theft, carrying weapons, and gang activity.[6] I view delinquency infractions as one indicator of problem behavior.

ANY PROGRAM PARTICIPATION

As shown in Table 23, any program participation was not associated with a lower rate of delinquency as measured by school reports. The program coefficient indicates that participation was associated with a 1.8-point reduction in delinquency. This translates in prevalence rates of 12.4% for the program group and 14.2% for the comparison group. Likewise, the adjusted group difference for delinquency infractions over ages 13 to 15 favored the program group but was not significant ($b = -.025, p = .407$).

ANY PRESCHOOL PARTICIPATION

Similarly, preschool participation was not associated with the delinquency

Table 23. Estimated Program Effects on School-Reported Delinquency Infractions

Intervention group	Age 13–4		Age 13–5	
	Unadj. mean diff.	Adj. mean diff.	Unadj. mean diff.	Adj. mean diff.
1. Any CPC vs. none	-0.018	-0.018	-0.021	-0.025
2. Any preschool vs. none	-0.005	0.001	-0.007	-0.0003
3. Any follow-on vs. none	-0.049*	-0.053*	-0.048t	-0.059*
4. Years of intervention	-0.010*	-0.010*	-0.006	-0.007
5. Extended vs. less extended	-0.053*	-0.049*	-0.025	-0.029

Note: Values are percentage points. Negative values favor the program group.
Unadj. = Unadjusted, Adj. = Adjusted for sex and risk status.
$t = p < .10$, * $p < .05$, ** $p < .01$.

Fig. 8. Delinquency Infractions for 3 Program Comparisons

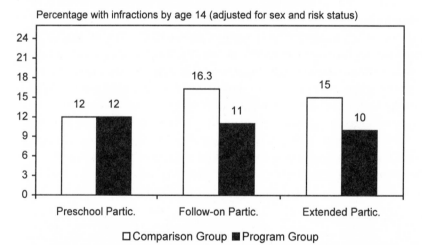

Percentage with infractions by age 14 (adjusted for sex and risk status)

□ Comparison Group ■ Program Group

infractions at ages 13 or 14 and ages 13 to 15. For example, 12% and 23% of each group had delinquency infractions, respectively, during these time periods. There was little difference between the adjusted and unadjusted program coefficients (see Figure 8).

FOLLOW–ON PARTICIPATION

Any participation in CPC follow-on intervention was associated with significantly lower rates of delinquency infractions at ages 13 or 14 and at ages 13 to 15. Adjusted for preschool participation, risk status, and sex, 11% of follow-on participants committed delinquency infractions at ages 13 or 14 compared to 16.3% for the comparison group, a 33% reduction. Through age 15, 20.4% of the follow-on group had delinquency infractions, compared to 26.3% for the non-follow-on group.

YEARS OF INTERVENTION

Similar to the scholastic outcomes, years of program participation were associated with a significantly lower likelihood of delinquency infractions at ages 13 or 14. Each year of participation contributed to a 1-point reduction in delinquency. Rates of school-reported delinquency at ages 13 or 14 showed a similar pattern. As shown in Figure 5, from 6 years of participation to 0 years respectively, the rates were 6.9%, 9.3%, 11.7%, 15.1%, 13.9% (1 and 2 years), and 13.8%. Years of CPC participation were unrelated to delinquency infractions at ages 13 to 15. Each additional year of participation was associated with just a 0.7-point reduction in infractions.

EXTENDED VERSUS LESS EXTENDED PARTICIPATION

Categorizing youth by their participation in extended intervention yielded findings consistent with years of intervention. Controlling for sex and risk status, youth who participated in all components of the CPC program up to second or third grade had a significantly lower rate of delinquency infractions than youth who had less extensive intervention exposure. The adjusted mean difference of about 5 percentage points translated into a prevalence rate of 10% for the extended group and 15% for the comparison group, a 33% reduction. The age 13–15 results, while favoring the extended group, were not significant (rates were 21% and 24%, respectively).

Perceived School Competence

Self-perceptions of competence were used to measure effects of program participation on academic self-concept. Competence perceptions are moderately associated with scholastic performance; they index the psychological domain of adjustment. Overall, children had positive competence perceptions. For the 12-item scale, the mean score was 37.4 (range of 12 to 48). Three in five children had an average item rating of 3 (satisfied) or higher. Table 24 shows the relation between different measures of program partici-

Table 24. Estimated Program Effects for
Perceived School Competence at Age 12

Program indicator	Unadj. mean diff.	Adj. mean diff.
Any participation	.36	.30
Any preschool	.81*	.78*
Any follow-on	.16	-.002
Years of participation	.23**	.18*
Extended participation	.98**	.76*

Note: N = 788. * p < .05, ** p < .01.

pation and age 12 perceptions of school competence. Findings are high-lighted below for the 788 youth who completed the survey.[7]

ANY PROGRAM PARTICIPATION

Any program participation was unrelated to perceptions of school competence. Program participants had only a slightly higher adjusted mean score ($M = 37.5$) on perceived competence than the comparison group ($M = 37.2$).

ANY PRESCHOOL PARTICIPATION

Children who participated in the CPC preschool and kindergarten program had significantly higher self-ratings of competence than the non-CPC comparison group ($b = .79, p = .04$) above and beyond the influence of sex, risk status, and follow-on intervention. The adjusted means were, respectively, 37.7 and 36.9.

FOLLOW-ON PARTICIPATION

Neither any participation or years of follow-on participation were independently associated with self-perceptions of competence above and beyond preschool participation, risk status, and sex of child.[8]

YEARS OF INTERVENTION

A dosage-response relation was detected between years of participation and self-perceptions of competence ($b = .18, p = .03$). Five years of participation, for example, were associated with a 0.85-point increase and 6 years with about a 1-point increase. This association, however, was weaker than for the above outcomes.

EXTENDED VERSUS LESS EXTENDED PARTICIPATION

Youth with extended participation for at least 4 years during preschool to third grade had, on average, higher self-perceptions of school competence than youth with less extensive intervention. The adjusted means were, respectively, 37.8 and 37.1. Due to the absence of effects of follow-on intervention, preschool and kindergarten intervention contributed most to this effect. This finding provides additional evidence that the effects of program participation extend beyond academic performance per se.

Robustness of Estimated Effects on Youth Outcomes

I estimated the effects of different measures of program participation using parent involvement in first grade (teacher ratings) and program site indicators as additional control variables. The inclusion of parent involvement addresses the potential validity threat that the observed group differences are due to family self-selection into the CPC program. This is a plausible hypothesis because parent involvement is an eligibility requirement, and parents who enroll children in the program may be more interested in their children's education than other parents. If true, their children could be better adjusted regardless of program participation. Parent involvement in school is a good indicator since it symbolizes family interest and values toward education. First grade was the earliest available time of measurement. The measure was a dichotomous variable indicating if teachers rated parent participation in school "average/a fair amount" or above.[9] Because of the first-grade measurement, estimates of program effectiveness are likely to be conservative, especially for participation in the follow-on program. Findings were interpreted as the effect of program participation above and beyond that of parent involvement and youth's sex and risk status.

In a separate analysis, indicators for each site of program or comparison group enrollment were included to measure the influence of school-level attributes that are independent of program participation. Twenty-four dummy variables representing enrollment in the 25 total sites were included along with risk status, sex of child, and the indicators of program participation.

Table 25 provides estimates of effects of preschool, follow-on participation, extended participation, and years of program participation for reading achievement, consumer skills, grade retention, and special education

Table 25. Estimates of Program Effects for Selected Age 15 Youth Outcomes Controlling for Sex of Child, Risk Status, and Parent Involvement in School or Program Sites

Program measure	Reading achievement		Consumer skills		Grade retention		Special ed. placement	
	Parent involv.	Sites	Parent involv.	Sites	Parent involv.	Sites	Parent involv.	Sites
Any preschool participation	4.2*	5.6*	2.8*	3.3*	-.077*	-.116*	-.052*	-.095*
Any follow-on participation	0.9	2.8	1.1	2.0*	-.064*	-.087*	-.015	-.071*
Extended participation	4.6*	4.6*	3.0*	2.5*	-.114*	-.120*	-.079*	.104*
Years of participation	1.1*	1.6*	0.8*	1.1*	-.035*	-.050*	-.015*	-.035*

Note: Consumer skills was measured at ages 14/15.
* $p < .05$.

placement. Only the findings for age 15 are displayed; age 14 findings were similar but showed an even more robust pattern of findings (see Appendix D for all estimates). The estimated effects of program participation were largely robust after adding parent involvement and site variables. Interestingly, the inclusion of parent involvement caused a reduction in the program coefficient, whereas inclusion of the site variables caused an increase in the coefficients. Generally, the change in estimated effects was approximately 10% (higher or lower).

As expected (due to time of measurement), the largest changes in effect sizes after the inclusion of parent involvement were for participation in the follow-on intervention. When parent involvement as well as risk status, sex of child, and preschool participation were controlled for, any follow-on participation remained significantly associated only with consumer life skills, grade retention, and special education placement. The most robust findings occurred for years of intervention, extended intervention, and preschool intervention. I do not interpret the lack of robustness of follow-on participation in affecting school achievement to mean that follow-on intervention is unrelated to these indicators, only that its influence is not usually independent of parent participation during the first year of the follow-on program.

Additional evidence supporting the robustness of the findings in Tables 19–25 was obtained by taking into account the nested nature of the data (children within schools and programs). Whereas the inclusion of site variables is one method, another is hierarchical modeling, which involves estimating child-level error terms within each site. Results based on this approach were consistent with findings reported above. Thus, program effects were robust against alternative model specifications.[10]

Summary of Findings for Youth Outcomes

The pattern of findings provides consistently positive evidence that measures of program participation were significantly associated with most youth outcomes up to age 15. The measures of years of participation and extended participation yielded the most consistent effects across outcomes. Preschool participation also yielded consistently significant benefits across outcomes, especially for school achievement, special education placement and grade retention, and perceived competence. Any program participation and any follow-on participation yielded somewhat weaker effects and were most consistent for grade retention and consumer life skills. The general pattern of findings was robust even after parent involvement in school and sites were included as control variables. These findings are largely consistent with the theory of the CPC program discussed in Chapter 2.

FAMILY SOCIALIZATION OUTCOMES

Table 26 shows the estimated effects of different measures of program participation on three family socialization outcomes assessed when children were 10 to 12 years of age (up to sixth grade). As with the youth outcomes, the covariates were risk status and sex of child. In general, parents (almost always mothers) had high educational expectations for their children: one half expected them to earn a college degree, and 15% a graduate degree. Eighty percent reported being satisfied with their children's education at school. This proportion is similar to national statistics (National Center for Educational Statistics, 1995). Parental school participation was typically rated as low to moderate by teachers and parents. About one half of the parents had two or more ratings of average or higher parent involvement from ages 8 to 12. Rather than reporting the findings for each program measure, I summarize findings across family outcomes.

Parent Educational Expectations

Four measures of program participation were significantly associated with higher expectations for children's educational attainment: (a) any program participation, (b) any preschool participation, (c) years of participation,

Table 26. Program Coefficients for 3 Family Outcomes

Program indicator	Educational expectations		Satisfact. school		Parent involvement	
	Coeff.	p	Coeff.	p	Coeff.	p
1. Any participation	.235	.012	.258	.005	.188	.044
2. Any preschool	.237	.010	.271	.003	.213	.019
3. Any follow-on	.043	.624	-.030	.724	.229	.009
4. Years of intervention	.062	.002	.047	.017	.110	<.001
5. Extended participation vs. less extended	.208	.016	.087	.307	.580	<.001

Note: N is 756 for educational expectations and satisfaction and 1,164 for parent involvement. Estimates are adjusted for differences in sex and risk status. Preschool and follow-on are adjusted for each other's influence. Extended participation estimates are adjusted for differences in reading achievement in kindergarten. Scale for parent expectations: 1–5, scale for satisfaction with school: 1–5, scale for parent involvement: 0–5.

and (d) extended participation. Preschool participation was common to these measures of program participation ($b = .237, p = .01$). The coefficients for both years of participation ($b = .062, p = .002$) and extended participation ($b = .208, p = .016$) also suggested that the combined program also contributed. Parents of the CPC program group were more likely than parents of the non–CPC comparison group to have higher educational expectations for their children. This contrasts with findings for children's reports of their own educational expectations (see endnote 7). Follow-on participation was unrelated to parent educational expectations.

When results are coded dichotomously, 52% of parents with any program participation expected their children to graduate from college compared to 43% for the non–CPC comparison group (controlling for sex of child and risk status). As shown in Figure 9, group means for preschool and extended program participation were of similar magnitude. There was no difference for follow-on participation. The addition of first-grade parent involvement in school did not affect the results. For example, the coefficient for years of intervention was robust ($b = .053, p = .009$).

Parent Satisfaction with Education

Only years of participation, preschool participation, and any program participation were significantly associated with parent satisfaction with children's education. The coefficient for preschool/kindergarten participation

Fig. 9. Parent Educational Expectations for 3 Program Comparisons

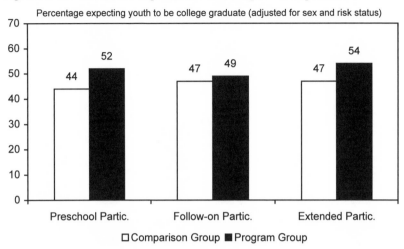

Percentage expecting youth to be college graduate (adjusted for sex and risk status)

□ Comparison Group ■ Program Group

was the largest in size ($b = .271, p = .003$). Measured categorically, 82% of program parents reported they were satisfied with their children's education, compared to 74% for the comparison group. Rates of satisfaction were also higher for preschool participants. These coefficients were unaffected by the addition of first-grade parent involvement. Extended program participation was statistically unrelated to parent satisfaction with education, though the direction of influence favored program participants. As with parent expectations, follow-on participation was unrelated to parent satisfaction with children's education.

Extent of Parent Involvement in School

All five program measures were significantly associated with ratings of parent involvement in school when children were aged 8 to 12.[11] Program parents were significantly more likely than the parents in the comparison group to participate in school activities after the end of the CPC program. As shown in Figure 10, the preschool and follow-on groups had a mean number of positive ratings of 1.8 compared to 1.6 for their respective non-CPC comparison groups. Likewise, the means for extended versus less extended intervention were, respectively, 2.2 and 1.6. These are by no means high ratings given that a score of 5.0 was possible. For years of participation, each additional year was associated with a 0.11-point increase in ratings of school involvement.

III

Fig. 10. Parent Participation in School for 3 Program Comparisons

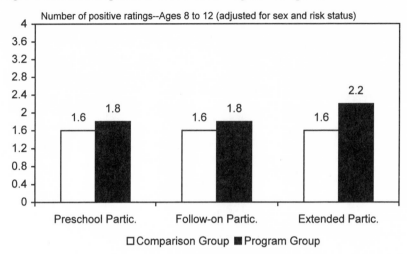

Number of positive ratings--Ages 8 to 12 (adjusted for sex and risk status)

☐ Comparison Group ■ Program Group

When parent involvement in school at the first-grade level is controlled for, follow-on participation was not associated with parent involvement during the elementary grades. This finding may be overly conservative because this control measure was taken at the end of the first year of the follow-on program.

Summary of Findings for Family Outcomes

Preschool participation, years of program participation, and any program participation were most often associated with indicators of family socialization. Preschool participation, however, appeared to contribute most to parent educational expectations, satisfaction with education, and school involvement. Support for an independent relation between follow-on participation and family outcomes was limited to school involvement during the elementary grades. Extended program participation was not associated with parent satisfaction with children's education.

Extended Program Participation versus
Participation Ceasing in Kindergarten

The above analyses show the consistently positive relation between measures of program participation and youth and family outcomes up to age 15. Relative to participation up to 4 years, CPC program participation in preschool/kindergarten and at least 2 years in the primary grades was associated with a 6- to 7-month increase in reading achievement and math achievement, nearly a 30% increase in passing the consumer life skills, and sizable reductions in cumulative grade retention and special education placement by age 15 as well as delinquency infractions by age 14.

None of these results, however, addresses the specific question of whether participation in extended early childhood intervention is more effective than participation that stops in kindergarten. Nor did analyses separate the effects of extended participation among 4-year, 5-year, and 6-year groups. To address these issues, I analyzed the performance of youth who participated in at least the preschool and kindergarten component. In other words, I estimated the effects of duration of program participation, holding constant the timing of program entry. The performance of the following groups were contrasted with that of children who participated only in preschool and kindergarten (nonextended program group):

The total extended program group included all children who participated in extended early childhood intervention for 4 to 6 years. This group is identical to the extended program group reported in the previous section.

The 6-year program group participated for the maximum amount of intervention in the 6 original Child-Parent Centers.

The 5-year program group participated for the maximum amount of intervention in the 14 later Child-Parent Centers.

The 4-year program group enrolled in any of the centers at age 4 and participated for 2 years during the primary grades.

The other 5-year group enrolled in the original centers but did not participate in the maximum amount of intervention either because they entered at age 4 or left after the second grade.

The question addressed is, Does extended early childhood intervention promote better adjustment than intervention that ceases in kindergarten? Group differences were adjusted for sex of child, risk status, and kindergarten prereading achievement (equation 2, expanded model specification; see Chapter 3). End-of-kindergarten math achievement was included as the pretest for adolescent math achievement. Note that inclusion of kindergarten achievement in the model restricts interpretation to the added value of CPC primary-grade intervention above and beyond preschool and kindergarten intervention. Thus, the possibility of synergistic or cumulative

Fig. 11. Reading Achievement at Age 15 for Extended Program Groups

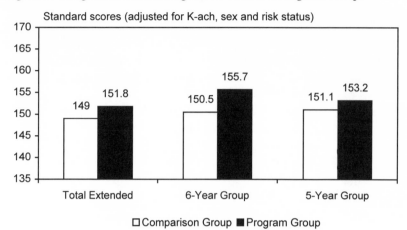

Standard scores (adjusted for K-ach, sex and risk status)

□ Comparison Group ■ Program Group

effects of extended intervention was removed in order to calculate the value added by extended intervention. Hence they may be conservative estimates.

Table 27 displays the adjusted group differences by outcome, which are further described below. Given the relatively small sample sizes of the groups, precise probability values of the significance of group differences were provided. Differences at the .10 level of significance or beyond were interpreted as meaningful.

YOUTH OUTCOMES

School Achievement in Reading and Math

The total extended intervention group scored significantly but modestly higher in reading achievement than the nonextended group at age 14 ($b = 3.1, p = .056$) but not at age 15 ($b = 2.8, p = .134$). The 6-year intervention group from the original CPCs displayed the best reading performance, scoring 5.7 points higher than the comparison group at age 14 and 5.2 points higher at age 15. The latter coefficient was only marginally significant. The 5-year extended intervention group also surpassed the reading achievement of the comparison group but only at age 14. The 4-year and other 5-year group (less than maximum participation) were indistinguishable from the comparison group. (See Figure 11.)

Findings for math were similar to those of reading. The estimated effects of extended intervention were limited to age 14 for the total group ($b = 3.4$,

Table 27. Estimated Effects of Extended Program Participation Relative to Preschool and Kindergarten Participation

	N	Age 14 Coeff.	p	Age 15 Coeff.	p
Reading achievement					
Total extended group	461/421	3.1*	.056	2.8	.134
6-year group	72/66	5.7**	.035	5.2*	.095
5-year group	175/154	3.9**	.050	2.2	.349
4-year group	124/116	3.0	.177	3.7	.139
Other 5-year group	90/85	-0.3	.909	0.9	.758
Mathematics achievement					
Total extended group	461/421	3.4***	.010	1.4	.353
6-year group	72/66	5.7***	.009	2.8	.268
5-year group	175/154	3.8**	.022	0.7	.713
4-year group	124/116	3.3*	.069	2.1	.326
Other 5-year group	90/85	1.2	.566	0.7	.769

	N	Consumer skills (age 14–15) Raw score	p	Rate of passing	p
Total extended group	461/421	2.0**	.015	.086*	.054
6-year group	72/66	3.0**	.023	.090	.184
5-year group	175/154	2.2**	.030	.085*	.083
4-year group	124/116	2.5**	.024	.110**	.033
Other 5-year group	90/85	-6.21E-04	.999	.009	.993

	N	Years placed in special education Coeff.	p	Coeff.	p
Total extended group	461/421	-.296**	.027	-.363**	.025
6-year group	72/66	-.192	.386	-.203	.449
5-year group	175/154	-.307*	.062	-.349*	.085
4-year group	124/116	-.376**	.038	-.493**	.025
Other 5-year group	90/85	-.241	.235	-.326	.182

	N	Ever placed in special education Coeff.	p	Coeff.	p
Total extended group	461/421	-.072**	.015	-.064**	.036
6-year group	72/66	-.044	.368	-.021	.779
5-year group	175/154	-.082**	.024	-.075*	.056
4-year group	124/116	-.101**	.012	-.097**	.025
Other 5-year group	90/85	-.030	.500	-.027	.647

Table 27 (*continued*)

	N	Age 14 Coeff.	p	Age 15 Coeff.	p
		Retained in grade			
Total extended group	461/421	-.100***	.003	-.097***	.007
6-year group	72/66	-.166***	.003	-.168***	.005
5-year group	175/154	-.099**	.016	-.087*	.052
4-year group	124/116	-.066	.152	-.062	.188
Other 5-year group	90/85	-.103*	.067	-.114**	.039
		School-reported delinquency			
		Ages 13–14		Ages 13–15	
Total extended group	461/421	-.074***	.006	-.075**	.038
6-year group	72/66	-.112**	.048	-.078	.195
5-year group	175/154	-.076**	.035	-.070	.120
4-year group	124/116	-.058	.118	-.119**	.015
Other 5-year group	90/85	-.072	.109	-.018	.791

	Perceived school competence		
	Age 12		
	N	Coeff.	p
Extended group (total)	328	0.54	.265
6-year group	52	1.40*	.075
5-year group	123	0.05**	.932
4-year group	87	0.78	.222
Other 5-year group	66	0.49	.482

Note: Adjusted for kindergarten reading achievement, sex, risk status, and alternative intervention indicators.
$* p < .10, ** p < .05, *** p < .01.$

$p = .01$) as well as the 6-year, 5-year, and 4-year groups. Again, the 6-year program group had the highest average math achievement at age 14 and age 15 relative to the comparison group (5.7 and 2.8 points, respectively).

Consumer Skills

Relative to the nonextended group, extended program participation was significantly associated with higher scores and a higher passing rate in consumer life skills. Three of the four extended program groups had signifi-

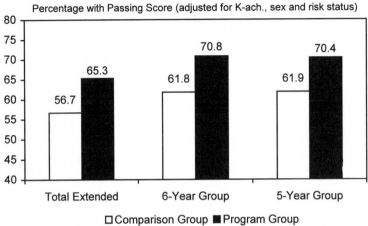

Fig. 12. Consumer Skills for Extended Program Groups

Percentage with Passing Score (adjusted for K-ach., sex and risk status)

□ Comparison Group ■ Program Group

cantly higher scores than the nonextended comparison group including the 6-year group (by 3.0 points), the 4-year group (by 2.5 points), and the 5-year group (by 2.2 points).

Only the 4-year and 5-year groups, however, had a higher passing rate in consumer life skills adjusted for the covariates; their respective advantages were 11.0 and 8.5 percentage points (see Figure 12). The 9.0-point advantage of the 6-year group did not reach statistical significance because of its relatively small sample size.

Grade Retention and Special Education Placement

Overall, the extended program group was significantly less likely than the comparison group to be retained in grade by age 15. Except for the 4-year group, all extended intervention groups had a lower rate of grade retention than the comparison group (see Figure 13). The 6-year group had the lowest retention rate by far. The difference of 16.8 percentage points translates to an adjusted rate of grade retention of 15.8% for the 6-year group and 32.6% for the nonextended group, a 50% reduction. The adjusted rates of grade retention for the 5-year maximum intervention group were, respectively, 23.9% and 21.4%. Some of these estimated effects may reflect the deemphasis on grade retention in the primary-grade program.

Extended program participants also had a lower rate of cumulative special education placement up to age 15 (by 6.4 percentage points) and spent fewer years in special education (0.36 years) than the nonextended compar-

Fig. 13. Grade Retention by Age 15 for Extended Program Groups

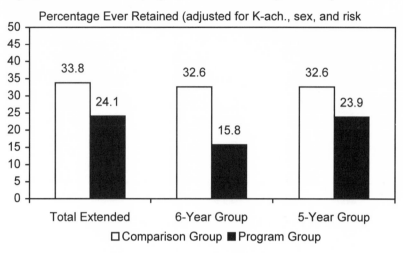

Fig. 14. Special Education by Age 15 for Extended Program Groups

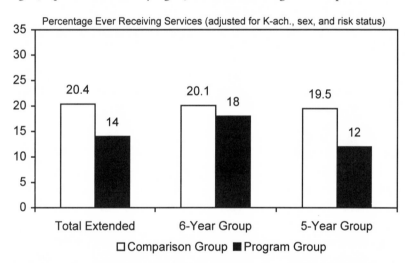

ison group (see Figure 14). Interestingly, it was children from the later CPCs (4-year and 5-year groups) who were less likely to receive special education services. In contrast, the 6-year group was more likely to avoid retention than special education. They spent less time in special education, on average, than the comparison group, but these differences were not significant.

Fig. 15. Delinquency at Ages 13–15 for Extended Program Groups

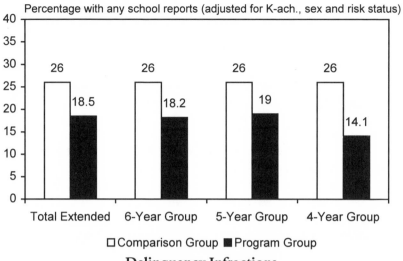

Percentage with any school reports (adjusted for K-ach., sex and risk status)

□ Comparison Group ■ Program Group

Delinquency Infractions

Overall, youth who participated in extended early intervention had a significantly lower rate of school-reported delinquency at ages 13 or 14 than the nonextended comparison group. Their rate of delinquency was 7.4 percentage points lower than the comparison group. Most of the effect was due to the 6-year and 5-year maximum intervention groups since the other two groups were indistinguishable from the comparison group.

The total extended intervention group also had a lower rate of delinquency than the comparison group from ages 13 to 15. As shown in Figure 15, the 7.5-point difference between groups translates, respectively, to adjusted rates of 18.5% and 26%. In contrast to ages 13 or 14, only the 4-year extended intervention distinguished themselves from the comparison group by age 15, though the direction of effects favored the extended intervention groups. The lack of consistent subgroup differences for both outcomes indicates that findings should be interpreted cautiously.

Perceived School Competence

As shown in Table 27, the total extended participation group did not have significantly higher ratings of school competence than the comparison group above and beyond kindergarten achievement, sex of child, and risk status. Of the four extended program groups, only the ratings of the 6-year group surpassed those of the nonextended comparison group ($B = 1.4$, $p = .075$), but only marginally.

FAMILY SOCIALIZATION OUTCOMES

I also investigated effects for the three family outcomes, again controlling for kindergarten achievement, sex of child, and risk status. Results indicated that extended program participation was significantly and positively associated only with parent participation in school ($b = .49$, $p < .001$). This estimated effect was specific to the 6-year and 5-year maximum intervention groups ($bs = .70$ and $.76$, respectively; $ps < .001$). These are youth who participated in the CPCs beginning at age 3 and ending at second or third grade. Adjusted group means for the 6-year and 5-year maximum intervention groups were 2.3 and 2.4, respectively, compared to 1.6 for the nonextended program group (controlling for sex of child, risk status, and kindergarten achievement).

None of the measures of extended program participation were independently associated with parent expectations for children's educational attainment and parent satisfaction with children's education up to age 12 ($ps > .10$). Sample sizes for the program groups were particularly small for these comparisons. This may have contributed to the absence of effects. Coded dichotomously, for example, parents of the extended program group were slightly more likely than those of the nonextended group to expect their children to graduate from college (52% versus 48%) and to be satisfied with their children's education (82% versus 79%).

In summary, the extended CPC intervention group performed significantly better than the nonextended group on all youth outcomes at the age 14 or age 15 follow-up. The most consistent findings occurred for grade retention, special education placement, and delinquency infractions. Effects for school achievement were largely limited to age 14. Yet the extended program groups exhibited significant advantages over their peers in consumer skills. Effects of extended program participation on family outcomes were specific to parent involvement in school. This is not surprising given that parent involvement is a distinguishing characteristic of the CPC program.

Consistent with the dosage-response relations reported earlier, the 6-year intervention group from the original CPCs consistently exhibited the best scholastic and social adjustment and had parents who were more involved in school after the program, although all extended groups surpassed the comparison group on at least one youth outcome. The direction of effects exclusively favored the extended program groups. These are improbable findings if extended program participation is unrelated to social competence.

Extended Participation to Third Grade Versus Second Grade

The above findings raise the question whether extended program participation to third grade offers an advantage over participation that ceases in second grade. This can be addressed because some centers offered services only through second grade while the six original centers offered services through third grade. This difference in years of service occurred due to administrative selection that was independent of family and child attributes. In a previous study by Reynolds and Temple (1998), 3-year follow-on participants had higher reading achievement and less grade retention than the two-year group at ages 9 and 13.[12]

Two sets of analyses were conducted to determine the value added by the third year of follow-on intervention. First, I contrasted the performance of the 6-year and 5-year maximum intervention groups shown in Table 27. Both groups of children enrolled in the CPC program at age 3 and completed the maximum number of years available at that site. Because youth received the same intervention experiences in each of these centers, a significant difference favoring the 6-year group would indicate an advantage of the third year of follow-on intervention. Because of this matching on program entry and available intervention, I compared raw group differences. Findings indicated significant differences only for grade retention. The 3-year extended group was less likely than the 2-year group to be retained in grade by age 14 (by 8.5 percentage points) and by age 15 (by 9.7 percentage points). Both coefficients were significant at the 7% level.

Because the above analyses did not include children who entered the CPCs at age 4 and continued their participation for the maximum number of years available in the center, all preschool participants were included in the model with years of preschool added as the lone covariate. Findings were consistent with the first set of analyses. Three-year participants were less likely to be retained up to age 14 (by 11.9 percentage points) and up to age 15 (by 12.9 percentage points). Both results were significant at the 0.2% level. Notably, children with extended participation through third grade had consistently better performance across the outcomes. For example, their average reading achievement scores were, respectively, 3.5 and 3.7 points higher than the 2-year groups ($ps = $ .117 and .128).

Effect of Primary-Grade Intervention Alone

Although across the total sample, years of participation in follow-on intervention was positively and significantly associated with several social competence outcomes, as was extended program participation, I investigated whether children who participated only in the kindergarten and primary-grade component of the CPC program showed performance advantages over the non-CPC comparison group. For the analysis, children who received CPC services from kindergarten to third grade ($N = 60$) were compared with the non-CPC intervention group ($N = 275$) on youth outcomes. Findings indicated that the kindergarten and primary-grade intervention group without preschool surpassed the non-CPC comparison group on two outcomes at ages 14 and 15. Participants in the follow-on program only had higher average scores on consumer skills (40.5 to 37.5, $p = $ .098) and had a higher rate of passing in consumer skills (62.4% to 49.8%, $p = $ .075). They also were less likely to be retained in grade by age 14 (24.4% to 35.8%, $p = $ .087) and by age 15 (23.2% to 39.1%, $p = $ .028). No significant differences were found for the remaining outcomes. These findings indicate that intervention beginning after preschool can lead to persistent advantages, though these advantages are not as large as interventions that begin in preschool. These findings continue the pattern reported by Reynolds (1994) that follow-on participation, after accounting for earlier intervention, did not lead to performance advantages in reading and math beyond the 1-year follow-up.

Timing of Intervention

Although participation in the primary-grade intervention alone provides some advantages over no participation in the CPC program, do these performance advantages also occur relative to children with early CPC participation? This addresses the effects of timing of program participation. For the analysis, I compared youth who participated only in the preschool and kindergarten component ($N = 220$) and youth who participated in only the kindergarten and follow-on component ($N = 93$). To equalize duration of participation as much as possible, those in the non-CPC comparison group who enrolled in the CPCs beginning in first grade were excluded. Because timing of program entry may be confounded with child and family attributes, I used youth's sex and risk status as covariates. Regression analysis indicated that the early entry group had significantly better performance only in reading achievement at age 14 ($b = 5.5$, $p = .039$) and marginally so at age 15 ($b = 4.9$, $p = .110$). Nevertheless, except for delinquency infractions, both youth outcomes and family socialization outcomes consistently favored the early entry group. These findings were unchanged when comparing youth who entered the program at age 3 (rather than ages 3 or 4) to youth who participated in kindergarten to at least second grade.

In a further analysis, I contrasted two groups who were matched on duration of program participation (4 years) but who varied in their timing of entry. This addresses the question of whether timing of entry into intervention influences youth social competence, controlling for duration of participation. To address this question, the performance of 124 children who participated in the program for 4 years beginning in preschool (PS + K + FO-2) was compared to the performance of 60 children who participated for 4 years beginning in kindergarten (NoPS + K + FO-3). Only one significant difference occurred: the early entry group had a significantly lower rate of delinquency infractions from ages 13 to 15 (by 12.6 percentage points, $p = .069$). The magnitude of the group difference for reading achievement at ages 14 and 15 (4.5 and 5.5 points) was consistent with analyses above, though because of smaller sample sizes it did not reach statistical significance. As above, the pattern of findings continued to favor the early entry group.

Summary
There was limited support for the positive effects of (a) 3 years of extended program participation relative to 2 years, (b) primary-grade intervention alone relative to no CPC intervention, and (c) early entry (timing) into the program. Extended participation for 3 years was associated with lower rates of grade retention, whereas primary-grade intervention was associated with lower rates of grade retention and with greater consumer skills. Although the pattern of findings favored the early entry group, only differences for reading achievement and delinquency infractions significantly favored early program participation alone over later intervention alone. Nevertheless, these comparisons were restricted by relatively small sample

sizes. As Figure 5 and Table 27 clearly demonstrate, the largest advantages occurred for children who had both early and extensive participation in the program.

DEVELOPMENTAL PATTERNS OF READING ACHIEVEMENT

I have restricted my analyses in this chapter primarily to outcomes at ages 13 to 15, with a major finding that while both preschool participation and follow-on participation were associated with youth or family outcomes, extended program participation provided the largest long-term effects. In this section, I highlight both the short- and long-term performance differences for program participants in reading achievement. Extensive longitudinal data are available in the CLS data set for charting patterns of individual growth. As indicated in Chapter 2, school achievement, especially reading, is a key outcome of the theory of the CPC program. Performance on standardized tests has been assessed yearly from age 5 (the beginning and end of kindergarten) to age 15 (the end of the ninth-grade year), the end point for the analysis in this monograph.

Figures 16.A, 16.B, and 16.C display the reading achievement of five intervention groups from kindergarten entry to age 15: the extended program group with three (PS + K + FO-3; max $n = 172$) and 2 years of follow-on intervention (PS + K + FO-2; max $n = 336$), the preschool and kindergarten group with no follow-on intervention (PS + K; max $n = 294$), the 3-year follow-on group with no preschool (NoPS + K + FO-3; max $n = 80$), and the non-CPC comparison group (zero years of intervention; max $n = 349$). The two vertical lines indicate the implementation of the primary-grade intervention.[13] The standard scores are unadjusted and are based on the available samples, not just the scores of the study sample. The age 5 score measures cognitive readiness (a composite of five subtests including language and word analysis). Several findings are highlighted in Figures 16.A to 16.C.

Figure 16.A clearly shows the powerful effects of CPC program participation, as both extended program groups were performing at the national average on the composite battery of the ITBS at the beginning of kindergarten (age 5) and above the national average at the end of kindergarten (age 6) in word analysis. In fact, the growth rate between the beginning and end of kindergarten was higher for the CPC groups. Each intervention group maintained its level of performance through the end of their respec-

Fig. 16. (A, B, & C) Patterns of Reading Achievement for Selected Program Groups

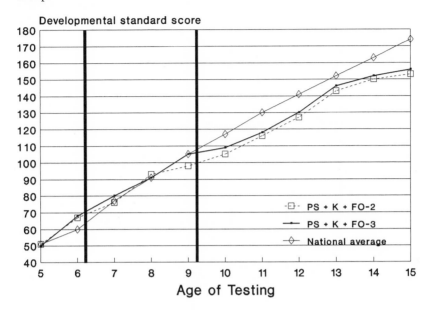

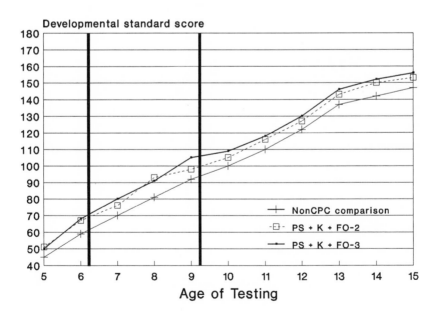

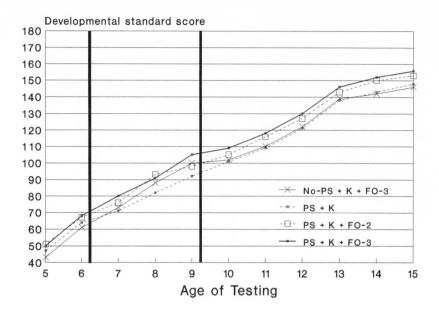

Developmental standard score

No-PS + K + FO-3
PS + K
PS + K + FO-2
PS + K + FO-3

Age of Testing

tive program durations—second grade (age 8) or third grade (age 9)—and then declined in the first year after completion of the program. The achievement gap widened following the program and up to age 12, narrowed at age 13, and then widened again at ages 14 and 15.

Figure 16.B shows that, relative to the non-CPC comparison group, the extended program groups had consistently superior reading performance over time. Not surprisingly, the gap was largest for the PS + K + FO-2 group at the end of second grade (age 8) and largest for the PS + K + FO-3 group at the end of third grade (age 9). Each was more than 10 standard-score points (1 year or more). After narrowing slightly from ages 10 to 12, the gap widened again during ages 13 to 15, with the extended program groups performing up to a year higher than their comparison cohorts. Also shown in 16.B is the advantage of 3 years of follow-on intervention after preschool and kindergarten over 2 years of follow-on intervention. Beyond age 10, however, the performance differences narrowed, but the 2-year group never surpassed the 3-year group (see Reynolds & Temple, 1998, for additional analyses).

Figure 16.C shows, as expected, that children who participated in the primary-grade intervention after preschool and kindergarten also outperformed both the CPC preschool group without follow-on intervention and the CPC group with no preschool but 3 years of follow-on intervention. Without preschool, the gains for the follow-on only group were lost by age 11 (grade 5). Without follow-on intervention, only the extended intervention groups (PS + K + FO-2 and PS + K + FO-3) maintained their performance advantage over the other groups.

The reading performance of youth who participated in only the follow-on group (NoPS + K + FO-3) was similar to that of the preschool plus kindergarten group (PS + K) and the non-CPC comparison group by age 15. Yet the early intervention group (preschool and kindergarten only) maintained a slight advantage in reading and math. These findings suggest that without earlier intervention, school-age intervention does not provide the optimal level of effectiveness over time. As shown, their performance advantage did not persist past age 10. This clearly shows the recency effect of follow-on participation. As shown earlier in this chapter, optimal performance appears to require both early and extensive program participation.

On a methodological note, Figures 16.B and 16.C also indicate that the intervention groups were growing at similar rates prior to the primary-grade intervention. All groups made substantial gains in cognitive performance from fall to spring of kindergarten. These findings lend support to the view that program groups were equivalent prior to entry into extended childhood intervention. These two pretests prior to later participation help to rule out selection-maturation (unequal growth prior to program) as an explanation of observed effects (see Reynolds & Temple, 1998). The large growth rate from the beginning to the end of kindergarten for the follow-on only group indicates the substantial impact of participation in the all-day kindergarten program associated with the Child-Parent Centers. This level of growth was not sustained, however. The follow-on only group and the non-CPC comparison group were performing below the national average at the beginning of kindergarten primarily because they had no systematic preschool experience.

Who Benefits Most from Participation?

For the final section of this chapter, I investigated if the estimated effects of different measures of program participation on youth outcomes varied by child, family background, and program attributes. Few previous studies have investigated such moderator effects, yet they would be predicted by both resilience theory and ecological systems theory (see Chapter 1). To determine which children benefited most from program participation, interaction terms for five sets of subgroup characteristics were included in the model. Five measures of program participation were investigated: (a) any CPC program participation, (b) duration of participation, (c) any preschool participation, (d) any follow-on participation, and (e) extended participation (relative to less extended participation).

The following questions were addressed:

Do girls benefit from program participation more than boys?

Do children who have experienced a relatively large number of risk factors benefit more than children experiencing a relatively low number of risks?

Do children whose parent(s) have graduated from high school benefit more than children whose parent(s) have not graduated from high school?

Do children who grow up in neighborhoods with relatively high poverty benefit more than children who grow up in neighborhoods with lower rates of poverty?

Do the program characteristics of instructional approach and parent participation in school lead to advantages for children?

Differential effects were estimated as follows for each youth outcome at ages 14 and 15 and each family outcome. Program interaction terms (e.g., program*sex and program*risk status) were added to the basic model specification (see Chapter 3) that already included the main effects of each variable included in the interaction. These terms were included sequentially for each program indicator. Only two subgroup characteristics were included in any one model specification. To determine if girls benefited more than boys, for example, program*sex and program*risk status were entered in the model after the main effects. Interactions involving program*parent education and program*school poverty were estimated separately and included sex of child and the sex by program interaction term. Effects for preschool participation and follow-on participation, however, were estimated simultaneously.

Results are summarized in Table 28 by outcome and program indicator for four interaction effects: girls versus boys, parent education (high school graduates versus nongraduates), risk status (index from 1 to 8 risks), and

Table 28. Subgroup Attributes Associated with Differential Program Effects

	Who benefits more from participation?			
Program participation	Girls or boys	High/Low risk status	HS grad or not	High/Low sch. poverty
Reading achievement				
1. Any participation	—	—	—	High .003r
2. Any preschool	Boys .023r	—	—	—
3. Any follow-on	Girls .006r	—	—	High .018r
4. Years of participation	—	—	—	High .012r
5. Extended participation	—	—	—	—
Mathematics achievement				
1. Any participation	—	—	—	High .000r
2. Any preschool	—	—	—	—
3. Any follow-on	Girls .034r	—	—	High .004r
4. Years of participation	—	—	—	High .001r
5. Extended participation	—	—	—	High .05
Consumer skills				
1. Any participation	—	—	—	High .000
2. Any preschool	—	—	—	High .018
3. Any follow-on	—	—	—	—
4. Years of participation	—	—	—	High .004
5. Extended participation	—	—	—	—
Grade retention				
1. Any participation	—	—	—	—
2. Any preschool	Boys .027r	—	—	Low .042
3. Any follow-on	Girls .006r	—	—	High .009
4. Years of participation	—	—	—	—
5. Extended participation	—	—	—	—
Any special education placement				
1. Any participation	—	—	—	High .002r
2. Any preschool	Boys .041	—	—	—
3. Any follow-on	—	—	—	—
4. Years of participation	—	—	—	—
5. Extended participation	Boys .024r	—	—	—
Delinquency infractions				
1. Any participation	—	—	—	Low .020
2. Any preschool	—	—	—	—
3. Any follow-on	—	—	—	Low .015
4. Years of participation	—	—	—	Low .031
5. Extended participation	—	—	—	—

Note: r = coefficient was significant ($p < .05$) at both ages 14 and 15; — = no interaction effect detected at the .05 level. Follow-on = primary-grade intervention.

school poverty in kindergarten (60% or more children in low-income families versus less than 60% low-income).[14] The advantaged group is noted in the table along with its corresponding level of significance.

Results indicated only modest support for differential program effects. Only 36 of 275 interaction terms for youth outcomes at ages 14 and 15 were significant at the .05 level.[15] The most frequently detected differential effects were for school poverty and sex of child. Notably, the interaction terms increased the variance explained in the outcomes by no more than 1 to 1.5%. These findings are summarized below. I emphasized the interaction effects that were robust for ages 14 and 15, that is, were significant at the .05 levels at ages 14 and 15. These are denoted by "r" in Table 28.

MODERATORS OF YOUTH OUTCOMES

SCHOOL POVERTY

School poverty was the most consistent moderator of the effects of program participation. For all outcomes except delinquency, children who attended programs in the highest poverty neighborhoods (i.e., more than 60% of children from low-income families) benefited more than children who attended programs in lower poverty neighborhoods. The most robust findings were for reading and math achievement and the program indicators of any program participation, follow-on participation, and years of participation. School attendance in a high-poverty neighborhood was associated with a greater preschool effect only for consumer life skills.

Alternatively, attendance in a neighborhood with a lower rate of poverty was associated with a lower rate of delinquency infractions for three of five program indicators. This finding should be interpreted cautiously since none of these coefficients were robust for both measures of delinquency.

SEX OF CHILD

Girls appeared to benefit more than boys from participation in the follow-on program in reading and math achievement and grade retention. The effects of extended program participation on grade retention also were greater for girls than boys.

Boys were more likely to benefit from preschool participation for reading achievement, grade retention, math achievement, and special education placement. Effects were not robust for the latter two outcomes, however. In addition, the effects of extended program participation also favored boys with regard to special education placement.

RISK STATUS

The effects of program participation on youth outcomes did not vary by the number of risk factors children experienced. A notable and marginally significant finding ($p = .055$) was that children experiencing relatively few risk factors were more likely to benefit from preschool participation by having a lower rate of grade retention.

PARENT EDUCATION

Likewise, no significant pattern of effects emerged for parent education. Children with and without parents who graduated from high school benefited equally from program participation. The effect of extended program participation on reading achievement and on consumer life skills somewhat favored children of high school graduates. Neither coefficient was significant at the .05 level, however.

PARENT PARTICIPATION IN SCHOOL

The effects of different measures of program participation on youth outcomes did not vary as a function of parent participation in school, at least as rated by first-grade teachers. This program-related attribute was measured dichotomously as "average" or "satisfactory" or better versus "below average" or no participation. Thus, program participants whose parents participated in school often were no more likely to have better social competence than program participants whose parents participated less often in school. Nevertheless, parent participation in school had a significantly positive effect on youth outcomes.

INSTRUCTIONAL APPROACH

Finally, to determine whether instructional approach in preschool was associated with differential group performance, I compared social competence among children in teacher-oriented, developmental, and non-differentiated (mixed) program implementations.[16] Analyses were based only on children with CPC preschool experience and included follow-on intervention plus risk status and sex of child as covariates. As reported in Table 29, the adolescent adjustment of children who attended centers with a relatively teacher-oriented preschool program had higher reading and

Table 29. Preschool Instructional Approaches Associated with Differential Program Effects

Relative instructional focus	More beneficial instructional approach					
	Reading achiev.	Math achiev.	Life skills	Spec. ed.	Grade retain	Delinq. infract.
Teacher-oriented vs. developmental	TO .025	TO .007	—	—	TO .067	—
Robust at age 15	no	no	no			
Developmental vs. undifferentiated	—	DV .074	DV .028	—	—	—
Robust at age 15		no	no			
Teacher-oriented vs. undifferentiated	TO .004	TO .000	TO .002	—	TO .053	—
Robust at age 15	yes	yes	yes		yes	

Note: Significance levels are for age 14 outcomes. Robustness based on same outcome one year later. TO = Teacher-oriented, DV = developmental, — = no interaction effect detected at the .10 level.

math achievement and a lower rate of grade retention than children in centers having a more developmental approach. However, none of these differences were robust at ages 14 and 15. Children in both developmentally oriented and teacher-oriented centers had more positive adolescent outcomes than children in centers with no distinct instructional focus. Only the advantages of children in teacher-oriented centers was robust at age 15.

That participation in centers implementing teacher-oriented instructional activities was associated with better adolescent adjustment indicates that in a climate of family involvement, opportunities for diverse learning experiences with relatively low teacher-child ratios, structured and academically oriented curriculum approaches can promote children's scholastic development without negative side effects. The within-study classification used in this study warrants cautious generalization, however.

MODERATORS OF FAMILY OUTCOMES

Similar to youth social competence, the effects of program participation on family socialization did not vary much by subgroup characteristics. Only 7 of the 75 interaction terms involving sex of child, parent education, risk status, and school poverty were significant at the .05 level, and 13 were significant at the .10 level of significance. Below, I emphasize findings at the .05 level of significance.

In contrast to the youth outcomes, risk status and parent education were more likely to moderate the effects of program participation on family socialization outcomes. The effects of preschool and any participation on parent satisfaction with children's education were greater for children with higher levels of risk than with lower levels of risk ($ps < .05$).[17] Likewise, school poverty in kindergarten moderated the effect of preschool and any participation on parent satisfaction with children's education: program parents in higher poverty settings were more satisfied than program parents in lower poverty settings ($ps < .07$).

On the other hand, parents who were high school graduates and who had children with fewer risk factors were more likely than parents without these attributes to benefit from preschool participation through higher expectations for children's educational attainment ($p = .067$) and any program participation through greater participation in school ($p = .001$).

With regard to instructional approach, the parents of children who attended teacher-oriented centers had greater satisfaction with their children's education than parents who attended centers that were developmentally oriented centers. No differences between groups occurred in parent expectations for children's educational attainment and parent involvement in school. Teacher and developmentally oriented instructional approaches were associated with greater participation in school than undifferentiated approaches.

Overall Summary of Findings

To summarize the wide range of findings across the measures of program participation, Table 30 displays a comprehensive set of effect sizes for three program measures: maximum intervention exposure versus no CPC intervention (6 years versus none), preschool participation versus none, and extended participation versus participation ceasing in kindergarten (above and beyond kindergarten achievement). These three were chosen because they represent the full spectrum of effects of CPC program participation. Participation in the maximum amount of intervention indexes the direct effect of the total CPC program (implied but not directly tested above). Preschool participation provides a middle-level index for the independent effect of early intervention. The effect of follow-on intervention after pre-

Table 30. Summary of Effect Sizes in Standard-Deviation or Percentage-Change Units for 3 Measures of CPC Program Participation

Program outcome	Child-Parent Center participation		
	Maximum (6 yrs. vs. none)	Preschool (vs. none)	Extended (vs. no extended)
School achievement			
Reading achievement at age 14	.43	.25	.14
Reading achievement at age 15	.33	.18	.12
Math achievement at age 14	.45	.24	.18
Math achievement at age 15	.31	.17	.07
Consumer life skills at age 14/15	.57	.27	.19
% increase in passing consumer life skills test at age 14–15	44	21	15
School competence			
% reduction in grade retention by age 15	68	22	28
% reduction in special ed. placement by age 15	48	25	31
% reduction in grade retention or special ed. by age 15	54	19	26
Years in special ed. by age 15	.42	.21	.18
Social-psychological behavior			
% reduction in delinquency infractions at ages 13–14	41	(1)	51
% reduction in delinquency infractions at ages 13–15	17	0	29
Perceived competence at age 12	.23	.17	.11
Family socialization			
Parent participation in school at ages 8–12	.48	.15	.36
Parent expectations for children's ed. attainment at age 10–12	.33	.21	.01
Parent satisfaction with children's ed. at ages 10–12	.26	.25	.07

Note: Standard deviations are the adjusted mean group difference divided by the total-group standard deviation. % change is the percentage of increase or reduction divided by the comparison-group baseline. All effects were adjusted for sex and risk status. Kindergarten achievement was included for estimating effects of extended intervention. Value in parentheses = gain.

school and kindergarten shows the added value of primary-grade intervention above and beyond earlier intervention.

The effects are presented in two forms. The continuous and ordinal outcome measures use effect sizes (ESs) in standard deviation units. ESs are calculated as the ratio of adjusted mean group difference to the total standard deviation of the program outcome. Values of .20 or above were interpreted as beyond the level of practical significance. An ES of .20 is equivalent to a correlation of .10 between program participation and outcome. It also is equal to a 22% improvement in success rate over the comparison group in the binomial effect size display (Rosenthal, 1991). For the dichotomous outcomes, effect magnitudes were reported as a percentage change (increase or decrease) from the adjusted rate of the comparison group. Thus, it is the ratio of the adjusted rate difference between groups to the adjusted rate of the comparison group. I interpreted a percentage change of 20% or more as practically significant for the outcomes measured in this study. As with statistical significance, thresholds of practical significance are inherently arbitrary. These identified thresholds, however, are consistent with those used in prior studies of this data set (Reynolds, 1995; Reynolds & Temple, 1995) and with other analyses of social programs (Lipsey & Wilson, 1993).

The first column in Table 30 reports the effect sizes of maximum intervention exposure of 6 years versus no participation in the CPC program on youth and families. As expected, this measure yielded the largest ESs, ranging from .23 (perceived school competence) to .57 (consumer life skills) and percentage changes ranging from a 17% reduction in age 13–15 delinquency to a 68% reduction in grade retention during the elementary grades. These are pervasive and sizeable effects.

The estimated effects of CPC preschool participation were smaller in magnitude but were largely beyond the level of practical significance. The largest percentage changes in performance were in the range of 21% (passing life skills test) to 25% (reduction in special education placement). The largest effect sizes were for consumer life skills (.27), reading achievement at age 14 (.25), and parent satisfaction with children's education (.25). Translated to months of performance, preschool participants scored, on average, 4 to 5 months higher than their comparison-group peers in school achievement at both ages. These are meaningful differences. Preschool par-

135

Fig. 17. School Remedial Services by Age 15 for 3 Program Contrasts

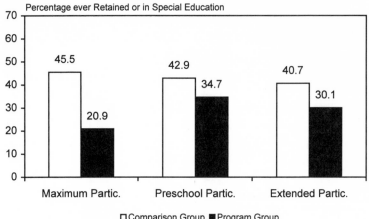

Percentage ever Retained or in Special Education

Maximum Partic.   Preschool Partic.   Extended Partic.

□ Comparison Group ■ Program Group

ticipation was not associated with school-reported delinquency infractions.

Also reported in Table 30 are effect sizes for a combined measure of special education placement and grade retention—the percentage of youth who were retained in grade or who received special education services by ages 14 and 15. This indicator of social competence takes into account that some schools may use special education more than grade retention or visa versa. Thus, it generally indexes remedial school services. Because this outcome was not reported earlier in this chapter, I highlight group comparisons in Figure 17. Each measure of program participation was associated with significantly lower rates of remedial school services.

Preschool participation was associated with a 19.1% reduction in remedial services, for 34.7% of the preschool group was so identified compared to 42.9% for the no-preschool group. Extended participation was associated with a 26% reduction in remedial services over the nonextended group (30.1% versus 40.7%), whereas maximum intervention was associated with a 54% reduction in remedial services (20.9% versus 45.5%). Any program participation and follow-on participation also were significantly associated with lower rates of remedial school services.

The added effect of follow-on intervention was largest for delinquency, grade retention, special education, and parent involvement in school. It was smallest for parent expectations, parent satisfaction with children's education, and math achievement at age 15. The effect sizes for school achievement were relatively small (Min. = .07, Max. = .18) because of the large standard deviation in performance in adolescence and because of the nature of the contrast. Unlike preschool, both program and comparison groups were in full-time schooling. The effects on parent involvement, grade retention, and special education were consistent with the program theory.

In summary, the effects of participation in the Child-Parent Center Program consistently favored program participants across most measures of program participation regardless of model specification. Extensive program participation was most associated with positive youth and family development, yet both preschool and follow-on participation significantly contributed to the long-term effects of intervention. School competence, consumer skills, and school achievement were most consistently impacted by intervention. Extended program participation was associated with significantly lower rates of delinquency infractions. The only consistent pattern of differential effects of program participation was that participating youth in the highest poverty neighborhoods appeared to benefit more than youth in lower poverty neighborhoods. No robust differences in social competence occurred between teacher-oriented and developmental instructional approaches in preschool, though the former was associated with better social competence at age 14. Given the consistent and substantial effects of CPC participation reported in this chapter, I now turn to the pathways through which these long-term effects come about.

5
Pathways of Program Effectiveness

A major question raised by the findings in Chapter 4 is how do the positive effects of participation in the CPC program come about? In other words, what are the pathways through which long-term effects are achieved? Identification of these pathways provides a rationale for explaining the observed program effects. As a central feature of the confirmatory program evaluation described in Chapter 1, causal inference is strengthened if the estimated program effects are explained by pathways predicted by the program theory.

Besides strengthening causal inference, investigation of the pathways of program effectiveness also helps identify intervening factors and processes that can be the focus of intervention for maintaining or enhancing the effects of earlier intervention. Identified pathways also aid program design and improvement by highlighting key components or active ingredients that require special attention. These pathways are mechanisms through which the long-term effects of intervention are realized.

A *mechanism* is defined as a "process in a concrete system, such that it is capable of bringing about or preventing some change in the system as a whole or in some of its subsystems" (Bunge, 1997, p. 414). In human development, mechanisms are often conceptualized as intervening variables within the major ecological systems of individuals, families, schools, and communities (Bronfenbrenner, 1979). Examples may include maternal responsiveness, parental monitoring, cognitive development, and school and community support. They also may be viewed as proximal processes (Bronfenbrenner & Morris, 1998) or developmental priming mechanisms

(Ramey & Ramey, 1998). In evaluation research, mechanisms are often called the "active" ingredients that give rise to and help maintain program impacts (Cook & Shadish, 1994; Reynolds, 1998b). They are key to theory-driven evaluations (Bickman, 1987; Chen, 1990; Reynolds & Walberg, 1998).

For this chapter, I investigated through structural equation modeling five theory-driven hypotheses of mechanisms that may explain the effects of CPC participation on youth social competence. As discussed in Chapter 1, the hypotheses are experiences associated with cognitive advantage, family support, motivational advantage, social adjustment, and school support. I first describe the confirmatory approach used to investigate the causal mechanisms that may promote long-term effects. This is followed by presentation of results of the structural modeling by youth outcome. The chapter concludes with a summary of major findings. As above, I use the terms *pathways*, *mechanisms*, and *processes* interchangeably.

A CONFIRMATORY APPROACH TO INVESTIGATING PROGRAM IMPACT

A common belief within some social science disciplines and program areas is that the only way to draw valid causal inferences is through experiments; anything less is insufficient. A careful reading of the postpositivist literature on program evaluation indicates that this view is a narrow interpretation of the nature of causal inference. As Donald Campbell (1984; Overman, 1988) and others have frequently observed, (a) all knowledge, however acquired, is fallible, (b) experiments only probe causal relations and theories; they cannot prove them, (c) the key to causal inference is to rule out *plausible* alternative hypotheses, and (d) while experiments are usually the most desirable means of inferring causality, quasi-experimental and observational studies also can probe causality (Abelson, 1995; Rosenbaum, 1995). Indeed, it is the overall pattern and coherence of empirical evidence that strengthens inferences. A major tenet of confirmatory program evaluation is that the plausibility of an estimated program effect can be strengthened through systematic testing of causal mechanisms and other aspects of the program-outcome relationship.

Confirmatory program evaluation (CPE) is a method for conducting a theory-driven evaluation in which the objective is to facilitate causal inference about the relationship between program participation and measured outcomes. It is an outcome or impact evaluation in which hypotheses about program effects are tested based on the program theory. Unlike theory-driven evaluation generally (Bickman, 1987; Chen, 1990), CPE specifically focuses on impact assessment. It can be applied to experimental, quasi-experimental, or nonexperimental data but enhances causal inference most in quasi-experimental and nonexperimental designs. See Reynolds (1998b) for details.

In CPE, causal uncertainty is reduced through an examination of the empirical pattern of findings against the expectations of the program theory. In contrast, traditional method-driven evaluations attempt to reduce causal uncertainty through control exercised during the research design phase. Alternatively, statistically oriented evaluations reduce causal uncertainty through control exercised during the data analysis phase. Of special interest in CPE is testing the causal mechanisms that may lead to long-term effects. The investigation of causal mechanisms is underutilized in evaluation practice (Cook, Anson, & Walchli, 1993; Cronbach, 1982; Rosenbaum, 1984, 1995).

The researcher in CPE investigates the empirical patterns of relationships among program, intervening, and outcome variables. Such systematic testing can be aided by the use of six criteria for interpreting findings. Causal inference is strengthened to the extent that these criteria about the relation between program participation and outcome are satisfied. Adapted from Anderson et al., (1980) and Susser (1973), the criteria are listed in ascending order of importance.

1. Temporality of program exposure. Program participation precedes the measurement of its consequences. Satisfaction of the temporality criterion is the most basic level of causal inference.

2. Strength of association. The larger the association between program participation and the intended outcome, the more likely the association reflects a real causal effect. Other factors being equal, a program that is associated with a one standard deviation change in performance as opposed to a one-third standard deviation change is more likely to represent a true as well as robust causal relation.

3. Gradient (dosage/response). A causal inference is more warranted if, other factors being equal, a monotonic relationship exists between program exposure (e.g., number of years or sessions) and

the program outcome. Of course, other linear or nonlinear forms of the relation do not rule out causality.

4. Specificity. If the program–outcome relation is limited to certain domains of behavior, as predicted by the program theory, causal inference is more straightforward. The effects of a delinquency prevention program, for example, are more interpretable if measures of delinquency and antisocial behavior are affected more than school achievement or truancy.

5. Consistency. If the program–outcome relation is found to be similar across sample populations and subpopulations, at different times and places, and under different analyses and model specifications, the more likely the observed effects are real. In a previous report in the Chicago Longitudinal Study, for example, Reynolds and Temple (1995) found consistent and positive effects of CPC preschool participation, regardless of model specification, analytic method, and underlying assumptions.

6. Coherence. At the highest level of causal interpretation is the extent to which the evaluation findings show a clear pattern of effects relative to the causes of behaviors the program is attempting to impact. A key indicator of coherence is whether the "active ingredients" of the program theory explain the observed relation between program participation and outcome.

Notably, the absence of one or more of the above conditions does not invalidate a causal relationship. To the extent that these conditions are satisfied, however, causal inference is strengthened for all types of research designs but especially in quasi-experiments (i.e., program is not assigned randomly). These criteria provide a foundation for assessing causal relationships. They emphasize that the pattern of empirical findings rather than the research design per se is crucial for causal assessment.

To illustrate, the most widely accepted causal relationship in the behavioral sciences is between smoking and lung cancer. Yet the evidence is based exclusively on observational studies, often without a comparison group. This is because the evidence satisfied several of the above criteria, most notably gradient and specificity. The risk of lung cancer increases monotonically as the number of cigarettes smoked increases (U.S. Department of Health, Education, & Welfare, 1964). Rates of lung cancer among smokers also are substantially higher than for other types of cancer (specificity). Over time, the strength and consistency of the evidence and the coherence of the findings (e.g., the carcinogenic effect on lung tissue) also supported a causal relationship. Other widely accepted causal relationships (e.g., quality of instruction and school achievement, prenatal nutrition and low birth weight, flouride and tooth decay) have been demonstrated in similar fashion.

The estimates of program effects reported in Chapter 4 support the criteria of gradient, consistency, and specificity. That is, the positive effects of program participation increased as a function of years of program participation, they were consistent under different model specifications and across different subgroups, and they most favored the outcomes predicted by the program theory—reduced grade retention and special education placement, increased achievement test scores and consumer skills, and greater parent involvement (see Table 30). In the rest of this chapter, the coherence of the program-outcome relationship is investigated with regard to the hypothesized causal mechanisms underlying the estimated program effects.

Hypothesized Mediators of Effects of CPC Participation

As discussed in Chapter 1 and reported in Figure 1, five hypotheses were tested to determine how and why participation in the CPC program has lasting effects. For this chapter, I investigated five sets of mediators to determine if the relationship between measures of CPC participation and youth outcomes can be explained by the program theory. CPC participation was measured by preschool participation and follow-on participation (both in years), total years of CPC participation, and extended program participation (dichotomously coded). They are restated from Chapter 1 as follows:

> *Cognitive advantage hypothesis:* Program participation is associated with greater social competence through its effect on children's early cognitive development. Cognitive development was measured by scores on the ITBS cognitive readiness battery at age 5 (kindergarten entry) and on reading and math-total subtests at age 9 (third-grade year). The age 5 measure was used as mediator of preschool participation; the age 9 scores were used as mediators of years of participation and extended program participation.

Family support hypothesis: Program participation affects children's social competence by enhancing family support behavior. The frequency of parent participation in school when children were aged 8 to 12, as rated by teachers and parents, indexed family support behavior.

Social adjustment hypothesis: Program participation affects children's social competence through enhancing social development. Teacher ratings of classroom adjustment at age 9 were used as an indicator of social-emotional adjustment to formal schooling. The scale included six items (e.g., "gets along well with others").

Motivational advantage hypothesis: Program participation is associated with greater social competence through enhanced motivational development. Child ratings of perceived school competence at age 9 indexed motivational development. This scale included 12 items, including "I do better in school than my classmates" and "I get good grades in school."

School support hypothesis: Program participation is associated with greater social competence by increasing the likelihood of attendance in good-quality schools and reducing the likelihood of school mobility. School support was measured by the number of years of participation in schools with a relatively large proportion of students performing at national norms (ages 10–14). As a secondary indicator, I also used the number of times the participants in the study changed schools between ages 10–13.

By definition, an intervening or postprogram variable must be significantly and simultaneously associated with (a) measures of program participation and (b) program outcomes to be a valid mediator or pathway of program effectiveness (Cohen & Cohen, 1983; Reynolds, 1998b). Satisfaction of only one of these criteria is *insufficient* for demonstrating a pathway of program effectiveness.

Descriptive Statistics for the Mediators

Table 31 displays mean scores of CPC preschool and comparison groups for each hypothesized mediator as well as correlations with the number of years of preschool (which was more associated with cognitive readiness and other intervening factors than was any preschool participation) and the total number of years of CPC participation. I report summary information

Table 31. Summary Statistics of Key Intervening Variables

Intervening measure	Hypothesis	Raw mean score		r with yrs. of preschool	r with yrs. of CPC
		CPC preschool group	Comparison group		
Cognitive readiness at age 5	CA	49.0	44.2	.28	.26
Reading achiev. at age 9	CA	98.6	93.7	.14	.25
Math achiev. at age 9	CA	102.1	97.9	.15	.25
Parent participa. in school	FS	1.9	1.5	.18	.21
% with 1 or more		82.3	75.3	—	—
% with 3 or more		30.9	21.0	—	—
Perceived competence	MA	23.8	23.2	.09	.12
Classroom adjustment at age 9	SA	19.2	18.5	.06	.14
No. of years in relatively "good" schools	SS	0.92	0.65	.15	.23
% with 1 or more		28.9	25.0	—	—
% with 3 or 4		20.8	13.2	—	—
No. of school changes	SS	0.9	1.2	-.18	-.24
% with no moves		47.2	31.1	—	—
% 2 or more moves		23.6	32.3	—	—

Note: Correlations are polychoric correlations estimated in the LISREL preprocessing program. Sample size = 1,164 with the following exceptions: cognitive readiness (n = 840), perceived competence (n = 914), classroom adjustment (n = 981), and reading and math achievement (ns = 1,081, 1,082). Except for classroom adjustment and years of preschool, all correlations were significant at the .05 level.

CA = cognitive advantage, FS = family support, MA = motivational advantage, SA = social adjustment, SS = school support.

for preschool groups rather than for any program participation because the findings in Chapter 4 indicated that preschool participation was more consistently associated with program outcomes than any participation. As hypothesized, preschool participants had significantly higher mean scores than the comparison group on all indicators of five hypotheses of intervention effects. Moreover, these indicators were significantly associated with both years of preschool participation and years of total CPC participation. Only the correlation between years of preschool and classroom adjustment was insignificant.

Preschool participants scored, on average, 5 standard-score points higher on the ITBS cognitive readiness battery at kindergarten entry and on ITBS reading and math total subtests at age 9. These are sizable differences. Notably, the average score of the program group was near the national average of 51; the average score of the program group at age 9 was somewhat lower than the national average of 108 for third graders in reading and math.

Parent participation in school also was more extensive for the preschool group, as 31% of CPC preschoolers had parents who participated in school frequently (three positive ratings or more) after the end of the program, compared to 21% for the comparison group. The advantage of preschool participation was lower for children's perceived school competence and teacher ratings of classroom adjustment but continued to favor the program group.

The final two mediators of CPC participation were postprogram school quality and school mobility. The CPC preschool group spent, on average, about one year ($m = 0.9$) in schools of relatively "good" quality from ages 9 to 13 compared to 0.65 years for the comparison group. Quality was defined as attendance in schools in which 25% or more of the student body were at national norms in reading and math achievement. Translated to percentages, less than 33% of CPC and comparison-group participants attended schools with such levels of student achievement. Twenty-one percent of the program group consistently attended schools judged "good" in quality, compared to only 13% of the comparison group.

Regarding school mobility, the CPC preschool group was significantly less likely than the comparison group to change schools after the end of the primary-grade program. This is consistent with prior studies in the Chicago Longitudinal Study (Reynolds, 1994; Reynolds & Bezruczko, 1993). For example, 47% of the program group were stable in the school they attended between ages 9 through 13, compared to only 31% for the comparison group. In addition, the program group was less likely than the comparison group to change schools two or more times after completion of the program (24% versus 32%).

These findings are summarized in Figure 18. They indicate that although program participants had higher rates of parental involvement in school, higher attendance in high-achieving schools, and lower rates of school mobility than did nonparticipants, the overall pattern revealed that relatively few youth had persistently positive school experiences after the end of intervention. This may explain the lower achievement patterns of program participants relative to national norms (see Table 18 and Figures 16.A–16.C).

STRUCTURAL MODELS OF PATHWAYS OF PROGRAM EFFECTS

I used structural equation modeling (SEM) to investigate the pathways of

Fig. 18. Postprogram Experiences by Preschool Participation

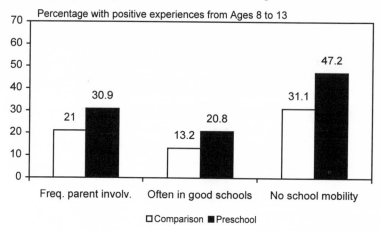

program effectiveness for youth outcomes. SEM is a broad identifier for a variety of techniques (e.g., path analysis) for testing models with intervening variables. Structural modeling is particularly appropriate for theory-driven tests of hypotheses of causal mediation such as those in Figure 1. Among its advantages over traditional path analyses are the following, all of which were utilized in the analyses reported in the chapter: (a) more accurate estimation of correlations of variables measured on an ordinal scale, (b) incorporation of multiple indicators of latent variables, (c) adjustments of model estimates for measurement error in observed variables, (d) simultaneous estimation of regression equations with fit statistics of overall model fit, and (e) estimation of indirect effects of model variables (here program participation). Thus, coefficients provide more accurate estimates of the relations between variables because they are corrected for measurement error and restriction of range.[1] See Appendix E for the correlation matrices of the models.

The pathway models for explaining the effects of program participation were estimated through LISREL (Joreskog & Sorbom, 1993a) as a system of hierarchical regression equations with one equation for each intervening and outcome variable. To be a pathway of program effectiveness, a variable has to be significantly associated with both (a) program participation and (b) the respective program outcome above and beyond the influence of other model variables. The magnitude of the effect of the mediating variable is calculated as the product of the standardized coefficients along the paths of influence. This product term is called an *indirect* (mediated) effect. An indirect effect indexes the extent to which the influence of an explanatory variable is transmitted through (or mediated by) other model variables. For example, if the estimated effect of preschool participation on parent participation is .10 and the estimated effect of parent participation on school achievement is .10 (controlling for preschool participation and other model variables), then the indirect effect of preschool participation on school achievement is .01 (.10 X .10). This means that the effect of preschool participation on school achievement is explained, in part, by parent participation. Note that parent participation would not be a mediator or pathway of preschool participation if either coefficient was insignificant.

Findings of the model are reported below by outcome domain. Figures 19 through 23 display the coefficients of the pathways through which program participation affects social competence outcomes at age 14.[2] Major indirect effects are reported in Tables 32 and 33. Given their consistent effects as reported in Chapter 4, I emphasized three program measures: (a) preschool participation (measured in years), (b) duration of program participation (measured in years), and (c) extended program participation for 4 to 6 years. The mediated effects of preschool participation take into account participation in follow-on participation, though the pathways of effects of the latter variable also are reported. The coefficients associated with each path are standardized regression coefficients. Standardized coefficients are comparable across different measures so that the magnitude of indirect effects (mediators) can be ordered. The models were estimated by maximum likelihood, and only coefficients of program and intervening variables significant at the .01 level are reported.[3] For clarity, the predictors and intervening pathways of grade retention and special education placement are shown in separate figures.[4]

Pathways of School Achievement

For parsimony and because program effects were similar for reading and math achievement, these subtests were combined to form a latent variable of school achievement at age 14.[5]

PRESCHOOL PARTICIPATION

As displayed in Figure 19.A and summarized in Table 32, the cognitive advantage hypothesis provided the best single explanation for the significant

Fig. 19.A. Primary Pathways from Preschool Participation to Adolescent School Achievement

(Values are standardized coefficients significant at the .01 level)

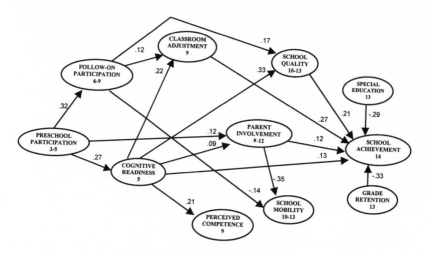

relation between preschool participation and adolescent school achievement. Preschool participants started kindergarten more cognitively ready to learn than no-preschool participants ($b = .27$), and this advantage directly carried over to later school achievement ($b = .13$), above and beyond the effects of other intervening variables. Apparently, this cognitive advantage diffuses throughout the schooling process by also promoting positive classroom adjustment and by preventing school mobility, grade retention, and special education placement (paths for the latter two variables are provided in Figures 22 and 23).

Several other pathways also contributed to the explanation of preschool effects, but their magnitudes were substantially lower than that of cognitive readiness at kindergarten entry. The dual mechanism of cognitive readiness and school quality ($b = .019$, or $.27 \times .33 \times .21$) had the second largest indirect effect on school achievement. This means that the effect of preschool participation on school achievement also occurred because the cognitive advantage at school entry led children to enroll in schools of relatively high quality (as defined by the proportion of the student body at or above national norms). Thus, this pathway supports a cognitive advantage–school support explanation of preschool effects.

Parent participation in school also was a pathway through which pre-

Table 32. Major Intervening Pathways (Mediators) of Effects of Preschool Participation (Standardized Indirect Effects)

	Program outcome					
	School achiev.	Consumer skills	Delinq. infract.	Grade retain	Special educa.	Hypothesis supported
1. Cognitive readiness at age 5	.035 (1)	.038 (1)	—	-.035 (1)	-.041 (1)	Cognitive advantage
2. Cognitive readiness & school quality	.019 (2)	.013 (4)	.009 (2)	—	.009 (2)	Cognitive advantage & school support
3. Cognitive readiness & social adjustment	.016 (3)	.015 (2)	-.007 (3)	.009 (3)	.007 (3)	Cognitive advantage & social adjustment
4. Parent involvement	.014 (4)	.014 (3)	-.017 (1)	-.020 (2)	—	Family support
5. Cognitive readiness & parent involvement	.003	.003	.003	-.004 (4)	—	Cognifive advantage & family support
6. Parent involvement & school mobility	—	—	-.007 (3)	—	—	Family support & school support
Indirect-effect magnitude (standardized)	.17	.13	-.07	-.11	-.05	

Note: Values in parentheses are rank order.

school participation affected school achievement. This provides support to the family support hypothesis. Controlling for other model variables, preschool participants were more likely to have parents who participated in school activities after the end of the program ($b = .12$), and this participation independently contributed to school achievement in adolescence ($b = .12$). As reported in Table 32, two other pathways involved the dual mechanisms of cognitive readiness and classroom adjustment as rated by teachers ($b = .014$) and cognitive readiness and parent involvement ($b = .003$). The latter pathway was relatively weak in magnitude, however.

Although included largely as a control variable, participation in CPC follow-on intervention (measured in years and controlling for preschool participation) affected school achievement through classroom adjustment ($b = .12 \times .27$ and school quality ($b = .17 \times .21$)). This supports both the social adjustment and school support hypotheses of program effectiveness.

Fig. 19.B. Primary Pathways from Years of Total Program Participation to Adolescent School Achievement

(Values are standardized coefficients significant at the .01 level)

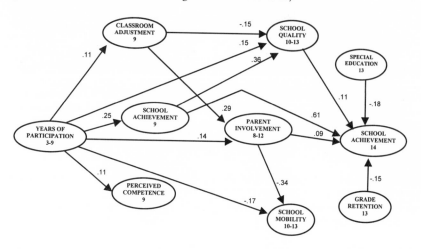

YEARS OF PARTICIPATION

The dominant pathway through which the years of program participation affected school achievement at age 14 was end-of-program school achievement at age 9. As shown in Figure 19.B and reported in Table 33, program participation led to greater school achievement in adolescence through the early cognitive advantage engendered by program enrollment. The indirect effect of .15 derived from the corresponding pathways linking years of participation to early school achievement at age 9 ($b = .25$) and early school achievement to adolescent achievement ($b = .61$). Thus, the cognitive advantage hypothesis provided the best single explanation for the relation between program participation and later school achievement.

Several other pathways also contributed to the explanation of effects of years of CPC intervention, but they were each smaller than the cognitive explanation by a factor of nine or more (see Table 33). Two involved the single mechanisms of school quality ($b = .017$) and parent involvement in school ($b = .013$) such that long-term program effects were more likely to be observed if children attended higher quality schools or if parents were more frequently involved in school. Complex pathways involving cognitive readiness and school quality, classroom adjustment and parent involvement, and classroom adjustment and school quality also helped explain the dosage-response effect of duration of participation and school achievement. Notably, classroom ad-

Table 33. Major Intervening Pathways (Mediators) of Effects of Duration of Program Participation (Standardized Indirect Effects)

	School achiev.	Consumer skills	Delinq. infract.	Grade retain	Special educa.	Hypothesis supported
			Program outcome			
1. Early school achiev. at age 9	.153 (1)	.170 (1)	—	-.135 (1)	-.110 (1)	Cognitive advantage
2. Parent involv.	.013 (3)	.013 (2)	-.017 (3)	-.017 (2)	—	Family support
3. School achiev. & school quality	.010 (4)	— —	.011 (4)	.009 (4)	.015 (3)	Cognitive advantage / School support
4. School mobility	—	—	-.029 (1)	—	—	School support
5. Classroom adjust. & parent involv.	.003	.003 (3)	-.004	—	—	Social adjustment / Family support
6. Classroom adjust. & school quality	.002	—	-.002	-.002	.003 (4)	Social adjustment / School support
7. School quality	.017 (2)	— —	.018 (2)	.015 (3)	.026 (2)	School support
Indirect-effect magnitude (standardized)	.26	.19	-.05	-.14	-.07	

Note: Values in parentheses are rank order.

justment, perceived school competence, and school mobility did not mediate the effects of years of participation.

Pathways of Consumer Skills

PRESCHOOL PARTICIPATION

The pathways through which preschool participation affected consumer skills at ages 14 and 15 largely mirrored those for school achievement. Indeed, only the ordering of pathways changed (see Figure 20.A). Cognitive readiness continued to be the greatest mediator of program effects ($b = .038$). The dual mechanism involving cognitive readiness and school quality was less important relative to school achievement, since the path from school quality to consumer life skills was smaller ($b = .15$). Parent partici-

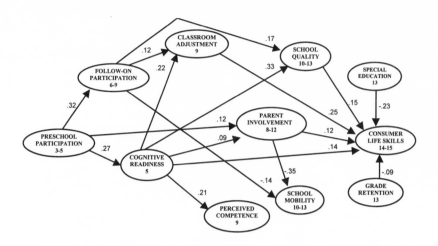

pation in school and the dual pathway of cognitive readiness and classroom adjustment also significantly contributed to the long-term effects of program participation. The pathways of the effects of follow-on participation remained as classroom adjustment and school quality but not school mobility.

Unlike school achievement, however, grade retention was associated with higher scores on consumer skills. Perhaps life skills are more affected by maturation than traditional school achievement.

YEARS OF PARTICIPATION

Although the pathways leading to higher scores in consumer skills overlapped those of school achievement, there were fewer of them. School achievement at the end of the follow-on program contributed the most, by far, to the mediation of program effects (see Figure 20.B). In fact, the respective coefficients along the paths of influence were moderate to large in size (bs = .25 and .68). Parent involvement in school was the next largest mediator of effects, as more extensive postprogram school participation helped to explain the effect of program participation above and beyond cognitive advantage and other factors. The third and final mechanism was the dual pathway involving classroom adjustment and parent participation in school, though the magnitude of its indirect effect was quite small (b = .003). These

Fig. 20.B. Primary Pathways from Years of Total Program Participation to Consumer Skills

(Values are standardized coefficients significant at the .01 level)

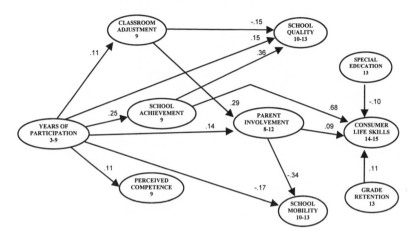

findings support the cognitive advantage hypothesis, the family support hypothesis, and, to a lesser extent, the social adjustment hypothesis.

Pathways of School-Reported Delinquency

Pathways leading to delinquency infractions as measured at ages 13 and 14 differed somewhat from the other outcomes. They are described below and are displayed in Figures 21.A and 21.B.

PRESCHOOL PARTICIPATION

Parent involvement in school was the primary source of the indirect effect from preschool participation to delinquency, as program participation was associated with more frequent parent involvement ($b = .12$), which led to a lower rate of delinquency infractions ($b = -.14$). Although cognitive readiness did not predict delinquency directly, it impacted delinquency indirectly through school quality, classroom adjustment, and parent involvement (see Figure 21.A). That school quality was positively associated with delinquency infractions should be interpreted with caution and may reflect that youth are monitored more closely in schools with higher achieving students and thus would be more likely to have infractions.

Note that because preschool participation was unrelated to delinquency

Fig. 21.A. Primary Pathways from Preschool Participation to Delinquency Infractions

(Values are standardized coefficients significant at the .01 level)

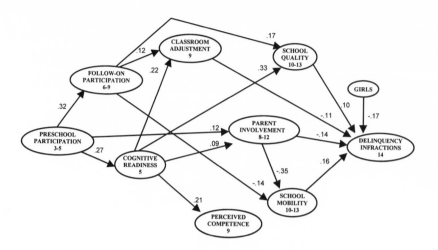

infractions (see Table 23 and Figure 8), pathways from preschool participation are not interpretable as mediators. Rather, these pathways identify intervention points for special consideration. For example, perhaps parent involvement was not sufficiently impacted by the program to result in a direct relationship between preschool and delinquency infractions. Unlike the CPCs, programs that have been associated with reduced delinquency (e.g., Perry Preschool, Yale Child Welfare) provided substantial home visitation (Reynolds et al., 1998; Yoshikawa, 1994).

The pathways from follow-on participation to delinquency are of greater interest since they are interpretable as pathways of effectiveness. As shown in Figure 21.A, participation in follow-on intervention was associated with a lower rate of delinquency by reducing frequent school mobility during elementary school (bs = -.14 and .16) and by promoting classroom adjustment at the end of the program (bs = .12 and -.11). Both of these pathways are consistent with the theory of extended early childhood intervention. Participants in CPC follow-on intervention after preschool also were significantly more likely to attend higher quality schools (b = .17), but attendance in such schools was associated with higher, rather than lower, rates of delinquency infractions. Again, this is most likely the result of more intensive monitoring of problem behavior in higher achieving schools.

Fig. 21.B. Primary Pathways from Years of Total Program Participation to Delinquency Infractions
(Values are standardized coefficients significant at the .01 level)

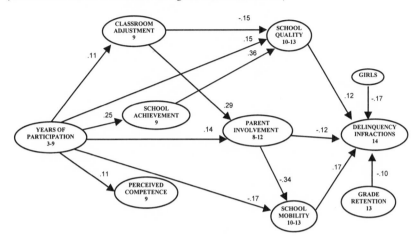

The primary mediators of the effects of years of CPC participation on delinquency infractions were school mobility and parent involvement (see Figure 21.B). More extensive program participation prevented delinquency because it reduced the likelihood of school mobility (b = -.17) as well as promoting postprogram parent involvement (b = .14). Both of these intervening factors predicted delinquency. These findings reinforce the school support and family support hypotheses of intervention effects. Classroom adjustment also mediated the effect of years of participation but only through its relation with parent involvement.

Also shown in Figure 21.B is that girls had a lower rate of delinquency than boys, as did youth who did not repeat a grade. Surprisingly, neither school achievement at age 9 nor perceived school competence was associated with delinquency infractions. School achievement was a significant predictor of school quality, however (b = .36). The pathways involving school quality alone and in conjunction with early school achievement should be interpreted with caution, given the positive sign of the school quality coefficient. Again, this could be because of greater monitoring or higher school standards.

Fig. 22.A. Primary Pathways from Preschool Participation to Cumulative Grade Retention

(Values are standardized coefficients significant at the .01 level)

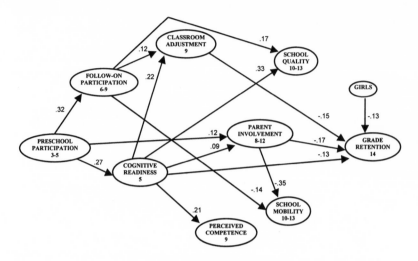

Fig. 22.B. Primary Pathways from Years of Total Program Participation to Cumulative Grade Retention

(Values are standardized coefficients significant at the .01 level)

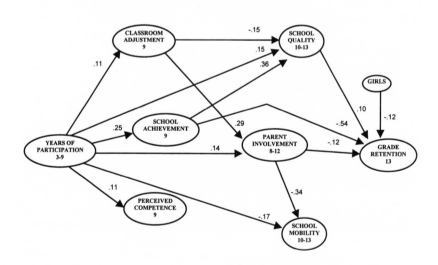

Fig. 23.A. Primary Pathways from Preschool Participation to Years in Special Education

(Values are standardized coefficients significant at the .01 level)

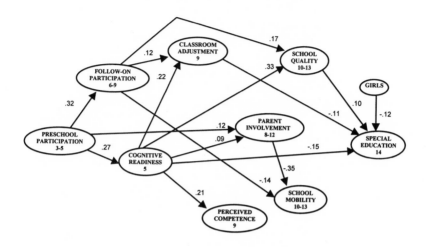

Mediators of Grade Retention and Special Education Placement

The mediators of the penultimate outcomes of grade retention and special education placement (in years) were investigated simultaneously with the primary outcomes. The pathways are reported separately in Figures 22.A, 22.B, 23.A, and 23.B.

GRADE RETENTION

As with school achievement and consumer skills, the cognitive advantage hypothesis best explained program-related reductions in grade retention. Figure 22.A shows that cognitive readiness at age 5 was the primary source of reductions in grade retention (b = -.035, or .27 ⋆ -.13). Figure 22.A also indicates that parent involvement in school also significantly contributed to the explanation of effects (b = -.20), as program participation led to greater parent involvement in school (b = .12) and then to a lower rate of grade retention (b = -.17).

Regarding the mediators of years of program participation, the cognitive advantage hypothesis was the dominant explanation, as early school achievement was the best predictor of grade retention (b = -.54). The family support hypothesis also helped explain the effects of years of program

Fig. 23.B. Primary Pathways from Years of Total Program Participation to Years in Special Education

(Values are standardized coefficients significant at the .01 level)

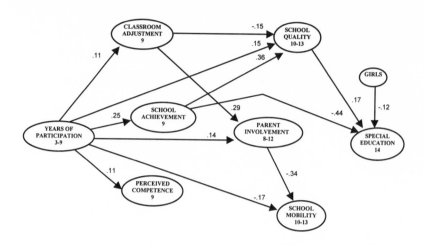

participation via the influence of parent involvement in school. Follow-on participation exerted its influence mainly through classroom adjustment.

YEARS IN SPECIAL EDUCATION

Like grade retention, the cognitive advantage hypothesis was the best explanation of the relation between preschool participation and years of special education during the elementary grades (b = -.041). As reported in Figure 23.A, cognitive readiness at age 5 was a substantial predictor of special education placement (b = -.15). Classroom adjustment (b = -.11) and sex of child, in favor of girls (b = -.12), also predicted special education placement.

Figure 23.B indicates that the cognitive advantage hypothesis also was the best explanation of the relation between years of program participation and special education placement (b = -.110). This was largely due to the strong relation between school achievement at age 9 and special education placement by adolescence (b = -.44).

Notably, school quality was positively associated with special education placement, with children spending more years in special education if they attended higher achieving schools. Thus, the cognitive advantage of program participation increased the likelihood of special education placement if children enrolled in higher achieving schools. This may partly explain why the 6-year intervention group did not have significantly lower rates of special education placement (see Table 27 in Chapter 4). Finally, school quality was unrelated to grade retention. Program-related reductions in grade retention came about, in part, through greater parent involvement in school.

Support for Five Hypotheses of Program Effects

Tables 32 and 33 summarize the major pathways of CPC program effects by youth outcome. Standardized indirect effects (and their associated rankings) are presented for each significant pathway through which program participation promoted adolescent development. The aggregate standardized indirect effect is reported in the last row of each table. This represents the extent to which program participation was mediated by all intervening factors. All of these coefficients were significant at the .01 level, which would be expected if the hypotheses explained the direct effects between program participation and outcomes. Note that the coefficients associated with pathways involving special education and grade retention are not reported in the tables. In several cases, they also contributed to the explanation of effects (see Figures 22.A, 22.B, 23.A, and 23.B).

For the most part, the tables indicated that the cognitive advantage hypothesis contributed the most to the explanation of intervention effects for school achievement, consumer skills, grade retention, and years in special education. Cognitive readiness alone accounted for about 20% to 33% of the aggregate indirect effects of preschool participation for the outcomes of school achievement, consumer life skills, and grade retention as well as almost all of the aggregate indirect effect of special education placement. Cognitive advantage made an even stronger contribution to the explanation of the effects of years of CPC participation. Indeed, it accounted for the vast majority of the aggregate indirect effect for all outcomes except delinquency.

Although the magnitude of its contribution was generally smaller, the family support hypothesis (as measured by parent participation in school) was also a consistent mediator of effects for both preschool participation and years of participation (up to 10–15% of indirect effects). Moreover, the family support hypothesis was a primary explanation of the effects of years of participation on delinquency and also contributed to the explanation of preschool influences.

Table 34. Fit Statistics for the Structural Models of Pathways of Effects

Models	Chi-square	df	Change in chi-square	AGFI	RMSEA
Preschool/follow-on participation					
1a. Exogenous Influence Model: Only sex, risk status included; no mediation	1091.3	61	—	.79	.120
1b. Direct Influence Model: All factors included; no mediation	298.1	40	793.2	.90	.074
1c. Full Mediated Model: Full mediation by five hypotheses	47.8	20	250.3	.97	.035
Years of participation					
2a. Direct Influence Model: Only sex and risk status included; no mediation	700.3	71	—	.87	.087
2b. Direct Influence Model: All factors included; no mediation	377.9	50	322.4	.90	.075
2c. Full Mediated Model: Full mediation by five hypotheses	104.9	30	217.5	.95	.046

Note: Values of .90 or above are indicative of good fit for the adjusted goodness of fit index (AGFI) and of .05 or lower for root mean square error of approximation (RMSEA).

The school support hypothesis provided a less consistent explanation of the effects of program participation. It helped explain the effects of years of program participation and follow-on participation but not preschool participation. School quality mediated the effects of both years of participation and follow-on participation on school achievement, whereas school mobility helped explain the link between years of participation and delinquency infractions. Although school quality also contributed to the explanation of the effects of years of participation on delinquency, grade retention, and special education, its influence on these outcomes was in the opposite direction expected. This suggests that attendance in schools with greater proportions of high-achieving students leads to greater achieve-

Table 35. Percentage of Variance Explained in Program Outcomes
for Full Model Specification

Model with	School achiev.	Consumer life skills	Grade retain	Years special ed.	Delinq. infract.
1. Preschool/ follow-on particip.	62	36	19	9	14
2. Years of particip.	76	52	34	17	14

Note: Because grade retention and delinquency infractions are dichomotous, variance explanations should be interpreted cautiously.

ment, and it also increases the risk of grade retention, special education, and delinquency; the former probably because of higher expectations (and standards) in higher achieving schools; the latter probably because of increased monitoring.

Substantial support also occurred for several hypotheses in combination. For example, cognitive readiness and school quality as well as cognitive readiness and social adjustment partially explained the long-term effects of preschool participation on school achievement, consumer skills, grade retention, and special education placement. The social adjustment hypothesis contributed to the explanation of the relation between follow-on participation and all outcomes except grade retention.

Nevertheless, the social adjustment hypothesis alone did not explain any of the effects of preschool participation and years of program participation. Neither did perceived school competence at age 9. As the figures show, years of program participation were significantly associated with greater perceived competence, but perceived competence did not predict any outcome.

Overall Model Fit

Table 34 shows the fit statistics of the structural models in Figures 19 to 23 for preschool and follow-on participation (1a-1c) and for years of total participation (2a-2c). Model A included only the exogenous influences of sex of child and risk status (all other coefficients set to zero). Model B included the direct effects of both exogenous and intervening variables (all indirect paths set to zero). Model C included the five sets of hypotheses of program effects shown in Figure 1 (i.e., both direct and indirect pathways were estimated).

Table 36. Percentage of Variance Explained in Intervening Variables for Reduced Model Specification

Model with	Cog. ready	School ach-9	Parent partic.	Class adjust.	Perceived comp.	School qual.	School mobil.
1. Preschool/ follow-on particip.	11	—	22	14	9	20	20
2. Years of particip.	—	14	21	9	5	19	18

As shown by rows 1c and 2c, model fit improved substantially after pathways associated with the five hypotheses of program effects were estimated. This improvement in model fit supports the significant contribution of the intervening variables in explaining the effects of intervention. Indeed, both the adjusted goodness of fit index (AGFI) and the root mean square error of approximation (RMSEA) were well within their respective ranges of acceptability (.90 or higher; .05 or lower) for the final models. These models fit the data well and provided good overall explanations for the long-term effects of program participation in Chapter 4.

Variation Explained in Outcome and Intervening Variables

Tables 35 and 36 show the percent of variance explained for each of the intervening and outcome variables estimated in Figures 19 through 23. Two sets of models were estimated, one for preschool and follow-on participation and one for duration of CPC intervention. Although percentages of variance explained are not the primary indicators of model fit, they nonetheless are informative in understanding the predictive power of the explanatory variables.

PRIMARY OUTCOMES

As shown in Table 35, the full model explained a majority of the variance in school achievement (62% and 76%, respectively, for the two models). Variation in performance on the consumer skills test also was well explained by the explanatory model (36% and 52%, respectively). The variances explained were smallest for years of special education placement (9% to 17%) and delinquency infractions (14%). Being a dichotomous outcome, the R-squared for delinquency is only a rough estimate. As shown, the variances explained were somewhat larger for the model including years of CPC intervention because this specification included school

Fig. 24. Primary Pathways from Extended Program Participation to School Achievement

(Values are standardized coefficients significant at the .01 level)

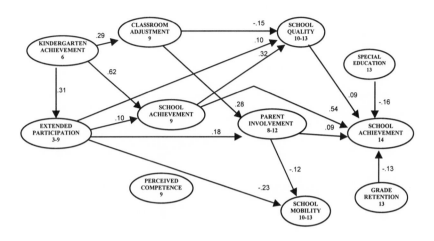

achievement at age 9 as a measure of cognitive advantage, instead of cognitive readiness at age 5.

INTERVENING OUTCOMES

As shown in Table 36, the explanatory power of the models in predicting the intervening variables was lower than for the primary outcomes. This is not surprising since the latter were the focus of the analysis. Proportions of variance explained ranged from 5% to 9% for perceived competence at age 9 to 21% to 22% for parent participation in school. Variances explained in cognitive readiness at age 5 (11%) and in school achievement at age 9 (14%) also were relatively low. These smaller values occurred because fewer predictors were specified. For example, only program participation, sex of child, and risk status were included as predictors of these cognitive variables. Indeed, the intervening variables were selected because of their hypothesized role as mediators of the effects of early intervention, not as ultimate outcomes.

Yet the relatively low variance explained in cognitive readiness at age 5 and reading and math achievement at age 9 raises the question of whether the strong support for the cognitive advantage hypothesis would be altered under a different model specification. Although the findings of both Reynolds (1995) and Reynolds and Temple (1995) suggest that the cognitive ef-

Fig. 25. Primary Pathways from Extended Program Participation to Delinquency Infractions

(Values are standardized coefficients significant at the .01 level)

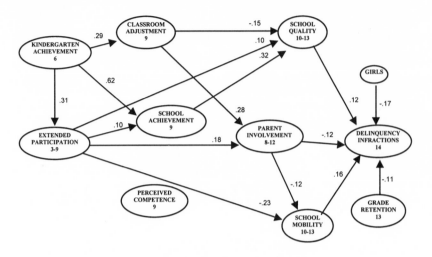

fects of program participation are the same under different model specifications, I probed this question further by including in the models indicators for the program and comparison sites in which children participated. These indicators index unmeasured factors associated with attending particular program sites (e.g., neighborhood characteristics). The pattern of findings remained the same.[6] These results further confirm the importance of the cognitive advantage hypothesis in explaining a substantial part of the relation between program participation and social competence outcomes.

Pathways of Extended Program Participation

As a final analysis of the pathways through which program participation affected youth social competence, I used extended program participation (1 = preschool plus follow-on for 4 to 6 years, 0 = otherwise) as the measure of CPC participation. The main advantage of including this indicator is that kindergarten achievement can be added as a pretest to follow-on intervention such that the identified mediators would be explanations of the effects of extended program participation relative to all other levels of intervention exposure. The significant pathways and associated coefficients for school achievement and delinquency infractions are displayed in Figures 24 and 25.[7]

The pathways leading to school achievement were largely similar to those reported above. That is, the cognitive advantage hypothesis accounted for the largest share of the indirect effect of extended participation. The path from extended program participation to school achievement at age 9 ($b = .10$) and the path from early school achievement at age 9 to school achievement at age 14 ($b = .54$) represented an indirect effect of .054. This is 45% of the aggregate indirect effect of extended participation. Parent participation in school ($bs = .18, .09$) and school quality ($bs = .10, .09$) also mediated the effects of extended program participation.

Although not displayed, pathways leading to consumer skills were very similar to those for achievement, as school achievement at age 9 was the primary mediator of the effect of extended program participation ($b = .58$ [school achievement to consumer skills]). Parent involvement in school, grade retention, and special education placement were secondary mediators. The major exception was that school quality did not mediate the effects of program participation ($bs = .10$ [program to school quality] and .01 [school quality to consumer skills]).

For delinquency infractions during ages 13 and 14, both family support shown by parent participation in school ($bs = .18, -.12$) and school support via school mobility ($bs = -.23, .16$) and via school quality ($bs = .10, .12$) mediated the effects of extended program participation. Like findings reported earlier in Chapter 5, school achievement at age 9 did not mediate the effect of extended program participation on delinquency ($b = -.07, t = 1.05$). Interestingly, grade retention was associated with a significantly lower rate of delinquency ($b = -.11$), and school quality was associated with a higher rate of delinquency ($b = .12$). While the former coefficient suggests that grade retention has positive benefits on social behavior, the latter should be interpreted with caution and may be an artifact of measurement.[8]

Although not shown, pathways leading to the penultimate outcomes of grade retention and special education were similar to those displayed for years of program participation. School achievement at age 9 ($bs = .10$ and $-.44$) and parent involvement in school ($bs = .18$ and $-.12$) were the primary mediators of grade retention; school achievement at age 9 ($bs = .10$ and $-.31$) and school quality ($bs = .10$ and $.18$) were the primary mediators of years in special education.[9]

SUMMARY

Path analyses of the five sets of mediators of program participation indi-

Fig. 26. Summary Pathways of Influence from Early Childhood Intervention
(The thicker the path, the more consistent the findings)

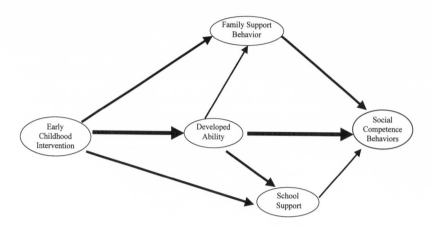

cated that long-term effects of the program occurred primarily because participation promoted early cognitive and scholastic advantages that culminated in better social competence in adolescence. Family support and school support hypotheses also confirmed the significant role of parent involvement and school quality as pathways of program effectiveness, but less strongly. In partial support of the social adjustment hypothesis, teacher ratings of classroom adjustment mediated independently only the effects of follow-on intervention. It helped explain the effects of preschool and years of participation only in combination with other hypotheses. The motivational advantage hypothesis (measured by perceived school competence) never explained the relation between program participation and adolescent competence. Only years of program participation were independently associated with perceived competence above and beyond other factors. These observed pathways are consistent with the program theory emphasizing school achievement and parent involvement and thereby strengthen the interpretation that the estimated effects in Chapter 4 represent real effects of CPC participation.

An overall summary of the major pathways of program effectiveness reported in this chapter is presented in Figure 26. For most outcomes and measures of early childhood intervention, developed ability, as measured by cognitive readiness or early school achievement, was the most consistent and strongest mediator of program effects. This is represented by the thick arrows from early childhood intervention to developed ability and from developed ability to social competence behaviors. Family support behavior was the next most consistent mediator of effects of intervention on social competence behaviors. This is reflected in the medium-thick paths connecting intervention, family support behavior, and social competence. The path from intervention to school support also was fairly consistent. As shown by the relatively thin path to social competence behavior, school support—measured by school quality and school mobility—was a less consistent mediator but nevertheless contributed to the transmission of program effects, especially for school achievement and consumer skills. As a secondary indicator of school support, school mobility mediated the effect of years of program participation on delinquency infractions in the expected direction.

6

Promoting Children's Success:
Lessons for the Future

I began this volume by noting that early intervention is based on the tenet that environmental conditions facing low-income families place children at risk for underachievement and school failure. With the advent of the War on Poverty in the middle 1960s, large-scale educational and social programs were developed with a major goal of preventing the development of problematic behaviors and promoting educational success beginning in preschool. Project Head Start and later programs also were based on the assumptions that the cognitive and social enrichment offered in early intervention can compensate for poverty-related risks, that long-term educational success will be more likely, and that interventions can be more effective if they focus on enhancing school transitions.

The 33-year-old Chicago Child-Parent Center Program was one of the earliest innovations under the 1965 Title I Act to promote children's success by providing comprehensive and extended educational and family support services spanning two sensitive periods of development—the preschool years and the transition to formal schooling. It is conceptually similar to Head Start plus Project Follow Through, which was designed to help continue the benefits of earlier intervention. Due to continual underfunding and changes in objectives, however, Follow Through never lived up to its promise as an extended intervention (Doernberger & Zigler, 1993).[1] Unlike most other programs subjected to extensive longitudinal analysis, the CPC program is federally funded and relatively large in scale, is administered through public schools, and serves children in the poorest Chicago neighborhoods. Thus, findings provide rare evidence about the efficacy of state and federally funded programs for children and families. This evidence is valuable to educators, parents, and policymakers since all have high expectations for such programs, and their effectiveness is a foundation upon which other programs and policies are made.

The purpose of this monograph is to investigate the comprehensive effects on youth and family development of participation in the CPC program implemented during 1983 to 1989. In this study 889 children (almost all African American) participated in the program for different lengths of time from ages 3 to 9. An additional 275 comparison-group children participated in an alternative early childhood intervention in kindergarten. In Chapter 1, I review the state of knowledge about early childhood intervention and the need for more comprehensive investigations of large-scale programs. The history and content of the CPC program is detailed in Chapter 2, and studies prior to and including the Chicago Longitudinal Study are reviewed. In Chapter 3, I describe the research design and measures with special attention to the comparability of groups and analytic methods. In Chapter 4, I report the relations between measures of program participation and social competence up to age 15 and the extent to which effects varied by subgroup attributes. The pathways through which program participation led to more positive youth outcomes, presented in Chapter 5, are based on five hypotheses derived from the program theory.

In this chapter, I summarize the overall study findings and discuss their significance for child development and education. The focus is on the unique contributions of the findings to the field of early intervention, for promoting youth and family development, and in explaining why the effects of the CPC program persist into adolescence. Finally, several policy implications of the findings are discussed in the context of changing social and economic conditions facing children and families.

Summary of Findings

The major findings of this study are summarized as follows.

1. All measures of program participation were significantly associated with at least one youth outcome at ages 14 or 15 above and beyond children's risk status and sex. Years of program participation, extended program participation, and preschool participation were most consistently associated with social competence outcomes, especially reading and math achievement scores, consumer skills,

and cumulative grade retention and special education placement. These relations did not vary by model specification. Only follow-on participation and extended intervention were consistently associated with delinquency infractions.

2. Any participation, years of participation, and preschool participation were consistently associated with the family socialization outcomes of expectations for children's educational attainment, satisfaction with school, and parent involvement in school. All program measures were significantly associated with parents' postprogram involvement in school, above and beyond the influence of the covariates (and alternative specifications).

3. Relative to children whose participation was limited to preschool and kindergarten, children who participated in extended intervention from preschool to second or third grade had significantly higher reading achievement at age 14, had significantly greater consumer skills, and were less likely to be retained in grade, to spend time in special education through age 15, and to have delinquency infractions. Extended participation for 3 years was significantly associated with all outcomes by age 15. These results took into account school achievement prior to participation in extended intervention.

4. The family effects of extended program participation were specific to parent involvement in school, as youth participating in extended intervention had more involved parents than youth with less extensive program participation. These family effects were largest for children having 6 years of CPC participation.

5. Both the timing and duration of program participation significantly contributed to long-term effects. Of children whose length of intervention was the same, those who began earlier tended to do better over time, especially in reading achievement, and they had a lower rate of delinquency infractions. Similar to result 2, of children who entered the CPC program in preschool, those with a longer length of intervention had consistently better outcomes in adolescence. Relative to 2 years of follow-on intervention, however, 3 years of intervention after preschool and kindergarten were associated with only a significantly lower rate of grade retention.

6. For the most part, the estimated effects of different measures of program participation did not vary by sex of child, parent education, risk status, and parent participation in school. The strongest evidence for differential effects was that children who attended programs in relatively high-poverty neighborhoods (more than 60% low income) benefited more than children who attended programs in neighborhoods with lower rates of poverty.

7. Children attending centers with a relatively teacher-oriented, academic emphasis had significantly higher reading and math achievement at age 14 than children attending centers with a more developmentally oriented focus. These children also were less likely to be retained in grade or to receive special education services. These findings, however, were not robust—they did not appear at age 15. Children experiencing either a teacher-oriented or developmental instructional program generally had better adjustment than those who experienced an undifferentiated preschool program.

8. With the exception of delinquency infractions, the cognitive advantage hypothesis provided the best explanation for the long-term effects of several measures of program participation. The family support hypothesis (via parent participation in school) and school support hypotheses (via school quality or youth school mobility) also contributed to the long-term effects of exposure. The family support hypothesis was the most consistent explanation for the effects of years of participation on delinquency. The social adjustment hypothesis contributed somewhat less to the explanation of effects but did help explain the relationship between follow-on participation and social competence outcomes. The motivational advantage did not mediate the effects of any measure of program participation. In magnitude and consistency, the hypotheses generally followed this order: cognitive advantage, family support, school support, social adjustment, and motivational advantage.

Unique Contributions

Overall, the findings of the Chicago Longitudinal Study presented in this book demonstrate that established large-scale early childhood programs can be successful for economically disadvantaged children. They can promote positive school adjustment and social behavior well into adolescence, as has been shown for model demonstration programs (Barnett, 1995; Schweinhart et al., 1993; Campbell & Ramey, 1995; Consortium for Longitudinal Studies, 1983; Lazar et al., 1982). These findings mollify the growing pessimism about the demonstrated long-term effects of early intervention as reported by publications as diverse as Herrnstein and Murray (1994) and the U.S. General Accounting Office (1997). Indeed, the consistency and breadth of findings presented in Chapter 4 would be highly unusual in absence of program effects (see Table 30). The estimated program effects on delinquency infractions and consumer skills are demonstrative of this breadth, and they have not been reported for federally funded, established programs. As with programs implemented in the 1960s and 1970s, including those of earlier CPC cohorts, this book shows that contemporary early childhood programs in the mid- to late 1980s can be just as effective as in earlier decades.

Consequently, the present study provides among the best evidence that large-scale early and extensive early childhood programs can promote positive outcomes for both children and families several years after program participation. The Child-Parent Center Program is unique in its integration of preschool, kindergarten, and primary-grade services within a single administrative system. This integration may be partly responsible for the consistent and robust effects. As shown in the pathway models of Figures 19 to 25, program participation provides a foundation for scholastic development that leads to better social competence in adolescence.

A second major contribution of the findings is that duration of exposure was significantly associated with all indicators of social competence regardless of model specification. Indeed, this dosage-response relationship was the most robust finding of the study. Given the 6- to 8-year time interval between program participation and the measurement of the outcomes, this relation was unlikely to have resulted from a recency effect of extended intervention. The interpretation of this monotonic relationship between intervention length and adolescent outcomes as a program effect was further strengthened by the findings reported in Chapter 5 that the pathways explaining this estimated effect were consistent with the CPC program theory. Indeed, no other study of the effects of early intervention has investigated such an array of pathways of program effects. I discuss this later in the chapter. Thus, as suggested in Reynolds (1994), duration of intervention may be just as important as timing of participation. The finding that follow-on only intervention was associated with some program outcomes suggests that interventions do not have to occur only in preschool for children to benefit from them.

Notably, participation in the follow-on intervention after preschool and kindergarten positively influenced performance above and beyond earlier intervention even after taking into account kindergarten achievement. The magnitude of effects of extended participation reported in this book were generally smaller than those at the 2- and 4-year follow-up, however, especially for school achievement (Reynolds, 1994; Reynolds & Temple, 1998). Nevertheless, they continued to favor CPC graduates. Empirical support is growing (Alexander & Entwisle, 1988; Reynolds, 1989, 1991) for the importance of intervening school-based and family support experiences in promoting successful adjustment. As reported in Chapter 4, at least 2 years of intervention beyond kindergarten was necessary to promote more lasting effects. I further discuss the importance of extended intervention later in the chapter.

Although duration of intervention exposure was an important element of later success, early entry into the program was crucial for long-term effects to occur. In fact, extensive participation in the CPC program is not possible without participation beginning in preschool. Indeed, children who participated in follow-on intervention without preschool performed better than the non-CPC comparison group only on grade retention. Preschool participation was more consistently associated with youth and family outcomes than follow-on intervention, and when the differential effects of early versus later participation were compared, the outcomes favored the early entry group (see Table 27).

Impacting Youth Social Competence

The most consistent long-term effects of the Child-Parent Center Program were to prevent grade retention and placement in special education and to promote school achievement and consumer skills. Although both preschool and follow-on intervention were associated with indicators of social competence, children who participated in extended intervention from preschool to second or third grade had the best adjustment. Overall, these findings are largely consistent with those of previous studies in the Chicago Longitudinal Study (Reynolds, 1994, 1995; Reynolds & Temple,

1998; Reynolds et al., 1995) and those of earlier CPC cohorts (Conrad & Eash, 1983; Fuerst & Fuerst, 1993; IDEA, 1973, 1974), though the later studies investigated only the effects of extended participation for subsamples of CPC graduates. The longitudinal effects of preschool participation reported here also are consistent with those of several model demonstration programs, including the Consortium for Longitudinal Studies (1983), the High/Scope Perry Preschool Project (Schweinhart & Weikart, 1980), and the Carolina Abecedarian Project (Campbell & Ramey, 1994, 1995), and are even stronger than many small- and large-scale programs (Barnett, 1995; Karoly et al., 1998; Reynolds et al., 1997).

The present study is the first to investigate the effects of a large-scale early intervention program on consumer skills and delinquency. The estimated effects of program participation (i.e., preschool and extended) on consumer skills yielded effect sizes that usually exceeded those for reading and math achievement. As reported in Table 19, for example, any participation in the follow-on program was unrelated to reading achievement but was significantly associated with better performance in consumer skills. These findings indicate that program effects (e.g., preschool, duration, extended) on school-content achievement generalize to important life skills beyond school, such as filling out job applications, identifying important community resources, reading maps and warning labels, and identifying government functions and services. These are practical skills, and many of these are prerequisite to good citizenship. Given the content of this instrument, consumer skills may be a truer measure of social competence than is school achievement. Moreover, the paths that led to long-term effects on consumer skills were consistent with school achievement.

The findings that duration of participation, follow-on participation, and extended program participation were associated with reductions in delinquency infractions of up to 51% are new and of major significance. Previous studies reporting reduced delinquency from participation in early intervention examined model programs in infancy or preschool, including the Perry Preschool, Yale Child Welfare Project, the Syracuse Family Development Research Program, and the Houston Parent-Child Development Center (cf. Reynolds et al., 1998; Yoshikawa, 1995; Zigler et al., 1992). In this study, most of the observed effects on delinquency appeared to derive from the follow-on program, even after adjusting for the effects of preschool participation, sex of child, risk status, and kindergarten

Table 37. Selected Effect Sizes for Four Early Childhood Interventions

Program	Program Type (sample N)	Estimated effects			
		Cognitive develop. (age 5)	Reading achiev. (age 15)	% reduct. retain	% reduct. spec. ed.
High/Scope Perry Preschool	Model (123)	.72	.48	ns	51
Carolina Abecedarian	Model (121)	.75	.43	44	48
Chicago Child- Parent Centers	Large scale (1,539)				
Preschool	—	.61	.17	22	25
Extended	—	—	.33	68	48
Consortium for Longitu. Studies	Model (3,656)	.50	n/a	18	29

Note: All values are statistically significant. Consortium N is based on 11 programs. Program group N is sample size at the beginning of the study. Percentage reductions are based on regression adjustments.

Ns = not statistically significant; n/a = not available but effects on math were detected until 5th grade and reading until 3rd grade (Lazar et al., 1982).

achievement. This is understandable because follow-on participation was significantly associated with increased parent involvement and reduced school mobility, both of which predicted delinquency. These two intervening factors are key ingredients of the CPC program theory. Not only do the CPCs provide a multitude of ways for families to get involved, but the length of the program is designed to foster stability of schooling experiences and thus lead to less mobility. Indeed, the CPC program shares with the above model programs an emphasis on parent involvement, but participation in school activities (e.g., parent room activities, classroom volunteering) rather than home visiting was the primary focus.

These findings indicate that large-scale programs can promote social behavior and consumer skills independent of classroom-based achievement tests. Continued investigation of these relations in late adolescence will reveal the stability of these effects and the extent to which other measures of delinquency lead to similar results. The measure of delinquency, for example, was based on school reports of infractions in a low to moderate range of severity (e.g., truancy, fighting, assault, carrying weapons). A recent study by Reynolds et al. (1998), for example, found that self-reports of delinquency and of arrest did not lead to a consistent pattern of program effects. The link to more serious criminal activity is uncertain, though criminal delinquency often follows from earlier problem behavior (Loeber & Stouthamer-Loeber, 1998; Sampson & Laub, 1993).

To gain some perspective on the magnitude and consistency of effects reported in this study and the extent to which they approximate findings from the early intervention literature, I compared the effect sizes of the CPC program with those from three well-known model programs: the High/Scope Perry Preschool Program (Schweinhart & Weikart, 1980), the Carolina Abecedarian Project (Campbell & Ramey, 1994, 1995), and the Consortium for Longitudinal Studies (1983). The effects of these model demonstration programs have been reported through at least age 15. Effect sizes in standard deviations are reported in Table 37 for cognitive development at age 5 (beginning of kindergarten) and for school achievement and school competence through age 15.

At school entry, the CPC preschool program had effect sizes on cognitive development within the range of these well-known model programs (.60 to .70 standard deviations).[2] By age 15, the effect sizes for the CPC preschool program were considerably smaller than those of the Perry and Abecedarian programs but slightly higher than the median effect sizes across the 11 Consortium projects. In both the Perry and Abecedarian programs, preschool participants showed greater reductions in special education placements than in the CPCs. Relative to their comparison group, the CPC preschool group's rate of reduction in grade retention was between that of the Perry Preschool and Abecedarian programs.

As indicated in the information provided in Table 37, long-term effects of extended program participation in the CPCs (versus none) were much closer to findings of the model programs for school achievement and special education placement. Given the different time periods and differences in school policies, the comparisons of grade retention and special education should be interpreted cautiously. In the latter case, placements depend, in part, on the availability of funds, and passage of the Education for All Handicapped Children Act in 1975 led to mainstreaming of students in special education.

There are two explanations for the generally smaller long-term effects of the CPC program. Being model programs implemented in single sites, the Perry and Abecedarian programs provided more intensive services;

their adult-to-child ratio did not exceed 1 to 6, compared to 1 to 8 for the CPC preschool program. Their yearly costs per pupil were also higher—$7,252 and $11,000, respectively, compared to $4,350.[3] Second, the CPC program was implemented in more economically disadvantaged contexts—central-city Chicago—than the other programs. Neither model program was located in the central city, whereas the CPC program was implemented in the poorest Chicago neighborhoods, in which over 40% of the residents were below the poverty line and almost all children were eligible for free lunches. Certainly, this economic context could have reduced the magnitude of effects over time, especially as related to school quality and family economic hardship. Nevertheless, the CPC program as implemented from 1983 to 1989 showed persistent effects on several measures of social competence into adolescence that were more positive, on average, than those of the Consortium for Longitudinal Studies (1983) and followed a similar pattern as the Perry Preschool and Abecedarian programs. CPC program effects on consumer skills and parent participation in school were even larger than those reported in Table 37.

Impacting Family Socialization

Although relatively modest and less consistent than for youth outcomes, the positive effects of the CPC program on parent expectations for children's educational attainment, parent satisfaction with school, and parent involvement in school were generally consistent with the theory behind the Child-Parent Center Program. Relatively few previous studies of large-scale programs have investigated family outcomes, and no prior studies of the Chicago Longitudinal Study have investigated family effects beyond parent participation in school. That preschool participation was significantly associated with greater parent satisfaction with children's education dovetails with the finding by Lazar et al. (1982) that parents of program participants in the Consortium for Longitudinal Studies were more satisfied with their children's school success than were the parents of the comparison group. Several other studies have reported a positive relationship between participation in early childhood intervention and family outcomes (Karoly et al., 1998; Lally, Mangione, Honig, & Wittner, 1988; Schweinhart et al., 1993; Seitz, Rosenbaum, & Apfel, 1985). In this volume, preschool participation also was associated with significantly higher parent expectations for children's educational attainment.

More than most other early childhood interventions, CPC staff provide a diversity of educational activities for parents in the centers. The separately staffed parent-resource room in each center is designed to provide more intensive family support activities including workshops on parenting and home economics, cooperative activities such as craft projects, and personal and social support. Parents also volunteer in the classrooms and assist on field trips. This extensive set of activities may explain why all measures of program participation were significantly associated with more frequent parent involvement in school, even after earlier parent involvement was taken into account (see Appendix D).

Not surprisingly, participation in the preschool component was more consistently associated with family outcomes. This reflects the greater program intensity in the early years. In contrast to the primary grades, parent involvement is required in preschool and kindergarten, and there is a separate parent-resource teacher. The mean frequency of parent participation in school when their children were ages 8 to 12 was relatively low (2.1 out of a maximum score of 6). Levels of parent expectations and satisfaction with children's education were similar between children who participated in extended intervention and children who participated in only preschool and kindergarten. This finding also may reflect the relatively lower intensity of parent involvement in the primary grades. Overall, study findings support the positive effects of program participation on family socialization 3 to 6 years after completion of the program. Continued follow-up of the sample will be conducted to investigate long-term effects on family education and employment outcomes, and whether parent involvement contributes to these outcomes.

The Status of Subgroup Effects

With regard to differential program effects within the sample, findings were mixed at best and lead to the tentative conclusion that most children appear to benefit equally from participation in the CPC program. The majority of tests to detect subgroup differences were nonsignificant, and even the effects that were statistically significant contributed only 1% to 1.5% extra variance to youth outcomes. The prediction from ecological and resilience theory that children experiencing a large number of environmental risk factors are more likely to benefit from program participation was not supported. There was some support for the notion that boys benefited more from preschool participation and girls benefited more from follow-on participation. The relatively uniform program effects are consistent with consortium studies (Consortium for Longitudinal Studies, 1983; Lazar et al., 1982) as well as more recent studies (cf. Barnett, 1995). Thus, findings provide little support in favor of targeting programs to particular child and family demographic groups, at least for those measured in this study.

The most consistent subgroup effect that emerged was at the level of the school neighborhood. Children attending programs in the highest poverty neighborhoods (where more than 60% of children in the school attendance area are low income) benefited more from participation than did children in lower-poverty settings, primarily for reading achievement, math achievement, and consumer skills. This finding indicates that the effects of the Child-Parent Center Program may be compensatory at the neighborhood level. In the relative absence of economic resources and social support, systematic interventions like the CPCs may be especially beneficial. This was the major justification for the development of the program in the middle 1960s and why it is funded by Title I. Neighborhood poverty may be a general indicator of neighborhood disadvantage (i.e., disorganization, absence of role models, low social support), which can influence children and families in complex ways. It also had greater variation than other child and family background factors; the percentage of children residing in low-income school neighborhoods ranged from 44% to 88%. Because no other studies have reported the neighborhood-moderated effects of early intervention, continued investigation is warranted.

Findings concerning the differential effects of program participation by instructional approach also warrant discussion. Although social competence outcomes generally favored children who experienced a teacher-oriented and academically oriented preschool program rather than a developmentally oriented program, this advantage was not robust at ages 14 and 15. Teacher-oriented approaches were more effective than undifferentiated instructional approaches in promoting school achievement and consumer skills and preventing grade retention. Centers characterized as having a teacher-oriented approach were more likely than other centers to emphasize whole-class activities and academic skills through a structured but diverse set of instructional activities. Those classified as developmental were more likely to emphasize small-group activities and activity-based language approaches. Interestingly, children experiencing a teacher-oriented approach had similar rates (slightly lower) of delinquency infractions as those experiencing a developmentally oriented approach. This indicates that academically oriented instructional approaches do not inherently lead to greater adolescent delinquency, a major negative side effect in the literature (Schweinhart, Weikart, & Larner, 1986).

Studies of the long-term effects of preschool curricula have found either no differences between approaches (Consortium for Longitudinal Studies, 1983) or differences in favor of a child-centered (developmental) approach (Marcon, in press; Schweinhart et al., 1986), especially with regard to misconduct and delinquency (Schweinhart & Weikart, 1997). Some studies, however, have found that teacher-directed approaches can have positive short-term effects on school achievement (Becker & Gersten, 1982; Meyer, 1984). My finding that undifferentiated instructional approaches (no distinct instructional emphasis or mixed emphasis) were the least effective method of instruction is consistent with Marcon's (in press) study of a similarly disadvantaged sample in the District of Columbia.

Overall, my findings support the general proposition that there is no single instructional model that is best for low-income children. The caveat is that undifferentiated or mixed models may be counterproductive. This conclusion is similar to that of the Consortium for Longitudinal Studies (1983). Examining the results from 11 model programs, the consortium determined that home-based or center-based programs that were structured or less structured and that used different curricula were equally associated with child outcomes. Indeed, Lazar (1983) concluded that "any well-designed professionally supervised program to stimulate and socialize infants and young children from poor families will be efficacious" (p. 462).

Two points are relevant in interpreting the findings on instructional approach in this study. Even the centers classified as using a teacher-directed approach did not exclusively rely on any one curriculum or method. Although some centers used the direct instruction program called DISTAR during the late 1960s and 1970s (Fuerst & Fuerst, 1993), they were more eclectic in the early 1980s and used a variety of materials including the activity-based EARLY (Early Assessment and Remediation Laboratory) described in chapter 2. Consequently, the instructional approaches of the Child-Parent Centers in the mid-1980s are best characterized along a continuum from structured and teacher oriented to less structured and developmental. Most of the centers would be classified as right of center or left of center, with none at the ends of the continuum.

A second point is that effects of instructional approaches must be viewed in the context of the total program that was implemented. The CPC program provided comprehensive services, parents were extensively involved, class sizes and adult-child ratios were relatively small, and field trips were frequent. Under these conditions, the effects of structured, teacher-oriented programs focused on school readiness may be beneficial, especially for high-risk children in central cities. Of course, the findings reported are limited primarily to urban African-American children. In addition, the classification of centers was based largely on retrospective reports by head teachers and other program professionals and could be subject to error. The results were similar across a number of different groupings, however, and the decision to classify centers into each of the categories was based on reports of instructional philosophy and use of specific materials, which are not easily forgotten or can be verified with other sources. A classroom-based study of a more recent CPC cohort (Bezruczko & Kurland, 1996) is also consistent with the findings presented here.

The Persistence of Effects

Why does the Child-Parent Center and Expansion Program lead to such persistent improvements in social competence? The beneficial effects of duration of participation indicate that program continuity is one key ingredient. Duration and intensity of services are believed to be key attributes of effective interventions (Ramey & Ramey, 1992, 1998; Zigler & Styfco, 1993). Unlike almost all early childhood programs, the CPCs integrate preschool and kindergarten components and coordinate the primary-grade component with the affiliated elementary school, all within a single administrative system. Second, the program begins prior to formal schooling (ages 3 or 4) so that children can develop a strong foundation for learning. Scholastic and cognitive performance beginning in kindergarten presages later performance (McLoyd, 1998; Walberg, 1986), and, based on many previous studies, early intervention can contribute significantly to this relation.

A third likely reason for persistent effects is that parent involvement is a major focus. An array of support services is provided, from basic parent education to volunteer activities in and out of the centers. Compared to

Head Start and other government-funded programs, the parent program in the CPCs is intense. Each center employs a full-time noninstructional parent-resource teacher who runs a separate parent-resource room. The fourth key ingredient of the program associated with persistent effects is the relatively structured, basic skills emphasis of the curriculum. Although curricula vary across centers, the primary objective shared among staff is to facilitate reading and math achievement. Moreover, the value of reduced class size in the primary-grade component should not be underestimated. A typical primary-grade classroom in Chicago has at least 30 students and no teacher aide, whereas the CPC program limits class sizes to 25 and does include teacher aides, which reduces the staff-to-child ratio to 1 to 12. Viewed in the context of the parent program and the variety of learning experiences (e.g., field trips) that are provided, such an approach can provide a strong foundation for success.

Nevertheless, the school achievement of CPC graduates, even those with 5 or 6 years of participation, was still below the national average for 14- and 15-year-olds. The mean reading achievement for youth with extended intervention who were never retained was 8.0 in eighth grade and 8.2 in ninth grade, or at the 37th and 33rd percentile, respectively. Thus, early childhood intervention can make a significant difference in children's lives, but it is not a panacea for all challenges facing low-income children. Children's postprogram experiences are key to maintaining as well as promoting scholastic development, and judging by the overall rates of school mobility, parent involvement, and school quality displayed in Figure 18, their later experiences typically do not have these consequences and thus interfere with learning.

Pathways of Effects

Another perspective on the estimated causes of the persistence of effects of the CPC program is through interpretation of results of the structural modeling reported in Chapter 5. A distinguishing characteristic of this study was the systematic testing of several hypotheses of how the long-term effects of the program come about. This is a unique feature of confirmatory program evaluation. Although the pathways of program effectiveness were diverse, findings largely supported cognitive advantage as the major initiator of long-term effects for all program outcomes except delinquency. This is largely consistent with previous analyses in the Chicago study (Reynolds, 1992a; Reynolds, Mavrogenes, et al., 1996) and in others (Berrueta-Clement et al., 1984; Consortium for Longitudinal Studies, 1983; Schweinhart & Weikart, 1980; Schweinhart et al., 1993). Program participation appears to enhance children's early cognitive and language development so that they are more likely to begin school ready to learn, and this greater readiness provides advantages in adjusting to school. As shown in Figures 19 to 25, these children are often rated higher by classroom teachers, are more likely to attend schools with a higher level of student achievement, are less likely to be retained or spend time in special education, and are less likely to change schools. This process is central to the theory behind the CPC program, in which the stability of the early childhood learning environment provides opportunities for cognitive and social development that lead to cumulative advantages over time.

A second but less powerful explanation for long-term program effects is that the intervention encourages parent involvement in school and in children's education; when the intervention ends, parents are more likely to continue to provide the nurturing necessary to maintain learning gains, which makes later school success more likely. This is consistent with ecological systems theory (Bronfenbrenner, 1979; Bronfenbrenner & Morris, 1998). Indeed, parent involvement in school was the only common mediator, albeit a modest one, of reading and math achievement, life skills competence, and delinquency at ages 13 or 14. Examining a sample of children from the six original CPCs, Reynolds, Mavrogenes, et al. (1996) also found corroboration for the family support and cognitive advantage hypotheses of program effects. The contribution of family support was greater in that study than in the present one, however.[4] Although cognitive functioning at school entry and parent involvement foster long-term program effectiveness, two other factors appear to inhibit the transmission of long-term gains: (a) frequent school mobility and (b) grade retention. Avoidance of these two life events after the end of the intervention helps maintain learning gains. Both experiences are associated with lower academic success (McCoy & Reynolds, in press; Temple & Reynolds, in press) and are a cause for concern.

That the quality of the schools in which children were enrolled mediated the effects of the duration of program participation on youth outcomes and was an independent predictor of achievement indicates that school quality can help reinforce and extend the effects of early intervention. Previous studies of the school support hypothesis (Currie & Thomas, 1998; Lee & Loeb, 1995; Reynolds, Mavrogenes, et al., 1996) have provided suggestive but indirect evidence that school-related factors mediate the long-term effects of intervention. This study is the first to directly investigate the long-term effects of program participation with the quality of schools, especially with regard to school achievement. Both school mobility and school quality contributed to the transmission of effects. Thus, another benefit to improving the quality of schools, as indexed by achievement levels of the school body, is to help maintain the effects of early intervention. The direction of effects of two pathways, however, were not in the expected direction. Youth attending schools with a higher proportion of the student body performing above national norms were more likely than others to have delinquency infractions and were more likely to receive special education services. These pathways should be interpreted with caution since higher achieving schools are more likely to regularly monitor students and provide remedial services to students who need them.

Finally, study findings revealed less support for the social adjustment and motivational advantage hypotheses of program effects. That social adjustment partially mediated the effects of duration of program participation on school achievement and consumer skills suggests that program participation provides social as well as cognitive advantages in adjusting to school. The social adjustment hypothesis directly mediated the effects of follow-on intervention on school achievement, however. Children's perceived school competence at age 9—an indicator of motivation—did not mediate the effects of any measure of program participation, though it was associated with program participation. Of course, other measures of motivation may yet contribute the transmission of effects. Certainly, achievement motivation is a part of, and is required for, good cognitive and social development (Zigler & Butterfield, 1968). Thus, its contribution may be more complicated and overlapping than that tested in the recursive structural models.

Figure 27 shows just how consistent the cognitive and social mediators of effects are between this study of the Child-Parent Centers and a past study of the High/Scope Perry Preschool Project (Berrueta-Clement et al., 1984)—the two studies that have investigated pathways of program effects in detail (see also Consortium for Longitudinal Studies, 1983). The coefficients reported are standardized regression weights. The figures reveal a

Fig. 27.A. Selected Pathways of CPC Program Effects
(Coefficients are standardized)

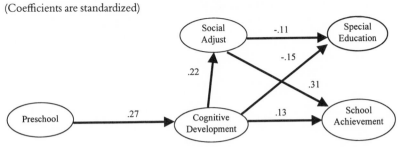

Fig. 27.B. Selected Pathways of Perry Preschool Effects

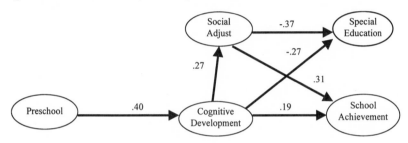

strikingly similar pattern of findings up to age 15 in support of the cognitive advantage hypothesis despite differences in time frame (i.e., two decades), geography, sample composition, program content, and model specification. Only the path from social adjustment to years in special education was substantially different, and this may be due to the unique operationalization of the measures in each study. This degree of consistency strongly indicates the primacy of early cognitive and scholastic development in the transmission of effects. Of course, the present study also corroborated the family support hypothesis as well as the school support hypothesis.

I note two limitations of pathway models. First, the measures of parent involvement and school quality were relatively narrow. Parent involvement was restricted largely to teacher reports of school participation albeit over several years. Certainly, alternative measures (e.g., home involvement, parenting style, and parenting attitudes) also are important and may have contributed to the model. The measure of school quality—aggregated achievement test scores—is only one of several indicators of school quality. Ratings of school climate, achievement gains, and other school resources and characteristics are complementary indicators. Likewise, delinquency infractions were based on school reports and did not include all acts of delinquency, especially those occurring after school hours or off school grounds. Other complementary measures should be investigated in future studies including self-reports and police records (see Reynolds et al., 1998).

A second limitation is that although the hypotheses were the most plausible for explaining intervention effects, others are possible. For example, physical health status could be a mediator of long-term effects, or pathways of influence could be reciprocal. In addition, alternative measures of intervening variables (e.g., family support at home) could have produced a different pattern of findings. To be valid, however, these mediators or measures would have to contribute above and beyond those of the present model. Nevertheless, no prior studies have investigated simultaneously the five hypotheses considered here. Based on the research literature and the theory of the CPC program, these hypotheses are the most plausible ones. Other programs, of course, may show a different pattern of support for the hypotheses, and these should be investigated in future studies.

Methodological Considerations

All research studies have to contend with the tradeoff between internal and external validity. This study is no different. A major methodological strength of this monograph is the large sample and large-scale nature of the program under study. The CPC program was developed in the Chicago public schools and has been implemented successfully in multiple sites for 33 years. Findings are thus more likely than previous studies to be generalizable to Head Start and other government-funded programs. I am aware of no other studies that provide such extensive support for established public service programs.

The tradeoff was that random assignment to the program was not possible. Given the long history of successful implementation and the focus of the program to serve families most in need on a first-come, first-served basis, an experimental study at this stage would be difficult to undertake and might be considered by some to be unethical because services already believed to be effective would have to be denied to some families. Although findings should be interpreted in the context of the quasi-experimental design that was implemented, several aspects of the study strengthen the validity of findings. First, the internal validity of findings has been investigated extensively over the years through analysis of attrition, selection bias, alternative comparison groups, multiple outcome variables, and duration of treatment participation (see Chapter 2). Findings have been consistent across these analytic approaches. Such in-depth sensitivity analysis is rare in intervention and evaluation research. I am aware of no other studies that have probed this issue further.

I found substantial evidence that the groups were well matched at the beginning of the study and at the age 14 and 15 follow-up (see also Chapters 2 and 3). The CPC group and non-CPC comparison group were similar on a number of background variables, were equally eligible for participation, and provided contrasts that were ecologically valid in the sense that the non-CPC comparison group participated in "treatment as usual" (e.g., full-day kindergarten) rather than no intervention. Several recent analyses indicate that under some conditions quasi-experimental designs can lead to conclusions that are consistent with those of randomized experiments or that approximate those of randomized experiments (Lipsey & Wilson, 1993; Reynolds & Temple, 1995; Shadish & Ragsdale, 1996). The keys seem to be that (a) the groups are reasonably well matched, (b) they come from similar populations, (c) the program selection process is well known, (d) measures are reliable, and (e) findings are robust to alternative model specifications. All of these conditions were met in the study. Yet as Popper (1959) has noted, research findings—regardless of the design upon which they are based—can only corroborate hypotheses, not prove them to be true in any absolute sense.

Second, the confirmatory program evaluation approach used to investigate effects moved well beyond main effects and toward explanation of how and why long-term effects occur. As indicated in Chapter 1, this is a major research need, and thus Chapter 5 was devoted entirely to it. In this study, I used confirmatory program evaluation to investigate the extent to which the pathways of the effects matched those predicted by the program theory. This approach is especially designed for longitudinal quasi-experimental studies and can increase confidence that the pattern of results is valid. Overall, many of the hypothesized pathways in Figure 1 were supported (see Figures 19 to 25). Pathways of program effectiveness included early developed abilities (i.e., cognitive readiness, early school achievement), family involvement in school, and school support factors, as well as the practices of grade retention and special education placement. These were similar to the sixth-grade analysis of Reynolds, Mavrogenes, et al. (1996) and provide confirmatory evidence of the efficacy of the CPC program. Because these mediators are central to the program theory as well as the assumptions of early intervention, confidence is increased that the estimated effects are attributable to the program.

Another strength of the study is the prospective longitudinal design and comprehensive data collection in the project. This has provided the opportunity for investigating year-to-year changes in outcomes and comparisons between outcomes. For example, the pattern of effects is most coherent in the scholastic domain rather than in the social or psychological domain. This is consistent with the program theory's emphasis on school achievement and competence. If the reverse occurred or if the pattern of effect sizes were similar across outcomes, interpretation would be more difficult. The pattern of findings over time also is similar to many other studies as determined by reviews of research (Bryant & Maxwell, 1997; Karoly et al. 1998; also see Table 1). The largest effects on cognitive development and school achievement occurred early and carried over to several indicators of school competence, including consumer skills.

How Good Is the Child-Parent Center Program?

The Child-Parent Center Program is not perfect. Far from it. The findings reported here clearly indicate that the effects on several of the outcomes, while statistically reliable and educationally meaningful, were not unusually large. Effect sizes for most program indicators were in the moderate range (.20 to .50 standard deviations), and the percentage reductions in problematic behavior varied between about 20% and 60%. The magnitude of effects of the CPC program also have declined over time for some outcomes, especially reading and math achievement. These findings and the accumulated literature on social programs (Crane, 1998) certainly refute the "naive" environmentalism of the 1960s in which it was believed that early interventions could result in massive and permanent individual change. Rather, this evidence leads to a more realistic portrait of environmental influence in which programs vary in their effectiveness, depending on a variety of individual, program, and context factors. The CPC program is no different than other programs in this regard, but nevertheless it has continued to demonstrate performance advantages. Program features have changed over the years, however, with some not necessarily for the better.

Based on the implementation history reported in Chapter 2 and the 1983–89 implementation period investigated in this study, three features of the program could be strengthened and may result in even larger effects. First, although the program does provide basic health screening and nurse visitation, health services are meager compared with those offered by Head Start. Unlike Head Start, physical and dental exams, immunizations, and mental health services are not provided as part of the CPC program. Rather, children and families are given referrals for most health services prior to program entry and during program participation. Health services were more comprehensive during the first 15 years of the CPC program, for a half-time nurse was located in each center, and other services were provided routinely.

Second, the level of coordination between the preschool/kindergarten and primary-grade components is modest at best. Although the close proximity and the conceptual similarity of the two components facilitate a relatively smooth transition, cooperation and communication between the two sites is relatively limited. Some of this has to do with the split funding of the program between federal and state sources. Another is the extra demands placed on the primary-grade component within the elementary school to share some resources with other programs or activities. School principals' commitment to the primary-grade program also is crucial, and some have scaled back program services over the years. This is because of the desire to implement programs and activities for the whole school rather than just for CPC graduates.

A third area that could be strengthened is parent education. Although program personnel encourage parents to further their education and job training, funds are not set aside for such activities, and many centers do not regularly provide GED and other courses. A greater commitment to parent education and training could further strengthen an already strong parent component. A survey of parents in the Child-Parent Centers in 1997 found that only 19% reported receiving a home visit when their child was in preschool or kindergarten.[5] In an age of welfare reform and mandated work requirements, parent involvement activities may become difficult to implement successfully without innovation. The press for full-day preschool services also will likely increase. The Child-Parent Centers and other programs must keep up with these changing times to continue to be effective.

On the other hand, the child education component of the program has probably improved over the years. Although the focus remains on enhancing basic literacy skills in reading and math, instructional materials and activities are relatively diverse compared to earlier years. The introduction of the activity-based EARLY materials as a standard supplement to preschool instruction in the early 1980s increased uniformity of objectives and activities across centers.

These areas for improvement, however, do not change the most important finding of this study and those of prior program implementations. The Child-Parent Center Program is effective in improving children's social competence in the short- and long-term. It has all the features that are optimal for success. The program is implemented early, before serious academic difficulties emerge. It is comprehensive, its length spans two key stages of development, and parents are integral to successful implementation. It provides systematic educational and family support services within a single administrative system. Indeed, the CPC program is similar to that envisioned by the planners of Head Start over 30 years ago (Zigler & Muenchow, 1992). That is, early intervention should occur throughout the preschool and primary grade years. Relative to what most other economically disadvantaged children experience, the CPC program, as shown in this volume, provides a solid foundation for learning that pays dividends for many years.

The effectiveness of the CPC program is further strengthened by comparing its demonstrated success with that of other social programs. Durlak and Wells (1997) reviewed the effects of 177 evaluations of mental health prevention programs for children and youth and reported an average effect size of .34 standard deviations at the end of the program or soon after. Only 25% of the studies reviewed had any follow-up assessment, and less than 10% had follow-up assessments beyond one year. Such findings are well short of those for the CPC program and those reported in Table 36. Lipsey and Wilson (1993) reviewed 156 meta-analyses of the effects of a wide range of educational, psychological, and behavioral treatments and found a mean effect size of .47 standard deviations. Posttest, short-term, and long-term effects were not distinguished, however. Given the near universal pattern that the effects of social programs dissipate over time, it is likely that the average short- and long-term effects would be substantially smaller. Moreover, program participation in the CPCs was significantly associated with eight different measures of social competence by age 15. This broad level of impact is unique among social programs.

Compared to many other social programs, the effects of the CPC program are relatively large and have effect sizes that are large and meaningful. In fact, as reported by Durlak and Wells (1997), the short- and long-term effects of most other interventions have yet to be documented. Investigation and demonstration of long-term effects of early interventions are commonplace, and the CPC program is one of the most notable of these. Based on this evidence, funding priority for early childhood interventions like the Child-Parent Centers should be even higher than it is currently.

Policy Implications

Based on the findings presented in the monograph and those of previous studies in the Chicago Longitudinal Study, early and extended childhood interventions like the Child-Parent Center Program should be implemented on a larger scale. After more than 30 years of government-funded early intervention, fewer than half of all low-income children who are eligible for preschool programs enroll in them (National Educational Goals Panel, 1995), and far fewer participate in enriched primary-grade programs designed to continue the benefits of earlier intervention. The findings of this study clearly indicate that federally funded early childhood programs can make a difference in the short and long term. One benefit of the CPC program is the joint preschool and kindergarten components. The reduced class sizes of the primary-grade component, the inclusion of teacher aides, and the presence of a curriculum parent-resource teacher also strengthen program continuity. Implementation of the Child-Parent Center Program has been exclusive to Chicago, however. Replication of the program in other schools and cities would be valuable in determining its impact within other contexts. Certainly, the findings presented in this monograph plus the principle of program continuity support its replication and diffusion (Ramey & Ramey, 1998; Zigler & Styfco, 1993, Chapter 5; also see Chapter 2 in this book). Evaluations of the National Head Start–Public Demonstration Project in 30 sites will add valuable information in this regard, though the CPC program differs in significant ways.[6]

One impediment to program diffusion is that the Child-Parent Center

Program and similar models are comprehensive and require preschool programs to be physically as well as conceptually connected to public elementary schools in a school-within-school framework. Funding for administrative centers such as this are often fragmented, and they often do not have high funding priority. In the past few years, several schools have decided to discontinue the state-funded primary-grade portion of the program. Unlike federal Title I funding, local schools have much latitude over state funds. A uniform funding mechanism would help avoid such difficulties. Funding decisions should favor programs like the Child-Parent Centers, which have demonstrated effectiveness. Based on the findings of this study, Title I funding should be targeted to early childhood programs from ages 3 to 9 rather than just to the preschool and kindergarten components. To enhance continuity of services, a single source of funding for all program-related services also is recommended.

The reasons that extended early childhood programs may be more effective are not just because they are longer in duration. They encourage stability in school and home learning environments and occur at an important time in children's development—the transition to formal schooling. School reform and social policy initiatives should take these issues into account. As shown in Figure 26 (Chapter 5), three alterable factors appear that promote the likelihood of long-term intervention effects: early cognitive development as impacted by preschool intervention, parental participation in children's education, and the quality of elementary schools. The strong support for the cognitive advantage hypothesis found in this study indicates that programs may be more likely to have long-term effects if they directly impact cognitive and scholastic development during the early childhood years. Cognitively oriented and structured approaches like those in the Child-Parent Centers, as well as in the Perry Preschool Program and Abecedarian Project, are illustrative of this focus. Thus, programs emphasizing early language development deserve high priority.

Since parent involvement in school appears to be a consistent pathway for promoting long-term success from early intervention, program and schoolwide efforts to involve parents in their children's education may benefit not only early childhood interventions but, more generally, family and child development. The amount of parent involvement in early intervention programs varies considerably, including in the Child-Parent Centers (Reynolds, 1994). Yet relative to other programs, parent involvement

Fig. 28. Eight Principles of Effective Early Childhood Programs

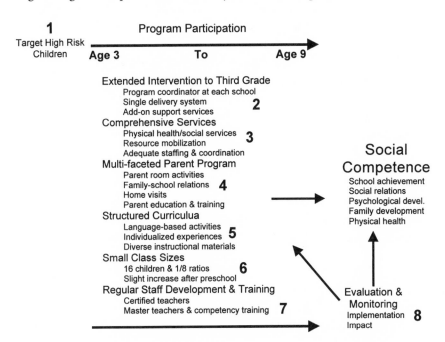

is greater in the CPC program (Schuster & Jennings, 1982). Based on the findings in this study, three ways to enhance parent participation include the following: (a) require that parents participate in the program for a minimum amount of time, such as two days per month; (b) each early childhood center should staff a parent-resource room; and (c) a diverse array of activities should be available in the centers, and the centers should accommodate family schedules.

Improvements in the quality of children's postprogram school environment may not only independently contribute to scholastic development but may also help maintain the effects of earlier intervention. Policies and practices to reduce the negative effects of school mobility, grade retention, and special education are especially important since all three were associated with lower achievement. Moreover, increasing the general quality of schools may promote long-term effectiveness. One striking finding of this study was that two thirds of the study sample *never* attended an elementary school in which one quarter or more of the student body performed at national achievement norms. Not surprisingly, Chicago children do not keep pace with their peers nationally. School reforms resulting in higher achievement levels in the elementary schools may have the further benefit of increasing the chances of long-term effects of early intervention.

The components of such early childhood interventions would be similar to the eight principles of effective early childhood programs displayed in Figure 28. Based on the findings in this study, as well as on previous research (see Barnett, 1995; Karoly et al., 1998; Guralnick, 1997; Ramey & Ramey, 1998), long-term effects of intervention will be more likely to occur if these eight features are emphasized.

Principle 1 is targeting children who are at high risk of experiencing school difficulties. Fewer than half of all eligible children participate in preschool education programs (National Educational Goals Panel, 1995). Preference in enrollment should be given to children who have the greatest learning needs. Findings in this monograph and in other studies (Zigler & Muenchow, 1992; Comer, 1993) indicate that the strategy of compensatory early intervention can be an effective one. Evidence in this study indicated that the effects of participation were greatest for children in the highest poverty neighborhoods.

Principle 2 concerns the timing and duration of program participation. Although early entry into programs, especially if prior to manifestation of problem behavior, has been a frequent characteristic of effective programs (Ramey & Ramey, 1992; Wachs & Gruen, 1982; Zigler & Styfco, 1993), duration or extensiveness of participation has been emphasized less. As shown in this study, long-lasting intervention can ease the transition to formal schooling so as to maintain the effects of earlier intervention and to provide further advantages in school adjustment. This enhances developmental continuity and is consistent with the ecological concept that experiences have the most impact if they occur "on a regular basis over extended periods of time" (Bronfenbrenner & Morris, 1998).

Principles 3 to 5 concern the scope and content of programs that lead to greater effectiveness for children and families. Programs that are comprehensive and focus on the whole child are more likely to impact one or more child and family outcomes. These should assist families in meeting their physical health, nutritional, social-emotional, and scholastic needs. This also means that typical programs providing curricula emphasis without sufficiently intensive health and family support services, such as those offered by many state and local school districts, are less likely to be effective.

Principle 4, active and multifaceted parent involvement, is a cornerstone of many early childhood programs, including the Child-Parent Centers and Head Start. Evidence is accumulating that early childhood programs involving parents in significant ways are most likely to show long-term effects on children and families (Miedel & Reynolds, in press; Reynolds, Mavrogenes, et al., 1996; Seitz, 1990; Yoshikawa, 1994). Easier to advocate than to implement well, some of the family activities and opportunities provided in many effective programs include (a) volunteering in the classroom and assisting with field trips, (b) attending workshops and social support activities in staffed parent-resource rooms, (c) receiving encouragement for support activities done at home, (d) providing educational and employment training on site or with cooperating agencies, and (e) receiving home visits from qualified staff.

Principle 5, a structured, language-based curriculum approach, appears to be particularly effective for low-income African-American children. As reported in this study and in others (Becker & Gersten, 1982; Madden et al., 1993; Rhine, 1981), instructional approaches that have a focus on language and reading appear to provide substantial benefits. The structured but diverse set of instructional activities provided in most of the Child-Parent Centers was associated with positive adjustment in adolescence without the side effects of increased behavioral problems. Debates about curriculum, however, continue to persist (see Schweinhart & Weikart, 1997).

Principle 6, small class sizes and low teacher-child ratios, encourages individualized learning and increases contact between teachers and children as well as among children. Most programs demonstrating long-term success with children have teacher-child ratios of 1 to 8 or lower. These ratios would be expected to rise in kindergarten and the primary grades. Without small class sizes and low teacher-child ratios, greater levels of intensity would not be possible. The teacher-child ratios in the CPC program averaged 2 to 17 in preschool and 2 to 25 in kindergarten and the primary grades.

Principles 7 and 8 include the provision of ongoing staff development and adequate funding of research and evaluation, respectively. These two activities are usually the first to be cut when funding is tight. The qualifications of staff are directly related to the quality of early childhood programs (Chafel, 1992; Frede, 1998), and ongoing professional training of all program staff is critical to program improvement initiatives. Among the recommendations of the Head Start advisory committee (U.S. Department of Health and Human Services, 1994) was establishing competency-based training for those who work with families and strengthening the availability of training and career development opportunities at the local levels.

The importance of Principle 8, full funding for research and evaluation, should not be underestimated. If there is a truism about social programs, it is that the most effective programs invest in research for program improvement. Private corporations devote as much as 10% of their annual expenditures to research and development. Yet school- and community-based programs for children devote very little. The National Science and Technology Council (1997) estimated that 2% of total federal expenditures on domestic programs went to research and development but that less than one third of 1% of the total expenditure on programs for children and youth was reserved for research and development. In 1996 the Head Start program expended one third of 1 percent of its federal expenditures on research and evaluation. Other programs are probably no different and may devote even less to evaluation. Given the widely accepted relationship between research and development and economic productivity, why should social programs spend so little on research? At a minimum, the annual expenditure devoted to research and evaluation for Head Start, Title I, and related programs should approach 2%, the proportion spent on domestic programs such as energy, transportation, and biomedicine. This ultimately could improve their effectiveness.

Current and Future Status of Children and Families

The force of the above implications is accentuated by recent demographic trends in the United States indicating that children and families are facing greater levels of social disadvantage than in the past two to three decades. Three indicators seem particularly important for consideration here:

> The number of young children under the age of 6 who are poor reached 6.4 million in 1993, its highest recorded level. This was 26% of all young children (Knitzer & Aber, 1995). The 1996 rate of 23% remains higher than for any other age group, and the poverty rate for young children in urban areas was 32% (National Center for Children in Poverty, 1998).

> The percentage of children living in single-parent families increased

by 130% from 1960 to 1994 (from 13% to 30%; U.S. Department of Health and Human Services, 1996).

The percentage of the nation's poor who live in central cities with high concentrations of poverty increased by 82% from 1972 to 1991 (from 33% to 60%; quoted in Wilson, 1996).

Unless families, schools, and social interventions are strengthened to counteract these increasing risk factors, children and families are likely to face even lower levels of preparation and achievement in the future. The consequences have been felt especially in the largest urban areas. In Chicago, about one half of all young children under age 3 experienced poverty between 1991 and 1995, a rate that has been consistently higher than both New York and Los Angeles (Chicago Public Schools, 1995; National Center for Children in Poverty, 1997).

As documented in Table 3 of Chapter 2, the concentration of poverty in the neighborhoods containing Child-Parent Centers increased by 40% from 1970 to 1990. The rate of unemployment increased by 30% during this same period. These trends already have impacted children's school readiness. A study by the Chicago Public Schools (1995) reported that the percentage of preschool children entering the Child-Parent Centers who exhibited a high level of mastery of skills declined by 29% from 1987 to 1995 (14% to 10%). The percentage of preschoolers who correctly named basic colors declined by 21% (from 28% to 22%). Moreover, the percentage of children in the state-funded prekindergarten program who scored below the third stanine on the Peabody Picture Vocabulary Test increased by 18% from 1988 to 1994 (67% to 79%).

An implication of these trends is that in order to successfully meet the needs of children, intervention programs today and in the future must be even better in quality, intensity, and comprehensiveness. If a 1- or 2-year preschool program would not immunize children from continuing disadvantages in the 1960s and 1970s, it most certainly will not do so today. The implementation and dissemination of programs like the Child-Parent Centers is one particularly promising strategy for addressing our nation's educational and social needs.

The costs of the program are low relative to those incurred by continuing the status quo. The annual cost per child of a CPC-type preschool or kindergarten program is about the same as Head Start, and about $1,000 more per child than a typical early childhood program (roughly $4,000

Table 38. Average Costs and Benefits of CPC Participation and Remedial Educational Interventions

Intervention approach	Annual expenditure per child	Average change in school achieve in months		% change in high school dropout
		Short-term	Long-term	
1a. CPC preschool particip.	4,350	+5	+5	-20%
1b. CPC extended particip. (two years)	3,000	+5	+4	-32%
2. Grade retention in elem. school	7,102	-7	-7	+35%
3. Special ed placement	9,000– 12,000	-2	-2	+6%

Note: All in1996 dollars. Short-term is 1–3 years, long-term is 4–9 years. Expenditure for grade retention is based on one additional year of school; that of special education placement is the average across many placements in Chicago (Chicago Public Schools, 1997). Values for high school dropout are derived from Temple, Reynolds, and Miedel (in press).

versus $3,000). The primary-grade component costs about $1,500 more annually per child than the regular school program. Certainly, the later costs of remediation, special education, and school dropouts are large multiples of these amounts. As shown in Table 38, the average expenditure for an extra year of schooling due to grade retention is over $7,000 per student in Chicago (not counting indirect costs associated with school dropouts); the expenditure for an addition year of special education services is about $9,000–12,000.[7] Yet both types of remediation are often associated with lower rather than higher levels of school achievement, as has been reported in recent analyses in the Chicago Longitudinal Study (McCoy & Reynolds, in press; Reynolds & Wolfe, 1997) and in other studies. Temple, Reynolds, and Miedel (in press), for example, reported that grade retention during elementary school significantly increased the risk of becoming an early school dropout by over 30%. In contrast, participation in the CPC preschool program or in the extended program to second or third grade lowered the risk of becoming an early school dropout by 20% to 30% (Temple et al., in press). The National Science and Technology Council (1997) estimated that the annual cost to society in lost wages and tax revenues of high school dropouts is $250 billion dollars. Thus, programs that help to prevent dropping out of high school and its predictors (school achievement, grade retention, mobility) can more than pay for themselves.

As reported in Table 38, the Child-Parent Center Program shows that large-scale early interventions are more effective than most alternatives in reducing the risk of grade retention, special education placement, and becoming an early school dropout. Certainly, their costs are lower, which reveals the benefits of intervention approaches that are preventive instead of remedial. Preventive interventions like the CPC program are not only more likely to be effective on a wider range of outcomes than remediation, but they often prevent the need for remediation in the first place.

Nevertheless, the dilemma for preventionists and policymakers is whether limited program funds should be distributed widely or targeted more selectively. It is the age-old question of quality versus expansion. Should schools provide 1 or 2 years of services to as many children as possible at some basic level of quality, or should they provide more intensive and longer lasting services to fewer children at a higher level of quality? The irony is that many more children need to be served, yet the level of quality and intensity that they often get needs improvement. The Silver Ribbon Panel on Head Start (National Head Start Association, 1990) made quality the top recommendation for the future. It stated that "program expansion should never occur at the expense of quality" (p. 35). Zigler and Styfco (1993) also addressed this issue by indicating "advocates must stop pleading for all of Head Start's needs and instead make some hard choices. Our choice is first to make every Head Start program a high-quality setting that guarantees known developmental benefits to every child enrolled and to his or her family" (p. 36).

Yet today many administrators and policymakers are deciding to serve as many children as possible at the lowest possible cost; "We'll make them better later" is a frequent response. But if only programs of high quality and intensity have lasting effects, is this the wisest decision? The findings of this study clearly show that modest and incremental investments in programs to increase comprehensiveness and duration can increase long-term effectiveness substantially. The eight principles of effective intervention provide guides for developing more effective strategies for early intervention. Even if all the principles cannot be fully implemented or the concept of early childhood education offered by the total CPC program is not possible, the following specific elements may help improve program effectiveness, although it should be noted that the findings of this monograph indicate that success is optimal with use of several of these elements:

Use one administrative system in implementing a comprehensive program from preschool through the primary grades. Public schools are an ideal institution for this and may improve continuity between program components.

Integrate preschool and kindergarten programs in one location. A single administrative structure can provide a more stable learning environment and eliminates the move from preschool to kindergarten.

Provide a parent-resource room in each center headed by a parent-resource teacher and teacher aide. Most early childhood programs do not have a parent-resource room in each center for education and training activities, yet having such space is a direct way to get families involved. Of course, this does not reduce the importance of home visitation.

Involve parents as classroom volunteers and as assistants on field trips and other activities.

Provide a school-community representative to conduct outreach activities such as identifying and enrolling the neediest families, conducting home visits, and making referrals to health, community, and employment agencies.

Use a common set of instructional materials and objectives that emphasizes the development of basic skills in language arts and arithmetic. The EARLY materials and a variety of other language- and activity-based materials also are valuable.

Offer reduced class sizes and lower staff-to-child ratios in the primary grades to help ease the transition to formal schooling. In the CPC program, class sizes are limited to 25 students in the first three grades, teacher aides are available, and an instructional coordinator—the curriculum parent-resource teacher—is responsible for organizing educational activities and has the resources available for individualized instruction.

Ideally, early childhood centers would be located in close proximity to elementary schools with enough space to fully staff preschool and kindergarten programs, to house a parent-resource room, and to accommodate other personnel such as a school-community representative, a nurse, and a noninstructional head teacher. The early childhood centers could be separate buildings or wings attached to elementary schools. While the availability of space may be an impediment to wide dissemination of the program, the concept of early childhood centers is consistent with recent federal, state, and local initiatives to invest substantially in school construction and renovation.

Conclusion

In many ways, the Child-Parent Center Program is a quintessential social program. It is both institutionalized and comprehensive in scope; it begins early and lasts long enough to make a difference; it is implemented in impoverished settings for children who need it most. The program is administered in cooperation with a public school system and is linked to neighborhood elementary schools, which function relatively independently in separate buildings or in wings. These features allow for better coordination between program components. Emphasis on children's educational development and on parent involvement is the cornerstone of the program. Such an intervention strategy provides for a smoother transition from preschool to kindergarten and from kindergarten to the primary grades than typically occurs for children today.

The findings presented in this volume attest to the beneficial effects of both early and extended intervention for children at risk envisioned by the planners of Head Start in the early 1960s. If nothing else, this volume supports the concept of early childhood intervention as including the ages from at least 3 to 9 and reinforces the idea that programs during these ages deserve funding priority, especially if they possess features that are linked to long-term success. To continue to be effective, however, the Child-Parent Centers and other programs must be better than in the past and must reflect the changing realities of family life and education.

In a larger sense, this volume reveals the promise of an intervention strategy whose time has come. Educators, policymakers, and school administrators should do as much as possible to disseminate it. Based on the findings presented here and the cumulative knowledge of the effects of other types of programs, the long-term benefits to children of early and extended intervention are worth the investment. Certainly, early interventions are not the only effective strategy for meeting the needs of children and families. But they provide a solid foundation upon which other efforts can build and child development can proceed with promise.

Appendix A
Descriptive Statistics for Study Sample in the Chicago Longitudinal Study

Appendix A

Descriptive Statistics for Study Sample in the Chicago Longitudinal Study

Variables	Original sample (N = 1,539)		Study sample (N = 1,164)		Attrition sample (N = 375)	
	N	M	N	M	N	M
Girls (%)	1531	50.2	1164	51.8	367	45.0
Blacks (%)	1530	92.9	1164	93.7	366	90.2
Parents HS graduate (%)	947	57.7	810	57.5	137	58.4
Missing on parent education	1539	38.5	1164	30.4	375	63.5
Free or reduced lunch (%)	977	92.8	818	93.0	159	91.8
Preschool participants (%)	1539	64.3	1164	66.3	375	57.9
Follow-on participants (%)	1539	54.8	1164	57.0	375	47.7
Total intervention (years)	1539	2.8 (2.0)	1164	2.9 (2.0)	375	2.3 (1.9)
Age at Kind. entry (months)	1525	63.4 (3.8)	1161	63.4 (3.7)	364	63.5 (4.0)
No. of children in family	945	2.5 (1.7)	810	2.5 (1.7)	137	2.6 (1.6)
Kind. word analysis	1531	63.8 (13.3)	1161	63.8 (13.4)	370	63.8 (13.0)
Kind. math achievement	1531	62.3 (13.6)	1161	62.3 (13.7)	370	62.2 (13.4)
School poverty (% of low-income children in school area)	1539	66.8 (9.5)	1164	66.6 (9.5)	375	67.1 (9.6)

Note: Standard deviations are in parentheses. Word analysis and math achievement are ITBS developmental standard scores.

Appendix B
Coefficients for Sample Recovery/Attrition and Selective Attrition for Youth and Family Outcomes

Appendix B Coefficients for Sample Recovery/Attrition and Selective Attrition for Youth and Family Outcomes

Sample Recovery/Attrition

Predictors	Model 1 b p	Model 2 b p	Model 3 b p
Age 14 outcomes (1 = in study sample)[a]			
CPC preschool	0.048 (.073)	0.045 (.123)	0.051 (.078)
CPC follow-on	0.051 (.033)	0.048 (.074)	0.050 (.062)
Risk index		-0.022 (.014)	-0.024 (.009)
Female vs. male		0.051 (.017)	0.054 (.012)
Kind. word analysis score			-0.001 (.164)
Age 15 outcomes (1 = in study sample)[b]			
CPC preschool	0.061 (.030)	0.058 (.051)	0.064 (.033)
CPC follow-on	0.036 (.164)	0.038 (.197)	0.040 (.173)
Risk index		0.003 (.621)	0.002 (.747)
Female vs. male		0.056 (.014)	0.059 (.011)
Kind. word analysis score			-0.001 (.242)
Perceived school competence (1 = in study sample)[c]			
CPC preschool	-0.0002 (.906)	-0.002 (.796)	0.005 (.975)
CPC follow-on	0.099 (.001)	0.092 (.002)	0.095 (.001)
Risk index		-0.036 (.001)	-0.038 (.000)
Female vs. male		0.016 (.535)	0.019 (.461)
Kind. word analysis score			-0.001 (.187)
Family socialization outcomes (1 = in study sample)[d]			
CPC preschool	0.034 (.256)	0.029 (.361)	0.031 (.345)
CPC follow-on	0.052 (.072)	0.041 (.185)	0.042 (.180)
Risk index		-0.058 (.000)	-0.058 (.000)
Female vs. male		0.064 (.010)	0.064 (.010)
Kind. word analysis score			-0.0003 (.789)

Appendix B (*continued*)

Selective Attrition

Predictors	Kindergarten word analysis			
	Age 14 sample		Age 15 sample[e]	
	b	p	b	p
CPC preschool	5.2	.000	5.2	.000
CPC follow-on	1.1	.450	1.1	.364
Sample status (1 = in sample)	-1.6	.234	-1.3	.313
Preschool x sample status	-0.2	.892	-0.3	.832
Follow-on x sample status	1.2	.465	1.2	.450

	Perceived school competence	
	b	p
CPC preschool	4.5	.000
CPC follow-on	3.0	.002
Sample status (1 = have competence score)	-0.4	.763
Preschool x sample status	1.2	.430
Follow-on x sample status	-2.3	.110

	Parent-reported family socialization	
	b	p
CPC preschool	3.3	.001
CPC follow-on	1.0	.299
Sample status (1 = have family score)	-3.3	.005
Preschool x sample status	3.5	.019
Follow-on x sample status	1.7	.241

Coefficients are B and (*p* values) from logit regression. B is transformed to linear.
[a]N = 1,164 for study sample and 375 for attrition sample.
[b]N = 1,070 for study sample and 469 for attrition sample.
[c]N = 788 for study sample and 751 for attrition sample.
[d]N = 756 for family study sample and 783 for attrition sample.
[e]Values for the covariates of sex and risk status are not shown.

Appendix C
Regression Analysis for Program Effects—
Ages 15 and 14

Appendix C Regression Analysis for Program Effects—Ages 15 and 14

Variables	Reading achiev.	Math achiev.	Yrs placed in spec. ed.	Retained in grade	School-reported delinq.
Age 15 outcomes					
Constant	155.3	156.8	1.05	-2.45	-1.12
Risk index	-3.5**	-1.9**	0.08*	0.17**	0.08
Female (vs. male)	8.8**	5.1**	-0.67**	-0.98**	-0.55**
Any CPC (vs. none)	3.5*	3.3*	-0.40**	-0.61**	-0.14
Multiple R	.240	.196	.196		
F	21.0**	13.8**	14.17**		
-2 log likelihood				1215.9	1134.4
Constant	153.3	155.9	1.22	-1.60	-0.95
Risk index	-2.4**	-1.8**	0.06	0.15**	-0.08
Female (vs. male)	8.7**	5.0**	-0.66**	-0.98**	-0.54**
Yrs of intervention	1.3**	1.0**	-0.14**	-0.22**	-0.04
Multiple R	.257	.209	.224		
F	24.4**	15.7**	18.8**		
-2 log likelihood				1193.4	1133.8
Constant	154.9	157.1	1.06	-2.73	-1.18
Risk index	-2.4**	-1.8**	0.06	0.16**	0.08
Female (vs. male)	8.8**	5.0**	-0.67**	-0.98**	-0.55**
Extended participa. (vs. less extended)	5.9**	4.4**	-0.60**	-0.80**	-0.17
Multiple R	.261	.213	.230		
F	25.2**	16.3**	19.9**		
-2 log likelihood				1201.2	1133.8

Appendix C (*continued*)

Variables	Reading achiev.	Math achiev.	Consumer skills	Yrs placed in spec. ed.	Retained in grade	School-reported delinq.
			Age 14 outcomes			
Constant	153.8	155.50	43.8	0.76	-2.95	-2.36
Risk index	-3.3**	-2.8**	-1.5**	0.08*	0.26**	-0.0001
Female (vs. male)	8.9**	6.1**	2.4**	-0.54**	-0.96**	-0.73**
Any CPC (vs. none)	4.1**	3.6**	3.0**	-0.29**	-0.54**	-0.16
Multiple R	.288	.269	.249	.186		
F	34.7**	29.9**	25.5**	13.8**		
-2 log likelihood					1277.2	873.3
Constant	151.3	153.3	42.8	0.92	-2.1	-2.01
Risk index	-3.1**	-2.6**	-1.4**	0.06t	0.24**	-0.01
Female (vs. male)	8.7**	5.9**	2.2**	-0.52**	-0.95**	-0.72**
Yrs of intervention	1.6**	1.4**	1.0**	-0.11**	-0.21**	-0.09*
Multiple R	.310	.296	.281	.213		
F	41.0**	36.9**	33.0**	18.4**		
-2 log likelihood					1253.3	870.2
Constant	153.3	154.8	44.2	0.811	-3.24	-2.54
Risk index	-3.1**	-2.6**	-1.4**	0.06t	0.24**	-0.02
Female (vs. male)	8.8**	5.9**	2.3**	-0.53**	-0.96**	-0.72**
Extended participa. (vs. less extended)	6.6**	6.2**	3.6**	-0.49	-0.83**	-0.47*
Multiple R	.312	.303	.273	.222		
F	41.5**	38.8**	31.0**	20.0**		
-2 log likelihood					1257.3	867.7

Note: $^*p < .05$, $^{**}p < .01$.

Appendix D
Estimated Effects for Measures of Program Participation Controlling for Sex of Child, Risk Status, and Parent Participation in School or CPC Site Enrollment

Appendix D Estimated Effects for Measures of Program Paricipation Controlling for Sex of Child, Risk Status, and Parent Participation in School or CPC Site Enrollment

	Age 14				Age 15			
	Parent involv.		CPC sites		Parent involv.		CPC sites	
	Adj. diff.	p	Adj. diff.	p	Adj. diff.	p	Adj. diff.	p
Reading achievement								
1. Any CPC vs. none	3.4	.019	4.8	.141	3.0	.069	4.0	.272
2. Any preschool vs. none	5.3	.000	7.2	.000	4.2	.011	5.6	.018
3. Any follow-on vs. none	0.4	.797	2.8	.086	0.9	.576	2.8	.138
4. Yrs. of follow-on	0.4	.458	1.7	.014	0.7	.727	1.8	.025
5. Yrs. of intervention	1.2	.000	2.0	.000	1.1	.004	1.6	.005
6. Extended vs. less extended	5.0	.000	5.0	.001	4.6	.002	4.6	.007
Mathematics achievement								
1. Any CPC vs. none	3.0	.014	3.3	.223	2.9	.036	4.5	.142
2. Any preschool vs. none	4.3	.000	5.3	.002	3.2	.019	3.7	.060
3. Any follow-on vs. none	0.8	.468	2.2	.107	0.9	.513	2.4	.132
4. Yrs. of follow-on	0.6	.213	1.5	.010	0.5	.385	1.4	.040
5. Yrs. of intervention	1.1	.000	1.5	.000	0.8	.010	1.1	.019
6. Extended vs. less extended	4.8	.000	4.2	.001	3.4	.006	3.5	.014

	Consumer skills rate of passing							
	Raw score				Rate of passing			
1. Any CPC vs. none	2.8	.000	3.7	.017	.113	.001	.155	.035
2. Any preschool vs. none	2.8	.000	3.3	.001	.101	.002	.115	.013
3. Any follow-on vs. none	1.1	.095	2.0	.012	.052	.099	.090	.015
4. Yrs. of follow-on	0.6	.023	1.2	.001	.029	.025	.051	.001
5. Yrs. of intervention	0.8	.000	1.1	.000	.033	.000	.042	.000
6. Extended vs. less extended	3.0	.000	2.5	.000	.125	.000	.111	.001

	Grade retention							
1. Any CPC vs. none	-.091	.002	-.076	.251	-.112	.000	-.104	.131
2. Any preschool vs. none	-.071	.012	-.115	.006	-.077	.012	-.116	.009
3. Any follow-on vs. none	-.051	.066	-.077	.021	-.064	.032	-.087	.014
4. Yrs. of follow-on	-.031	.002	-.047	.001	-.037	.002	-.052	.001
5. Yrs. of intervention	-.030	.000	-.046	.000	-.035	.000	-.050	.000
6. Extended vs. less extended	-.107	.000	-.119	.000	-.114	.000	-.120	.000

	Age 14				Age 15			
	Parent involv.		CPC sites		Parent involv.		CPC sites	
	Adj. diff.	P	Adj. diff.	P	Adj. diff.	P	Adj. diff.	P
Any special education placement								
1. Any CPC vs. none	-.029	.252	-.110	.053	-.031	.249	-.078	.181
2. Any preschool vs. none	-.051	.038	-.112	.002	-.052	.049	-.095	.012
3. Any follow-on vs. none	-.016	.517	-.065	.022	-.015	.550	-.061	.043
4. Yrs. of follow-on	-.011	.273	-.037	.002	-.012	.257	-.039	.003
5. Yrs. of interven.	-.015	.008	-.037	.000	-.015	.011	-.035	.000
6. Extended vs. less extended	-.079	.000	-.106	.000	-.079	.001	-.104	.000
Years in special education								
1. Any CPC vs. none	-.26	.024	-.72	.005	-.36	.010	-.74	.016
2. Any preschool vs. none	-.36	.001	-.68	.000	-.40	.004	-.67	.001
3. Any follow-on vs. none	-.06	.602	-.29	.026	-.14	.306	-.37	.017
4. Yrs. of follow-on	-.07	.128	-.18	.001	-.11	.044	-.24	.000
5. Yrs. of interven.	-.09	.000	-.20	.000	-.12	.000	-.22	.000
6. Extended vs. less extended	-.42	.000	-.52	.000	-.51	.000	-.62	.000

	School-reported delinquency infractions							
	Ages 13–14				Ages 13–15			
1. Any CPC vs. none	-.018	.440	-.014	.778	-.025	.408	-.089	.172
2. Any preschool vs. none	-.0004	.987	-.042	.189	-.061	.035	-.049	.250
3. Any follow-on vs. none	-.054	.014	-.064	.012	-.0001	.997	-.099	.003
4. Yrs. of follow-on	-.021	.022	-.021	.062	-.012	.329	-.028	.056
5. Yrs. of interven.	-.010	.058	-.014	.074	-.008	.258	-.019	.065
6. Extended vs. less extended	-.050	.015	-.053	.024	-.031	.258	-.044	.155

	Perceived school competence			
	Age 12			
	Parent involv.		CPC sites	
	Adj. diff.	p	Adj. diff.	p
1. Any CPC vs. none	.22	.570	.16	.856
2. Any preschool vs. none	.73	.056	1.30	.018
3. Any follow-on vs. none	-.14	.702	.11	.825
4. Yrs. of follow-on	.02	.897	.09	.642
5. Yrs. of interven.	.14	.095	.30	.031
6. Extended vs. less extended	.55	.111	.72	.079

Appendix E
Polychoric Correlations for Structural Models
Estimated in LISREL/PRELIS

Appendix E Polychoric Correlations for Structural Models Estimated in LISREL/PRELIS

I. Matrix including CPC preschool and follow-on participation

	1	2	3	4	5	6	7	8	9	10	11	12	13	14	15	16
1. CPC preschool	1.00															
2. CPC follow-on	0.33	1.00														
3. Cog. readiness	0.28	0.14	1.00													
4. Class adjust.	0.06	0.15	0.24	1.00												
5. Perceived comp.	0.09	0.11	0.23	0.47	1.00											
6. Parent involv.	0.18	0.17	0.22	0.36	0.21	1.00										
7. School quality	0.15	0.23	0.34	0.07	0.05	0.09	1.00									
8. Mobility	-0.18	-0.21	-0.21	-0.14	-0.11	-0.35	-0.21	1.00								
9. Special ed. yrs.	-0.14	-0.11	-0.18	-0.18	-0.12	-0.10	0.00	0.07	1.00							
10. Retention	-0.17	-0.19	-0.25	-0.30	-0.18	-0.29	-0.12	0.18	0.25	1.00						
11. Reading age 14	0.17	0.13	0.35	0.44	0.26	0.33	0.28	-0.18	-0.37	-0.48	1					
12. Math age 14	0.17	0.14	0.39	0.46	0.26	0.33	0.28	-0.19	-0.42	-0.53	0.78	1				
13. Consumer skills	0.19	0.17	0.35	0.41	0.28	0.29	0.23	-0.14	-0.33	-0.31	0.73	0.75	1			
14. Delinquency	-0.03	-0.07	-0.03	-0.10	-0.05	-0.13	0.01	0.12	0.06	0.04	-0.13	-0.13	-0.11	1		
15. Girls	0.08	-0.02	0.09	0.21	0.08	0.10	0.05	-0.06	-0.16	-0.19	0.19	0.15	0.10	-0.12	1	
16. Risk status	-0.05	-0.18	-0.17	-0.16	-0.15	-0.19	-0.24	0.14	0.06	0.14	-0.19	-0.20	-0.19	0.00	0.05	1

Note: See Chapter 3 for definition of variables.

Appendix E (*continued*)

II. Matrix including years of CPC participaton

	1	2	3	4	5	6	7	8	9	10	11	12	13	14	15	16
1. Yrs. of CPC	1.00															
2. Class adjust.	0.14	1.00														
3. Reading age 9	0.25	0.50	1.00													
4. Math age 9	0.25	0.50	0.79	1.00												
5. Perceived comp.	0.12	0.47	0.32	0.35	1.00											
6. Parent involv.	0.21	0.36	0.30	0.28	0.21	1.00										
7. School quality	0.23	0.07	0.31	0.26	0.05	0.09	1.00									
8. Mobility	-0.24	-0.14	-0.17	-0.12	-0.11	-0.35	-0.21	1.00								
9. Special ed. yrs.	-0.15	-0.18	-0.31	-0.34	-0.12	-0.10	0.00	0.07	1.00							
10. Rentention	-0.21	-0.30	-0.48	-0.48	-0.18	-0.29	-0.12	0.18	0.25	1.00						
11. Reading age 14	0.18	0.44	0.64	0.62	0.26	0.33	0.28	-0.18	-0.37	-0.48	1					
12. Math age 14	0.19	0.46	0.64	0.71	0.26	0.33	0.28	-0.19	-0.42	-0.53	0.78	1				
13. Consumer skills	0.21	0.41	0.59	0.63	0.28	0.29	0.23	-0.14	-0.33	-0.31	0.73	0.75	1			
14. Delinquency	-0.11	-0.20	-0.14	-0.13	-0.10	-0.21	0.02	0.20	0.10	0.07	-0.21	-0.21	-0.18	1		
15. Girls	0.04	0.21	0.16	0.10	0.08	0.10	0.05	-0.06	-0.16	-0.19	0.19	0.15	0.10	-0.19	1	
16. Risk status	-0.14	-0.16	-0.20	-0.20	-0.15	-0.19	-0.24	0.14	0.06	0.14	-0.19	-0.20	-0.19	-0.01	0.05	1

Note: See Chapter 3 for definition of variables.

Appendix E (*continued*)

III. Matrix including extended program participation

	1	2	3	4	5	6	7	8	9	10	11	12	13	14	15	16	17	18
1. Extended CPC	1.00																	
2. Class adjust.	0.16	1.00																
3. Ready age 9	0.28	0.50	1.00															
4. Math age 9	0.28	0.50	0.79	1.00														
5. Perceived comp.	0.12	0.47	0.32	0.35	1.00													
6. Parent involv.	0.26	0.36	0.30	0.28	0.21	1.00												
7. School qual.	0.20	0.07	0.31	0.26	0.05	0.09	1.00											
8. Mobility	-0.30	-0.14	-0.17	-0.12	-0.11	-0.35	-0.21	1.00										
9. Special ed. yrs.	-0.20	-0.18	-0.31	-0.34	-0.12	-0.10	0.00	0.07	1.00									
10. Retention	-0.23	-0.30	-0.48	-0.48	-0.18	-0.29	-0.12	0.18	0.25	1.00								
11. Reading age 14	0.21	0.44	0.64	0.62	0.26	0.33	0.28	-0.18	-0.37	-0.48	1							
12. Math age 14	0.24	0.46	0.64	0.71	0.26	0.33	0.28	-0.19	-0.42	-0.53	0.78	1						
13. Consum. skills	0.24	0.41	0.59	0.63	0.28	0.29	0.23	-0.14	-0.33	-0.31	0.73	0.75	1					
14. Delinquency	-0.15	-0.20	-0.14	-0.13	-0.10	-0.21	0.02	0.20	0.10	0.07	-0.21	-0.21	-0.18	1				
15. Pre-reading	0.27	0.26	0.47	0.47	0.20	0.18	0.26	-0.11	-0.24	-0.34	0.44	0.46	0.41	-0.10	1			
16. Pre-math	0.23	0.27	0.43	0.48	0.25	0.19	0.17	-0.13	-0.29	-0.35	0.45	0.48	0.45	-0.08	0.60	1		
17. Girls	0.03	0.21	0.16	0.10	0.08	0.10	0.05	-0.06	-0.16	-0.19	0.19	0.15	0.10	-0.19	0.09	0.08	1	
18. Risk status	-0.15	-0.16	-0.20	-0.20	-0.15	-0.19	-0.24	0.14	0.06	0.14	-0.19	-0.20	-0.19	-0.01	-0.18	-0.17	0.05	1

Note: See Chapter 3 for definition of variables.

Appendix F
List of Child-Parent Centers in Chicago:
Year Opened and Community Area

Appendix F
Child-Parent Centers in Chicago

Year opened	Community area
1967	Charles Dickens, 740 S. Campbell Ave. (Near West Side)
	Lorraine Hansberry, 4055 W. Arthington Ave. (West Garfield Park)
	Milton Olive, 1326 S. Avers Ave. (North Lawndale)
	Nathaniel Cole, 412 S. Keeler Ave. (West Garfield Park)
1969	Dorie Miller, 3030 W. Harrison St. (East Garfield Park)
	Phyllis Wheatley, 902 E. 133rd Pl. (Riverdale)
1970	Catherine Ferguson, 1215 N. Clybourn Ave. (Near North Side)
	George Donoghue, 707 E. 37th St. (Oakland)
	James Wadsworth, 6407 S. Blackstone Ave. (Woodlawn)
	Roswell Mason, 4216 W. 19th St. (North Lawndale)
	Sojourner Truth, 1409 N. Ogden Ave. (Near North Side)
1974	Alexander Dumas, 6615 S. Kenwood Ave. (Woodlawn)
	Anthony Overton, 4935 S. Indiana Ave. (Grand Boulevard)
	Carter Woodson, South, 4511 S. Evans Ave. (Grand Boulevard)
	James Johnson, 1504 S. Albany Ave. (North Lawndale)
	Joseph Stockton, 4425 N. Magnolia Ave. (Uptown)
	Theodore Herzl, 1401 S. Hamlin Ave. (North Lawndale)
1975	Bernice Joyner, 1315 S. Blue Island Ave. (Near West Side)
	Edward Delano, 3905 W. Wilcox St. (West Garfield Park)
	Francis Parker, 328 W. 69th St. (Englewood)
	George Dewey, 638 W. 54th Pl. (New City)
	John Farren, 5165 S. State St. (Grand Boulevard)
	Oneida Cockrell, 30 E. 61st St. (Washington Park)
1978	Alexander Von Humboldt, 1345 N. Rockwell St. (West Town)

Note: Some centers have changed locations since their opening. Addresses provided are for the years 1983–89. Truth, Herzl, Stockton, and Woodson South are not included in the Chicago Longitudinal Study.

Appendix G
Map of CPC Community Areas in Relation to U.S. Census Track Poverty Rates

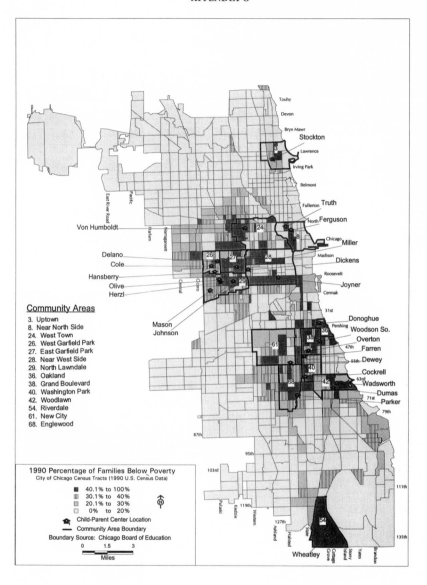

Community Areas

3. Uptown
8. Near North Side
24. West Town
26. West Garfield Park
27. East Garfield Park
28. Near West Side
29. North Lawndale
36. Oakland
38. Grand Boulevard
40. Washington Park
42. Woodlawn
54. Riverdale
61. New City
68. Englewood

1990 Percentage of Families Below Poverty
City of Chicago Census Tracts (1990 U.S. Census Data)

■ 40.1% to 100%
▥ 30.1% to 40%
▤ 20.1% to 30%
☐ 0% to 20%

🏠 Child-Parent Center Location
— Community Area Boundary
Boundary Source: Chicago Board of Education

0   1.5   3
Miles

Notes

1. The State of Early Intervention

Portions of this chapter are adapted from Reynolds, Mann, Miedel, and Smokowski (1997), primarily the reviews reported in Tables 1 and 2.

1. Poverty or low-income status is one of many risk factors that are associated with less than optimal development (e.g., school underachievement, delinquency). Biological risk (e.g., mental retardation) and family dysfunction (e.g., associated with child neglect or abuse, parental mental illness) are others.

2. The Child–Parent Center Program and Study

1. I use the term *Child-Parent Centers* throughout this monograph to refer to the overall program from preschool to the primary grades. This is the name most frequently used within the Chicago public schools. The original name, however, was Child-Parent Education Centers, and there are two separate programs, each with its own funding. The Child-Parent Center refers to the preschool and kindergarten component, and the Adaption/Expansion Program is the primary-grade component. I use the terms *follow-on intervention* and *primary-grade component* interchangeably to refer to services for children in the early school grades.

2. The Distinguished Schools National Recognition Program replaced the Joint Dissemination Review Panel. It is a partnership between the U.S. Department of Education and the National Association of State Title I Directors. The purpose of the Distinguished Schools program is to identify schools that are "ensuring that all children have access to effective instructional strategies and challenging academic content" and "demonstrating success in ensuring that all children, particularly educationally deprived children, make significant progress

toward learning that content." In 1997–1998, 109 schools in 39 states were included, though the CPC was the only across-school program chosen. Schools are selected for recognition by independent review panels based on six attributes: opportunity for children to learn at proficient and advanced levels, professional development, coordination with other programs, curriculum and instruction, partnerships with families and communities, and demonstration of effectiveness through 3 years of successful achievement data (e.g., test scores, performance-based assessments).

3. All 24 centers implemented the primary-grade component in 1986–1989, the time period of enrollment for children in this study. Because school principals have discretion in how to use these funds, many decided in the early 1990s to implement schoolwide programs rather than CPC programs.

4. They directed, respectively, Nathaniel Cole (Cluster 1 at 4346 W. Fifth Ave.), Charles Dickens (Cluster 2 at 605 S. Campbell), Lorraine Hansberry (Cluster 3 at 4059 W. Grenshaw), and Milton Olive (Cluster 4 at 1335 S. Pulaski) Child-Parent Education Centers. The Cole Center opened first on 12 May 1967, followed by the others at the end of May and in June 1967. Being mobile units, they are all in school buildings in different locations today. Hansberry, for example, is now at 4055 W. Arthington in the West Garfield Park community area.

5. The original program objectives as stated by the Board of Education were as follows: "1. To involve parents in the initial stages of the educational process of their children. 2. To provide educational experiences and develop verbal skills appropriate to the culture of an industrial-oriented, urban society. 3. To improve the self-concept and raise the operational level and motivational level of both parent and child" (quoted in Naisbitt, 1968, p. 1). Also, the centers have "relatively little emphasis on the development of social skills, outdoor play, dramatic play, etc. as are found in a typical, child-development oriented middle-class nursery school" (p. 1).

6. Low-income status is determined by eligibility for the National School Lunch Program funded by the U.S. Department of Agriculture. A full lunch subsidy is set at 130% of the federal poverty level and a reduced-price lunch is 185% of the federal poverty level. Another measure of school characteristics is percentage of enrolled students who are in low-income families. This was 90% or higher in the CPC sites and in the affiliated elementary schools.

7. A complete list of centers is in Appendix F; Figure 2 provides a map of the CPCs based on 1990 census data. Some of the centers have changed locations since opening. Hansberry CPC, for example, was originally located in North

Lawndale (on Grenshaw) but is currently in the southern part of West Garfield Park (on Arthington). Two centers have changed locations since the 1983–1989 implementation: Johnson (to a new building on Albany from Kedzie) and Parker (one block away on W. 69th). The new Ferguson CPC opened in 1998 at 1420 N. Hudson Ave.

8. The categorization was based primarily on answers to two open-ended questions: (a) Please describe the teaching philosophy of the center, and (b) Please list the most frequently used (no more than 5) instructional materials for the classroom. Ratings of the frequency (never too often) of child-initiated versus teacher-initiated activities also were used as criteria. The number of children classified in each instructional approach at follow-up was 479 who were developmentally oriented, 302 who were teacher oriented, and 196 who were undifferentiated.

9. Although parents enroll their children with the understanding that participation is required, they seldom are sanctioned for not participating, and program termination occurs only in unusual circumstances.

10. In a recent survey of family participation in the CPC program in the Chicago Longitudinal Study (Miedel & Reynolds, in press), 79% of responding parents indicated they participated in the centers two or more times per month during 1983–1986. Participation rates were highest for attending school assemblies (91% reported that they did), attending school meetings (90%), going on class field trips (79%), volunteering in the classroom (75%), and attending programs in the parent-resource room (74%). Only 15% of respondents reported receiving a home visit, however.

11. For students at grade level, age 14 corresponds to the eighth grade year. Ages 14 and 15 are used throughout this volume to denote the approximate ages of the study sample, recognizing that some youth have not turned exactly 14 or 15 by the end of the eighth- and ninth-grade school years.

12. Eighty (80) of the 389 children in the CESP group participated in Head Start (66 were active at age 14); 15 participated in the CPC preschool program for 1 or 2 years. They were counted as preschool participants.

13. Of this original non-CPC comparison group, 46 children participated in the CPC primary-grade component for 1 (n=13), 2 (n=27), and 3 years (n=6). Of course, in the analyses reported in chapters 4 and 5, these children were coded as CPC follow-on participants.

14. To account for both measured and unmeasured factors associated with program participation, Reynolds and Temple (1995) used simultaneous-equation

modeling and latent-variable modeling and found that these approaches led to program effect sizes that largely mirror those of classical regression analysis (see also Reynolds & Temple, 1998, for analyses of attrition).

3. Study Methods and Measures

1. Other youth and family outcomes include high school completion, total years of education, employment status, and welfare status. These outcomes and others will be investigated in follow-up studies.

2. Children with missing data for parent education, lunch eligibility, employment status, and single-parent status were assigned a minimum value of 1 and a maximum value of 3 depending on the number of values missing. The estimate was $X - 1$, where X = number of missing values. As expected, children with missing data were more likely than those with valid data to be economically disadvantaged. The number of children in the study sample at age 14 missing data on one indicator was 37 (3%), two indicators 559 (48%), three indicators 43 (4%), and four indicators 158 (14%). The pattern was the same for the study sample at age 15 and between program and comparison groups.

3. Principal components analysis showed that the underlying structure of the MPST consists of three discrete ability strata mediated by two cognitive mechanisms. These cognitive mechanisms—the capacity to recall and understand common everyday knowledge and the ability to conduct quantitative mental operations ranging from simple arithmetic to more complex analytical operations—account for approximately 30% of the test score variance on the MPST (Bezruczko, 1999). Psychometric analyses show that its first factor shares only 50% common variance with the ITBS, suggesting that the MPST construct successfully measures an aspect of human performance that differs from ordinary school achievement (Reynolds & Bezruczko, 1989).

4. Negatively worded items were reverse coded so that higher scores reflect more positive competence perceptions.

5. When children were at age 8, the question about parent participation was coded on a 7-point scale from 1 (never) to 7 (everyday). I used a rating of 4 (between monthly and weekly) or higher to denote average or better participation. At ages 10–12, the item was coded on a 3-point scale from 1 (never) to 3 (often). I used ratings of sometimes (middle category) or often to indicate average or better participation.

6. Prior to 1990, the ITBS used by the Chicago public schools was based on 1978 norms, and this covered the ages of 5 (kindergarten) to 9 (second or third

228

grade) for the study sample. From 1990 onward, the tests were based on 1988 norms. For comparability across years, all scores reported in this study were based on 1988 norms.

7. About one quarter of the non-CPC comparison did participate in Head Start. This fact reflects the cross-sectional nature of the comparison group. Indeed, the goal was not to select a "pure" comparison group with no preschool experience but a group that reflected the typical experiences of low-income children in Chicago.

8. The preprocessing program PRELIS (Joreskog & Sorbom, 1993b) was used to provide estimated correlations among variables, including polychoric and polyserial correlations for variables measured on an ordinal scale. Previous studies in the CLS (e.g., Reynolds, 1991; Reynolds, Mavrogenes, et al., 1996) have followed a similar approach.

9. See Appendix B for attrition analysis for the program outcomes. It shows that attrition from the original study sample was similar between preschool and no-preschool and follow-on and no-follow-on groups for the youth outcomes at ages 14 and 15. Due to selective attrition for the family outcomes, group differences on family outcomes should be interpreted cautiously.

4. Program Participation and Social Competence

1. Following Reynolds and Temple (1995, 1998), I also estimated the across-equation correlation between participation in the study sample and youth outcomes. The across-equation correlation (between model error terms), if statistically significant, would suggest bias in estimated program effects due to sample selection (i.e., attrition). Based on simultaneous equation modeling with a sample participation equation and an outcome equation, all correlations between the error terms were nonsignificant. That is, the estimated effects of different measures of program participation were unaffected by model misspecification due to differential attrition. The across-equation correlation for age 14 reading achievement, for example, was -.07 ($p = .88$) for the model including preschool participation and follow-on participation. It was -.06 ($p = .90$) for the model with extended program participation. Thus, the findings presented in the chapter are robust.

2. Similar to Reynolds (1995), youth with 2 years of preschool participation had higher reading achievement than those with 1 year, but this difference was not statistically significant. Thus, the effects of years of preschool participation were not reported.

3. For parsimony, the coefficients for years of follow-on participation are reported in this footnote rather than in the tables. At ages 14 and 15, each additional year of participation was associated, respectively, with a 1.1 and 1.3 standard-score point increase (adjusted scores) in reading achievement and 1.2 and 0.9 points in math achievement. The first and third coefficients were significant only at the .10 level, however. Accordingly, 3 years of participation in the follow-on program was associated with a 3.9-point (3 X 1.3) increase in reading achievement at age 15 relative to the nonfollow-on group above and beyond sex of child, risk status, and preschool participation. Adjusted coefficients for the remaining youth outcomes were as follows (level of statistical significance). Consumer skills raw score, 0.9 (p = .01) and percent passing, .039 (p = .01); grade retention age 14, -.055 (p = .01) and age 15, -.057 (p = .01); years placed in special education age 14, -.100 (p = .05) and age 15, -.148 (p = .05); ever placed in special education age 14, -.018 (p = .10) and age 15, -.019 (p = .10); school-reported delinquency infractions ages 13/14, -.022 (p = .05) and ages 13–15, -.011 (p .10); and perceived school competence at age 12, .09 (p .10).

4. For eighth graders only, the respective distribution in grade equivalents was 8.0, 7.8, 7.5, 7.3, 7.3, and 7.4 grade equivalents. The ninth-grade distribution was, respectively, 8.2, 8.0, 7.8, 7.6, 7.7, and 7.8.

5. When end-of-kindergarten achievement was added to the model, only years of follow-on intervention were associated with significantly lower rates of grade retention and years of special education placement.

6. I also investigated the number of delinquency infractions during these time periods. Since the number of infractions rarely exceeded two by age 14 and three by age 15, our dichotomous measure was chosen. For example, only 19 youth had three or more infractions at ages 13 and 14.

7. I further investigated the link between program participation and self-perceptions for the indicator expectations for educational attainment measured at age 10 (i.e., How far in school do you think you will get?). The categories ranged from "some high school" (1) to "go to college" (4). Ratings were obtained 4 years after preschool participation and 1 to 2 years after primary-grade participation. Analyses of 805 responding children indicated that any follow-on participation (b = .08, p = .006) and years of follow-on (b = .04, p = .002) were significantly associated with higher educational expectations, as were duration of participation (b = .02, p = .015) and extended program participation (b = .08, p = .02). In contrast to perceived competence, this could indicate a recency effect of intervention.

Any program participation and preschool participation were not associated with higher child-reported educational expectations.

8. The unadjusted and adjusted coefficients for years of follow-on participation were, respectively, .16 and .09. Both were not significantly different from zero.

9. This item had a 5-point scale from poor/not at all to excellent/much. I recoded to a dichotomous variable to increase reliability and to reduce halo effects or response bias since teachers may rate parental involvement partly on the basis of children's academic performance in school. For example, teacher ratings of parent involvement are more associated with school achievement than are parent ratings of performance (Reynolds, 1992b).

10. This approach is also called random effects estimation. It allows individual-level error terms in prediction to be correlated within each site. As explained by Raudenbush (1988), standard regression procedures such as multiple regression and logistic regression assume that individual observations are drawn independently of each other from a larger population. In the case of nested study designs, however, the observations within each site may be correlated. Failure to allow for the within-group correlation in errors may lead to inaccurate estimates of effect sizes. Results of the random effects estimation indicated that the within-site correlations in the error terms were very small, ranging from .01 to .02 youth outcomes at ages 14 and 15. Thus, they had no substantive effect on the findings. In percentage of variance terminology, less than 10% of the variation in youth outcomes was between sites and more than 90% was within sites.

11. Years of follow-on participation showed the same pattern of effects as did any follow-on participation. Adjusted coefficients for educational expectations, satisfaction with school, and school involvement were, respectively, .026 ($p = .454$), .005 ($p = .890$), and .102 ($p = .044$).

12. Because some of the later Child-Parent Centers did not include all-day kindergarten programs, this could complicate the interpretation of results even though lasting effects of all-day kindergarten would not be expected. Inclusion of the all-day/half-day kindergarten in the model did not contribute to the explanation of performance differences between groups.

13. For parsimony and because the pattern of findings was similar to reading achievement, trends for math achievement were not shown.

14. Because I was most interested in middle adolescent outcomes, differential program effects were not presented for perceived school competence at age 12. Those findings were similar to those in Table 28. Children attending the program in high-poverty neighborhoods, for example, had higher ratings of competence

than other children. The effects of preschool participation on perceived school competence were greater for boys than girls. In addition, perceived school competence was unaffected by preschool instructional approach. The direction of effects favored developmentally oriented and then teacher-oriented approaches.

15. Note that use of a more liberal definition of statistical significance ($p < .10$) resulted in 45 significant interactions. Of these 9 additional coefficients, 4 included sex of child and 4 included school poverty.

16. To classify the centers into instructional approaches, head teachers or other staff at the time of the study were asked to complete a short survey about the curriculum and organizational structure of the preschool and kindergarten program for the years 1983–1986. Ratings by a long-time evaluator of the Child-Parent Centers (and a founder of the Chicago Longitudinal Study) were used if head teachers or staff could not be located for these years. Teachers rated a number of curriculum attributes, including the extent to which the centers emphasized basic skills, small- and large-group activities, formal reading instruction, and child- and teacher-initiated activities. The teaching philosophy of the center and specific instructional materials in use also were reported. From these data, each Child-Parent Center was classified into the instructional categories of teacher-oriented, child-developmental, and undifferentiated programs. Inter-rater reliability (based on three raters) was .70.

Notably, the classrooms in each center were fairly homogeneous in their instructional activities so that the classification well represented the experiences of most participating children. Nevertheless, the classification was based largely on retrospective reports. To minimize reporting bias, I relied most heavily on the teaching philosophy and specific instructional materials used in the centers in determining the classifications. This information was more easily verifiable.

Moreover, the classification is relative, not absolute in terms of indexing a particular standard. Most of the centers, for example, used a diversity of instructional activities and curriculum materials.

17. Significance levels were as follows: preschool by risk status ($p = .017$), any participation by risk status ($p = .045$).

5. Pathways of Program Effectiveness

1. Measurement errors (1 minus reliability coefficient) for several intervening variables were estimated as follows (based on published reliabilities or previous research): cognitive readiness at age 5 (.06), classroom adjustment and consumer life skills (.05), parent participation in school, school mobility, school quality, and delinquency (.10),

and perceived school competence (.15). Also, the following were handled as ordinal variables in estimation of the polychoric correlation matrix in LISREL: preschool participation, follow-on participation, years of total program participation, risk status, parent participation in school, school quality, and school mobility.

2. Analyses were based on the age 14 study sample because it was larger and more representative of the original kindergarten sample. Nevertheless, findings based on the age 15 study sample were consistent with those at age 14—the pattern of pathways was largely the same. For example, the effect of preschool participation was transmitted primarily through cognitive advantage (*bs* = .26 and .12) as well as parent involvement (*bs* = .10 and .09). The influence of these pathways was even larger for consumer skills and grade retention. The best predictor of delinquency infractions (ages 13 to 15) was school mobility (*b* = .20), and participation in follow-on intervention was associated with significantly less school mobility (*b* = -.12). Contact the author for further findings concerning age 15 analyses.

Note that program-related pathways leading to perceived school competence were not investigated because the age at which it was measured (age 12) did not occur sufficiently after the measurement of the intervening variables. Family socialization outcomes (i.e., parent involvement in school) were conceptualized as intervening rather than outcome variables.

3. This level of significance is associated with a t-statistic of 2.58 or higher. I used the .01 level of significance to counteract the possible underestimation of the standard errors used to calculate statistical significance under maximum likelihood estimation (Joreskog & Sorbom, 1993a).

4. Note that the figures are displayed separately for clarity of presentation. For each program measure, the structural models were estimated for all youth outcomes simultaneously.

5. The factor loadings for reading comprehension and math-total achievement subtests were, respectively, .87 and .91 at age 14 (.87 and .83 at age 15). Respective factor loadings for age 9 school achievement and end-of-kindergarten pretest achievement were .87 and .90, and .77 and .77.

6. Twenty-four site dummy variables representing the 25 sites in which children participated were entered. These variables proxy both measured and unmeasured attributes that are specific to each site and that may be associated with cognitive development. Results indicate that the addition of these site variables increased the percent of variance explained in cognitive readiness at age 5 from 9% to 24%. Despite this substantial increase, the estimated effect of preschool participation on cognitive readiness was unchanged. In fact, it increased slightly (i.e., from .23 to .24, standard-

ized). Results for the model of years of CPC participation yielded a similar pattern as the variance explained in reading and math achievement increased from about 10% to 16% without affecting the magnitude of the effect of duration of intervention. Also note that kindergarten achievement was significantly associated with consumer skills ($b = .23$), but that teacher ratings of classroom adjustment ($b = .03$) and perceived school competence at age 9 ($b = -.01$) were not.

7. Fit statistics indicated this model reproduced the data well as chi-square = 143.01 ($df = 47$), RMSEA = .042, AGFI = .95. This level of fit is similar to that using other measures of program participation.

8. One potential artifact is that schools with greater proportions of high-achieving students may have higher expectations for students and retain them after poor performance. In addition, the coefficients for teacher ratings of classroom adjustment ($b = -.10$, $t = 2.14$), perceived school competence ($b = .02$), and kindergarten achievement ($b = -.04$) were not significant.

9. Other predictors of grade retention by age 14 were kindergarten achievement ($b = -.16$) and girls ($b = -.12$). The influence of school mobility was marginal ($b = .07$, $t = 2.34$). Other predictors for years in special education were kindergarten achievement ($b = -.18$) and girls ($b = -.12$).

6. Promoting Children's Success

1. Project Follow Through was intended to provide extended intervention to former graduates of Head Start Preschool from kindergarten to third grade. Funding shortfalls and changes in objectives prevented it from being a school-age version of Head Start. Preschool participation in Head Start was not required, and the evaluation design was not set up to assess the effects of timing and duration of participation in Head Start or Follow Through. Nevertheless, Project Follow Through's focus on the effects of alternative approaches to primary-grade instruction led to many valuable findings such as the positive effects of direct instruction on school achievement and the substantial variation in outcomes across schools. See Doernberger & Zigler (1993) and Rhine (1981) for further information.

2. I estimated this for the total available sample at age 5 of 1,102 children. The control variables were sex of child, risk status, and site dummy variables (24 for the 25 sites) representing school attributes associated with enrollment at each center. The average group difference, in standard scores, was 6.2, or .61 SD units (about 4 months of performance). The effect size without the site variables was .49 SD. Notably, preschool participants were, on average, scoring at the national norm on the composite battery at age 5. The effect size for extended program participation

relative to intervention ceasing at kindergarten was .56 SD in reading at second grade (.34 SD controlling for kindergarten pretest).

3. The costs for the Perry Preschool are in 1992 dollars as reported in Schweinhart et al. (1993); those for the Abecedarian Project are from C. Ramey, personal communication, 3 February 2000; see also Ramey, Campbell, & Blair (1998). It should be noted that most expenditures in these programs are due to program personnel and vary by location. Schweinhart et al. (1993) indicate that this fact explains most of the difference between Head Start and Perry. The annual per pupil expenditure for Head Start was $4,491 in 1994.

4. This 1996 study measured parent involvement differently than does the present study. Instead of computing a composite teacher and parent rating of parental involvement in school, the earlier study treated parent and teacher ratings as separate indicators of a latent variable, parent involvement. These measures were limited to grades 2 and 4. This plus the shorter time frame employed resulted in larger effects of family support than in the present study. For example, the coefficient for the pathway from preschool participation to parent involvement was .40; the pathway from parent involvement to school achievement was .29. The study did not investigate pathways involving other measures of program participation.

5. This survey was based on the responses of 500 parents when their children were about to graduate from kindergarten (spring 1997). This rate of home visitation differed dramatically from parent reports of participation in school, for more than 80% of responding parents reported attending school assemblies, going on class field trips, and attending parent-resource room activities. A 1997 retrospective survey of parents in the Chicago Longitudinal Study found a similar pattern of home visitation and participation in activities at the centers and schools.

6. The CPC program reflects a school organization approach to the transition to school in that class sizes are reduced, teacher aides are added, and the focus is on intensifying reading and math skills in the classroom, all within a single institutional arrangement. The Head Start–Public School Transition Program is more akin to a case-management model, for there are few attempts to alter the organization of the school in these ways. Head Start and the public school transition program also are embedded in different institutional structures, as the former are typically based in social service and community action agencies. The CPC program operates within a single organizational structure and centers located in or in close proximity to elementary schools.

7. These expenditures are reported in the Illinois State Board of Education (1997) and in Chicago Public Schools (1997).

References

Abelson, R. P. (1995). *Statistics as principled argument*. Hillsdale, NJ: Erlbaum.

Alexander, K. L., & Entwisle, D. R. (1988). Achievement in the first 2 years of school: Patterns and processes. *Monographs of the Society for Research in Child Development, 53* (2, Serial No. 218).

Anderson, S., Auquier, A., Hauck, W. W., Oakes, D., Vandaele, W., & Weisberg, H. I. (1980). *Statistical methods for comparative studies: Techniques for bias reduction.* New York: Wiley.

Barnett, W. S. (1992). Benefits of compensatory preschool education. *Journal of Human Resources, 27*, 279–312.

Barnett, W. S. (1995). Long-term effects of early childhood programs on cognitive and school outcomes. *Future of Children, 5*(3), 25–50.

Becker, W. C., & Gersten, R. (1982). A follow-up of Follow Through: The later effects of the Direct Instruction model on children in fifth and sixth grades. *American Educational Research Journal, 19*, 75–92.

Bendersky, M., & Lewis, M. (1994). Environmental risk, biological risk, and developmental outcome. *Developmental Psychology, 30*, 484–494.

Berrueta-Clement, J. R., Schweinhart, L. J., Barnett, W. S., Epstein, A. S., & Weikart, D. P. (1984). *Changed lives: The effects of the Perry Preschool Program on youths through age 19.* Ypsilanti, MI: High/Scope.

Bezruczko, N. (1999). Competency gradient for Child-Parent Centers. *Journal of Outcome Measurement, 3*, 35–52.

Bezruczko, N., & Kurland, M. (1996, April). *Longitudinal study shows elementary school classes influence preschool intervention effects.* Paper presented at the annual meeting of the American Educational Research Association, New York.

Bezruczko, N., & Reynolds, A. J. (1987). *Minimum proficiency skills test: 1987 item pilot report.* Chicago: Department of Research and Evaluation, Chicago Public Schools.

Bickman, L. (1987). The functions of program theory. In L. Bickman (Ed.), *Using program theory in evaluation* (New Directions for Program Evaluation Series No. 33, pp. 5–18). San Francisco: Jossey-Bass.

Bloom, B. S. (1964). *Stability and change in human characteristics.* New York: Wiley.

Bronfenbrenner, U. (1975). Is early intervention effective? In M. Guttentag & E. Struening (Eds.), *Handbook of evaluation research* (Vol. 2, pp. 519–603). Beverly Hills, CA: Sage.

Bronfenbrenner, U. (1979). *The ecology of human development: Experiments by nature and design.* Cambridge, MA: Harvard University Press.

Bronfenbrenner, U. (1989). Ecological systems theory. *Annals of Child Development, 6,* 187–251.

Bronfenbrenner, U., & Morris, P. (1998). Ecological processes of development. In W. Damon (Ed.), *Handbook of Child Psychology: Theoretical issues* (Vol. 1, pp. 993–1028). New York: Wiley.

Bross, I. D. J. (1967). Pertinency of an extraneous variable. *Journal of Chronic Disease, 20,* 487–495.

Bryant, D., & Maxwell, K. (1997). The effectiveness of early intervention for disadvantaged children. In M. Guralnick (Ed.), *The effectiveness of early intervention* (pp. 23–46). Baltimore: Paul H. Brookes.

Bunge, M. (1997). Mechanism and explanation. *Philosophy of the Social Sciences, 27,* 410–465.

Bureau of Early Childhood Programs. (n.d.). *The optimum in parent involvement.* Chicago: Chicago Public Schools, Department of Government Funded Programs.

Campbell, D. T. (1984). Can we be scientific in applied social science? *Evaluation Studies Review Annual, 9,* 26–48.

Campbell, F. A., & Ramey, C. T. (1994). Effects of early intervention on intellectual and academic achievement: A follow-up study of children from low-income families. *Child Development, 65,* 684–698.

Campbell, F. A., & Ramey, C. T. (1995). Cognitive and school outcomes for high risk African-American students at middle adolescence: Positive effects of early intervention. *American Educational Research Journal, 32,* 743–772.

Campbell, R., Marx, L. A., & Nystrand, R. O. (Eds.). (1969). *Education and urban renaissance.* New York: Wiley.

Carnegie Task Force on Meeting the Needs of Young Children. (1994). *Starting points: Meeting the needs of our youngest children.* New York: Carnegie Corporation of New York.

Carnegie Task Force on Learning in the Primary Grades. (1996). *Years of promise: A comprehensive learning strategy for America's children.* New York: Carnegie Corporation of New York.

Carter, L. F. (1984). The sustaining effects study of compensatory and elementary education. *Educational Researcher, 13*(7), 4–13.

Chafel, J. A. (1992). Funding Head Start: What are the issues? *American Journal of Orthopsychiatry, 62,* 9–21.

Chen, H. T. (1990). *Theory-driven evaluations.* Newbury Park, CA: Sage.

Chicago Board of Education. (1984). *Chicago Effective Schools Project.* Chicago: Author, Office of Equal Educational Opportunity.

Chicago Board of Education. (1988). *Chicago EARLY: Instructional activities for ages 3 to 6.* Vernon Hills, IL: ETA.

Chicago Department of Public Health. (1994). *Community area health inventory: Vol. 1. Demographic and health profiles.* Chicago: Author.

Chicago Fact Book Consortium. (Ed.). (1984). *Local community fact book: Chicago metropolitan area, 1980.* Chicago: Board of Trustees of the University of Illinois.

Chicago Fact Book Consortium. (Ed.). (1995). *Local community fact book: Chicago metropolitan area, 1990.* Chicago: Board of Trustees of the University of Illinois.

Chicago Public Schools. (1974). *Child Parent Centers.* Chicago: Author. (ERIC Document Reproduction Service No. ED 108 145)

Chicago Public Schools (1983). *Goals and suggested activities for parents: ECIA Chapter I Child-Parent Centers.* Chicago: Author, Department of Government Funded Programs, Bureau of Early Childhood Programs.

Chicago Public Schools. (1985). *Elementary school—Criteria for promotion.* Chicago: Author.

Chicago Public Schools. (1987). *Chapter 2 all-day kindergarten program final evaluation report: Fiscal 1986.* Chicago: Author, Department of Research and Evaluation.

Chicago Public Schools. (1992). *ECIA Chapter I application: Fiscal 1991.* Chicago: Author.

Chicago Public Schools. (1995). *Chicago's public school children and their environment.* Chicago: Author, Office of Accountability.

Chicago Public Schools. (1997). *1997–1998 proposed budget.* Chicago: Author, Office of Management and Budget.

Cohen, J., & Cohen, P. (1983). *Applied multiple correlation/regression analysis for the behavioral sciences.* Hillsdale, NJ: Erlbaum.

Comer, J. P. (1993). *School power: Implications of an intervention project* (Rev. ed.). New York: Free Press.

Conrad, K. J., & Eash, M. J. (1983). Measuring implementation and multiple outcomes in a Child Parent Center compensatory education program. *American Educational Research Journal, 20,* 221–236.

Consortium for Longitudinal Studies. (1983). *As the twig is bent: Lasting effects of preschool programs.* Hillsdale, NJ: Erlbaum.

Cook, T. D., Anson, A. R., & Walchli, S. B. (1993). From causal description to causal explanation: Improving three already good evaluations of adolescent health programs. In S. G. Millstein, A. C. Peterson, & E. O. Nightengale (Eds.), *Promoting the health of adolescents: New directions for the twenty-first century* (pp. 339–374). New York: Oxford University Press.

Cook, T. D., & Shadish, W. R. (1994). Social experiments: Some developments over the past fifteen years. *Annual Review of Psychology, 45,* 545–580.

Crane, J. (Ed.). (1998). *Social programs that work.* New York: Russell Sage Foundation.

Cronbach, L. J. (1982). *Designing evaluations for educational and social programs.* San Francisco: Jossey-Bass.

Crum, D. (1993). *A summary of the empirical studies of the long-term effects of Head Start.* Unpublished manuscript, Pennsylvania State University, University Park, PA.

Currie, J., & Thomas, D. (1998). School quality and the longer-term effects of Head Start (NBER Working Paper No. 6362). Cambridge, MA: National Bureau of Economic Research.

Danziger, S. K., & Danziger, S. (1993). Child poverty and public policy: Toward a comprehensive antipoverty agenda. *Daedalus, 122,* 57–84.

Doernberger, C., & Zigler, E. (1993). Project Follow Through: Intent and reality. In E. Zigler & S. J. Styfco (Eds.), *Head Start and beyond: A national plan for extended childhood intervention* (pp. 43–72). New Haven, CT: Yale University Press.

Dryfoos, J. G. (1990). *Adolescents at risk: Prevalence and prevention.* New York: Oxford University Press.

Duncan, G. J., & Brooks-Gunn, J. (Eds.). (1997). *Consequences of growing up poor.* New York: Russell Sage Foundation.

Durlak, J. A., & Wells, A. M. (1997). Primary prevention mental health programs for children and adolescents: A meta-analytic review. *American Journal of Community Psychology, 25,* 115–152.

Elementary and Secondary Education Act of 1965, Pub. L. No. 89–10, 79 Stat. 27 (1965).

Entwisle, D. R. (1995). Elementary school. *Future of Children, 5*(3), 10–15.

Farran, D. C. (1990). Effects of intervention with disadvantaged and disabled children: A decade review. In S. J. Meisels & J. P. Shonkoff (Eds.), *Handbook of early childhood intervention* (pp. 501–539). Cambridge: Cambridge University Press.

Frede, E. C. (1998). Preschool program quality in programs for children in poverty. In W. S. Barnett & S. S. Boocock (Eds.), *Early care and education for children in poverty* (pp. 77–98). Albany, NY: SUNY Press.

Fuerst, J. S., & Fuerst, D. (1993). Chicago experience with an early childhood program: The special case of the Child Parent Center program. *Urban Education, 28,* 69–96.

Goldring, E. B., & Presbrey, L. S. (1986). Evaluating preschool programs: A meta-analytic approach. *Educational Evaluation and Policy Analysis, 8*(2), 179–188.

Guralnick, M. (Ed.). (1997). The effectiveness of early intervention. Baltimore: Paul H. Brookes.

Haskins, R. (1989). Beyond metaphor: The efficacy of early childhood education. *American Psychologist, 44,* 274–282.

Haynes, N. M., Comer, J. P., & Hamilton-Lee, M. (1988). The effects of parental involvement on student performance. *Educational and Psychological Research, 8,* 291–299.

Herrnstein, R. J., & Murray, C. (1994). *The bell curve: Intelligence and class structure in American life.* New York: Free Press.

Hieronymus, A. N., & Hoover, H. D. (1990). *Iowa Tests of Basic Skills: Manual for school administrators* (Supplement). Chicago: Riverside.

Hieronymus, A. N., Lindquist, E. F., & Hoover, H. D. (1980a). *Iowa Tests of Basic Skills: Early primary battery.* Chicago: Riverside.

Hieronymus, A. N., Lindquist, E. F., & Hoover, H. D. (1980b). *Iowa Tests of Basic Skills: Primary battery.* Chicago: Riverside.

Hill, M. S., & Sandfort, J. R. (1995). Effects of childhood poverty on productivity later in life: Implications for public policy. *Children and Youth Services Review, 17,* 91–126.

Hunt, J., McVickers. (1961). *Intelligence and experience.* New York: Ronald Press.

Illinois State Board of Education. (1997). *Spending on elementary and secondary schools in Illinois: Fiscal year 1996–1997.* Springfield, IL: Author.

Institute for the Development of Educational Auditing (IDEA). (1973). *ESEA Title I, Child Parent Centers, 1971–1972: Final evaluation report.* Arlington, VA: IBEX.

Institute for the Development of Educational Auditing (IDEA). (1974). *ESEA Title I, Child Parent Centers, 1972–1973: Final evaluation report.* Arlington, VA: IBEX.

Janowitz, M. (1967). *How shall the school for the Model Cities Program be organized?* Center for Social Organization Studies, University of Chicago. (ERIC Document Reproduction Service No. ED 038 457)

Jordan, T. J., Grallo, R., Deutsch, M., & Deutsch, C. P. (1985). Long-term effects of early enrichment: A 20-year perspective on persistence and change. *American Journal of Community Psychology, 13,* 393–415.

Joreskog, K. G., & Sorbom, D. (1993a). *LISREL 8:* Structural equation modeling with the SIMPLIS command language. Chicago: Scientific Software.

Joreskog, K. G., & Sorbom, D. (1993b). *PRELIS: A program for multivariate data screening and data summarization (A preprocessor for LISREL).* Chicago: Scientific Software.

Karoly, L. A., Greenwood, P. W., Everingham, S. S., Hoube, J., Kilburn, M. R., Rydell, C. P., Sanders, M., & Chiesa, J. (1998). *Investing in our children: What we know and don't know about the costs and benefits of early childhood interventions.* Santa Monica, CA: Rand.

Karweit, N. L. (1994). Can preschool alone prevent early learning failure? In R. E. Slavin, N. L. Karweit, & B. A. Wasik (Eds.), *Preventing early school failure: Research, policy and practice* (pp. 58–77). Needham Heights, MA: Allyn and Bacon.

Knitzer, J., & Aber, J. L. (1995). Young children in poverty: Facing the facts. *American Journal of Orthopsychiatry, 65,* 174–176.

Lally, J. R., Mangione, P. L., Honig, A. S., & Wittner, D. S. (1988, April). More pride, less delinquency: Findings from the ten-year follow-up study of the Syracuse University Family Development Research Program. *Zero to Three,* 13–18.

Lazar, I. (1983). Discussion and implications of findings. In Consortium for Longitudinal Studies, *As the twig is bent: Lasting effects of preschool programs* (pp. 461–466). Hillsdale, NJ: Erlbaum.

Lazar, I., Darlington, R. B., Murray, H. W., & Snipper, A. S. (1982). Lasting effects of early education: A report from the consortium for longitudinal studies. *Monographs of the Society for Research in Child Development, 47* (2/3, Serial No. 195).

Lee, V. E., & Loeb, S. (1995). Where do Head Start attendees end up? One reason why preschool effects fade out. *Educational Evaluation and Policy Analysis, 17,* 62–82.

Linn, R. (1989). Iowa Tests of Basic Skills [Review]. In J. C. Conoley & J. J. Kramer (Eds.), *The tenth mental measurements yearbook* (pp. 393–395). Lincoln, NE: University of Nebraska Press.

Lipsey, M. W., & Wilson, D. B. (1993). The efficacy of psychological, educational, and behavioral treatment: Confirmation from meta-analysis. *American Psychologist, 48,* 1181–1209.

Locurto, C. (1991). Beyond IQ in preschool programs? *Intelligence, 15,* 295–312.

Loeber, R., & Stouthamer-Loeber, M. (1998). Development of juvenile aggression and violence: Some common misconceptions and controversies. *American Psychologist, 53,* 242–259.

Madden, N. A., Slavin, R. E., Karweit, N. L., Dolan, L. J., & Wasik, B. A. (1993). Success for All: Longitudinal effects of a restructuring program for inner-city elementary schools. *American Educational Research Journal, 30,* 123–148.

Marco, G. L., & Landes, S. R. (1971). *The evaluation implications of a survey of the 1969–70 Chicago ESEA Title I Program.* Princeton, NJ: Educational Testing Service. (ERIC Document Reproduction Service No. ED 054 225)

Marcon, R. A. (in press). Differential impact of preschool models on development and early learning of inner-city children: A three cohort study. *Developmental Psychology.*

Masten, A. S., & Garmezy, N. (1985). Risk, vulnerability, and protective factors in developmental psychopathology. In B. B. Lahey & A. E. Kazdin (Eds.), *Advances in clinical child psychology* (Vol. 8, pp. 1–51). New York: Plenum.

McCoy, A. R., & Reynolds, A. J. (in press). Grade retention and school performance: An extended investigation. *Journal of School Psychology.*

McKey, R. H., Condelli, L., Ganson, H., Barrett, B. J., McConkey, C., & Plantz, M. C. (1985). *The impact of Head Start on children, families, and communities* (DHHS Publication No. OHDS 85–31193). Washington, DC: U.S. Government Printing Office.

McLoyd, V. C. (1998). Socioeconomic disadvantage and child development. *American Psychologist, 53,* 185–204.

Mehana, M. (1997). *A meta analysis of school mobility effects on the achievement of elementary students.* Unpublished doctoral thesis, Pennsylvania State University, University Park.

Meyer, L. (1984). Long-term academic effects of the direct instructional Project Follow Thru. *Elementary School Journal, 84,* 380–392.

Miedel, W. T., & Reynolds, A. J. (in press). *Parent involvement in early intervention for disadvantaged children: Does it matter?* Paper presented at the 4th biennial National Head Start Research Conference, Washington, DC.

Miller, L. B., & Bizzell, R. P. (1983). The Louisville experiment: A comparison of four preschool programs. In Consortium for Longitudinal Studies, *As the twig is bent: Lasting effects of preschool programs* (pp. 171–199). Hillsdale, NJ: Erlbaum.

Naisbitt, N. (1968). *Child-Parent Education Centers, ESEA Title I, Activity I.* Unpublished report, Chicago, IL.

Naron, N. K., & Perlman, C. L. (1981, April). *Chicago EARLY Program: Initial implementation of a preventive prekindergarten program.* Paper presented at the annual meeting of the American Educational Research Association, Los Angeles. (ERIC Document Reproduction Service No. ED 201 382)

National Center for Children in Poverty. (1997, April). *Early childhood poverty: A statistical profile.* New York: Columbia University.

National Center for Children in Poverty. (1998, March). *Young children in poverty: A statistical update.* New York: Columbia University.

National Center for Education Statistics. (1995, July). *Use of school choice* (Educational policy issues: Statistical perspectives; No. 95–742R). Washington, DC: U.S. Department of Education.

National Education Goals Panel. (1995). *Data for the National Education Goals Report: Vol. 1. National data.* Washington, DC: U.S. Government Printing Office.

National Head Start Association. (1990). *Head Start: The nation's pride, a nation's challenge.* Alexandria, VA: Author.

National Science and Technology Council. (1997, April). *Investing in our future: A national research initiative for America's children for the 21st century.* Washington, DC: Executive Office of the President, Office of Science and Technology Policy, Committee on Fundamental Science, and the Committee on Health, Safety, and Food.

Olds, D. (1988). The prenatal/early infancy project. In R. H. Price et al. (Eds.), *14 ounces of prevention: A casebook for practitioners.* Washington, DC: American Psychological Association.

Overman, E. S. (Ed.). (1988). *Methodology and epistemology for social science: Select papers of Donald T. Campbell.* Chicago: University of Chicago Press.

Phillips, D. A., & Cabrera, N. J. (Eds.). (1996). *Beyond the blueprint: Directions for research on Head Start's families.* Washington, DC: National Academy Press.

Pierson, D. E. (1988). The Brookline Early Education Project. In R. H. Price et al. (Eds.), *14 ounces of prevention: A casebook for practitioners*. Washington, DC: American Psychological Association.

Popper, K. R. (1959). *The logic of scientific discovery*. New York: Basic Books.

Ramey, C. T., Campbell, F., & Blair, C. (1998). Abecedarian Project. In J. Crane (Ed.), *Social programs that work*. New York: Russell Sage Foundation.

Ramey, C. T., & Ramey, S. L. (1998). Early intervention and early experience. *American Psychologist, 53*, 109–120.

Ramey, S. L, & Ramey, C. T. (1992). Early educational intervention with disadvantaged children—To what effect? *Applied and Preventive Psychology, 1*, 131–140.

Raudenbush, S. W. (1988). Educational applications of hierarchical linear models: A review. *Journal of Educational Statistics, 13*, 85–116.

Reynolds, A. J. (1989). A structural model of first-grade outcomes for an urban, low socioeconomic status, minority population. *Journal of Educational Psychology, 81*, 594–603.

Reynolds, A. J. (1991). Early schooling of children at risk. *American Educational Research Journal, 28*, 392–422.

Reynolds, A. J. (1992a). Mediated effects of preschool intervention. *Early Education and Development, 3*, 139–164.

Reynolds, A. J. (1992b). Comparing measures of parental involvement and effects on school achievement. *Early Childhood Research Quarterly, 7*, 451–472.

Reynolds, A. J. (1994). Effects of a preschool plus follow-on intervention for children at risk. *Developmental Psychology, 30*, 787–804.

Reynolds, A. J. (1995). One year of preschool intervention or two: Does it matter? *Early Childhood Research Quarterly, 10*, 1–31.

Reynolds, A. J. (1998a). Resilience among black urban youth: Prevalence, intervention effects, and mechanisms of influence. *American Journal of Orthopsychiatry, 68*, 84–100.

Reynolds, A. J. (1998b). Confirmatory program evaluation: A method for strengthening causal inference. *American Journal of Evaluation, 19*, 203–221.

Reynolds, A. J. (1998c). Developing early childhood programs for children and families at risk: Research-based principles to promote long-term effectiveness. *Children and Youth Services Review, 20*, 503–523.

Reynolds, A. J. (1998d). The Child-Parent Center and Expansion Program: A study of extended childhood intervention. In J. Crane (Ed.), *Social programs that work* (pp. 110–147). New York: Russell Sage Foundation.

Reynolds, A. J., & Bezruczko, N. (1989). Assessing the construct validity of a life skills competence test. *Educational and Psychological Measurement, 49,* 183–193.

Reynolds, A. J., & Bezruczko, N. (1993). School adjustment of children at risk through fourth grade. *Merrill-Palmer Quarterly, 39,* 457–480.

Reynolds, A. J., Bezruczko, N., Mavrogenes, N. A., & Hagemann, M. (1996). *Chicago Longitudinal Study of children in the Chicago public schools: User's guide (Version 4).* Madison, WI: University of Wisconsin, and Chicago: Chicago Public Schools.

Reynolds, A. J., Chang, H., & Temple, J. A. (1998). Early childhood intervention and juvenile delinquency: An exploratory analysis of the Child-Parent Centers. *Evaluation Review, 22,* 341–372.

Reynolds, A. J., Mann, E., Miedel, W., & Smokowski, P. (1997). The state of early childhood intervention: Effectiveness, myths and realities, new directions. *Focus, 19*(1), 3–11. Institute for Research on Poverty, University of Wisconsin-Madison.

Reynolds, A. J., Mavrogenes, N. A., Bezruczko, N., & Hagemann, M. (1996). Cognitive and family-support mediators of preschool effectiveness: A confirmatory analysis. *Child Development, 67,* 1119–1140.

Reynolds, A. J., Mehana, M., and Temple, J. (1995). Does preschool intervention affect children's perceived competence? *Journal of Applied Developmental Psychology, 16,* 211–230.

Reynolds, A. J., & Temple, J. A. (1995). Quasi-experimental estimates of the effects of a preschool intervention: Psychometric and econometric comparisons. *Evaluation Review, 19,* 347–373.

Reynolds, A. J., & Temple, J. A. (1998). Extended early childhood intervention and school achievement: Age 13 findings from the Chicago Longitudinal Study. *Child Development, 69,* 231–246.

Reynolds, A. J., & Walberg, H. J. (Eds.). (1998). *Evaluation research for educational productivity.* Greenwich, CT: JAI Press.

Reynolds, A. J., & Wolfe, B. (1997). Special education placement and school achievement: An exploratory analysis of a central-city sample. Discussion paper, Institute for Research on Poverty, University of Wisconsin–Madison.

Rhine, W. R. (Ed.). (1981). *Making schools more effective: New Directions from Follow Through.* New York: Academic Press.

Richmond, J. B. (1997). Head Start: A retrospective view. In E. Zigler and J. Valentine (Eds.), *Project Head Start: A legacy of the war on poverty* (2nd ed., pp. 120–128). Alexandria, VA: National Head Start Association.

Rosenbaum, P. (1984). From association to causation in observational studies: The role of tests of strongly ignorable treatment assignment. *Journal of the American Statistical Association, 79,* 41–48.

Rosenbaum, P. (1995). *Observational studies.* New York: Springer-Verlag.

Rosenthal, R. (1991). *Meta-analytic procedures for social research.* Newbury Park, CA: Sage.

Rossi, P. H., & Freeman, H. E. (1993). *Evaluation: A systematic approach* (5th ed.). Thousand Oaks, CA: Sage.

Royce, J. M., Darlington, R. B., & Murray, H. W. (1983). Pooled analysis: Finding across studies. In *As the twig is bent: Lasting effects of preschool programs* (pp. 411–459). Hillsdale, NJ: Erlbaum.

Rutter, M. (1987). Psychosocial resilience and protective mechanisms. *American Journal of Orthopsychiatry, 57,* 316–331.

Sampson, R., & Laub, J. (1993). *Crime in the making: Pathways and turning points through life.* Cambridge, MA: Harvard University Press.

Scannell, D. P., Haugh, O. M., Schild, A. H., Ulmer, G. (1990). *Tests of Achievement and Proficiency: Multi-level battery.* Chicago: Riverside.

Schuster, F., & Jennings, J. (1982). *Child Parent Centers: 1967–1980.* Chicago: Department of Research and Evaluation, Chicago Board of Eduation.

Schweinhart, L. J., Barnes, H. V., & Weikart, D. P. (1993). *Significant benefits: The High/Scope Perry Preschool study through age 27.* Ypsilanti, MI: High/Scope Educational Research Foundation.

Schweinhart, L. J., & Weikart, D. P. (1980). *Young children grow up: The effects of the Perry Preschool Program on youths through age 15.* Ypsilanti, MI: High/Scope Educational Research Foundation.

Schweinhart, L. J., & Weikart, D. P. (1997). *Lasting differences: The High/Scope preschool curriculum comparison study through age 23.* Ypsilanti, MI: High/Scope Educational Research Foundation.

Schweinhart, L. J., Weikart, D. P., & Larner, M. B. (1986). Consequences of three preschool curriculum models through age 15. *Early Childhood Research Quarterly, 1,* 15–45.

Seitz, V. (1990). Intervention programs for impoverished children: A comparison of educational and family support models. *Annals of Child Development, 7,* 73–103.

Seitz, V., Apfel, N., Rosenbaum, L., & Zigler, E. (1983). Long-term effects of Projects Head Start and Follow Through: The New Haven Project. In Consortium for Longitudinal Studies (Eds.), *As the twig is bent: Lasting effects of pre-school programs* (pp. 299–332). Hillsdale, NJ: Erlbaum.

Seitz, V., Rosenbaum, L. K., & Apfel, N. H. (1985). Effects of family support intervention: A ten-year follow-up. *Child Development, 56*, 376–391.

Shadish, W. R., & Ragsdale, K. (1996). Random versus nonrandom assignment in controlled experiments: Do you get the same answer? *Journal of Consulting and Clinical Psychology, 64*, 1290–1305.

Sherman, A. (1994). *Wasting America's future: The Children's Defense Fund Report on the cost of poverty*. Boston: Beacon Press.

Stallings, J. (1975). Implementation and child effects of teaching practices on Follow-through classrooms. *Monographs of the Society for Research in Child Development, 40* (Serial No. 163).

Steinberg, L., Lamborn, S. D., Dornbusch, S. M., & Darling, N. (1992). Impact of parenting practices on adolescent achievement: Authoritative parenting, school involvement, and encouragement to succeed. *Child Development, 63*, 1266–1281.

Stenner, A. J., & Mueller, S. G. (1973, December). A successful compensatory education model. *Phi Delta Kappan*, pp. 246–248.

Stipek, D., Daniels, D., Galluzzo, D., & Milburn, S. (1992). Characterizing early childhood education programs for poor and middle class children. *Early Childhood Research Quarterly, 7*, 1–19.

Sullivan, L. M. (1970). Report on Child-Parent Education Centers. Chicago: Chicago Public Schools, Board of Education.

Sullivan, L. M. (1970). *Report on Child-Parent Education Centers.* Chicago: Chicago Foresman.

Susser, M. (1973). *Causal thinking in the health sciences, concepts and strategies of epidemiology.* New York: Oxford University Press.

Temple, J. A., & Reynolds, A. J. (in press). School mobility and achievement: Longitudinal findings from an urban cohort. *Journal of School Psychology.*

Temple, J. A., Reynolds, A. J., & Miedel, W. (in press). Can early intervention prevent high school dropout? Evidence from the Chicago Child-Parent Centers. *Urban Education.*

U.S. Department of Health, Education, and Welfare. (1964). *Smoking and health: Report of the advisory committee to the surgeon-general of the Public Health Service* (No. 1103). Washington, DC: Public Health Service.

U.S. Department of Health and Human Services. (1994, March). Creating a 21st century Head Start: Executive summary of the final report of the Advisory Committee on Head Start Quality and Expansion. *Young Children, 65*–67.

U.S. Department of Health and Human Services. (1996). *Trends in the well-being of America's children and youth: 1996*. Washington, DC: Author.

U.S. General Accounting Office. (1997). *Head Start: Research provides little information on impact of current program* (Report GAO/HEHS-97-59). Washington, DC: Author.

U.S. Senate. (1967). *Elementary and Secondary Education Act of 1965* (Report No. 146, pp. 1446–1461). Washington, DC: Author.

Wachs, T. D., & Gruen, G. E. (1982). *Early experience and human development*. New York: Plenum.

Walberg, H. J. (1986). Synthesis of research on teaching. In M. Wittrock (Ed.), *Handbook of research on teaching* (pp. 214–229). Washington, DC: American Educational Research Association.

Weissberg, R. P., & Greenberg, M. T. (1998). School and community competence-enhancement and prevention programs. In W. Damon (Ed.), *Handbook of child psychology: Child psychology in practice* (Vol. 4, pp. 877–954). New York: Wiley.

White, K. R. (1985). Efficacy of early intervention. *Journal of Special Education, 19*, 401–416.

Wilson, W. J. (1987). *The truly disadvantaged: The inner city, the underclass, and public policy*. Chicago: University of Chicago Press.

Wilson, W. J. (1996). *When work disappears: The world of the new urban poor*. New York: Knopf.

Woodhead, M. (1988). When psychology informs public policy: The case of early childhood intervention. *American Psychologist, 43*, 443–454.

Yeaton, W. H., & Sechrest, L. (1981). Critical dimensions in the choice and maintenance of successful treatments: Strength, integrity, and effectiveness. *Journal of Consulting and Clinical Psychology, 49*, 156–167.

Yoshikawa, H. (1994). Prevention as cumulative protection: Effects of early family support and education on chronic delinquency and its risks. *Psychological Bulletin, 115*, 27–54.

Yoshikawa, H. (1995). Long-term effects of early childhood programs on social outcomes and delinquency. *Future of Children, 5*(3), 51–75.

Zigler, E. (1994). Reshaping early childhood intervention to be a more effective weapon against poverty. *American Journal of Community Psychology, 22*, 37–48.

Zigler, E., Abelson, W., Trickett, P. K., & Seitz, V. (1982). Is an intervention program necessary in order to improve economically disadvantaged children's IQ scores? *Child Development, 53*, 340–348.

Zigler, E., & Berman, W. (1983). Discerning the future of early childhood intervention. *American Psychologist, 38*, 894–906.

Zigler, E., & Butterfield, E. C. (1968). Motivational aspects of change in IQ test performance of culturally deprived nursery school children. *Child Development, 39*, 1–14.

Zigler, E., & Muenchow, S. (1992). *Head Start: The inside story of America's most successful educational experiment.* New York: Basic Books.

Zigler, E., & Styfco, S. (Eds.). (1993). *Head Start and beyond: A national plan for extended childhood intervention.* New Haven, CT: Yale University Press.

Zigler, E., Taussig, C., & Black, K. (1992). Early childhood intervention: A promising preventive for juvenile delinquency. *American Psychologist, 47*, 997–1006.

Zigler, E., & Trickett, P. K. (1978). IQ, social competence, and evaluation of early childhood intervention programs. *American Psychologist, 33*, 789–798.

Author Index

Subject Index